Cork on Cork

Cork on Cork

Sir Kenneth Cork
takes stock

with
Hugh Barty-King

MACMILLAN
LONDON

First published 1988 by
MACMILLAN LONDON LIMITED
4 Little Essex Street London WC2R 3LF
and Basingstoke

Associated companies in Auckland, Delhi, Dublin, Gaborone,
Hamburg, Harare, Hong Kong, Johannesburg, Kuala Lumpur,
Lagos, Manzini, Melbourne, Mexico City, Nairobi, New York,
Singapore and Tokyo

British Library Cataloguing in Publication Data

Cork, *Sir* Kenneth
  The Cork report.
  1. Great Britain. Accountancy. Cork, Sir Kenneth
  I. Title
  657′.092′4

  ISBN 0–333–44479–5

Typeset by Wyvern Typesetting Ltd, Bristol, England
Printed by Richard Clay plc, Bungay, Suffolk

To Nina, with her unbelievable patience

Contents

Foreword

I have known and been a friend of Sir Kenneth Cork for many years. I knew him when he was on his way to great distinction but at a time when he was known to the world only as a name connected with insolvency matters. Knowing him as well as I do, I have always known that he is a kind and generous man. Those who know him personally will have no doubt about it, but the most satisfactory aspect of this book is that it will establish this agreeable fact to every reader.

At first blush the detailed story of the career of an accountant, largely, and in the early days almost exclusively, concerned with bankruptcy, would not suggest riveting reading. The surprise to me, as it will be to those wise enough to acquire a copy of this book, is that it *does* make interesting reading. It tells how a young man, regarded by his father as unequipped to do anything except enter a family business, emerged as the leading practitioner in his field; as a national authority advising governments; became Lord Mayor of London; and later, branching off into a totally fresh area of activity – the Arts – became Chairman of one of our two great theatrical companies, an authority on the economic aspects of the Arts, a Vice-Chairman of the Arts Council, and ultimately Chairman of a seminal enquiry into drama, the conclusions of which excited interest and had a considerable influence on the whole field of Arts finance.

It was a privilege to be asked to introduce to what will, I hope, deservedly be a large reading public, a book as unusual and informative as this. It tells the story of Sir Kenneth's life until now, but, although no longer a young sprite, I entertain the hope that further fruitful activities will produce at least a second volume, if not a third.

Lord Goodman
July 1988

Author's Preface

One man in his time plays many parts. I have been extremely fortunate that in my life I have had the opportunity to wear so many hats. Chartered Accountant; insolvency accountant; army officer; company doctor; chairman of the Royal Shakespeare Company (which required an expert on insolvency to keep it solvent!); thirty-five years in the City Corporation; Sheriff and Lord Mayor of London. Money-raiser for the arts and various charities. Now a venture capitalist. Possibly a Jack of all trades and master of none! That is for other people to judge. I don't want to know the answer! I have had great enjoyment playing these parts and have made countless friends and only a few enemies, I hope. When one chapter has closed another has always opened.

Without having had a father who created a business and whose name was well known, and a mother who ensured that I was sent to Berkhamsted School, all this would never have got off the ground. Without a marvellous and loyal wife, Nina, who unlike me is sensible and practical, and who thinks, quite understandably, that I have never grown up, and treats me accordingly, I would not have been able to stay the course; and without a dedicated secretary, Winifred Garner, who organises my life and picks up the pieces when I do not succeed in carrying out her plans, it would have fallen apart. Lastly, without my love of sailing and boats to blow away the worries, it would not have been worth the hassle.

To all these and my wonderful partners and friends in W. H. Cork Gully & Co. I extend my grateful thanks; not forgetting my brother Norman, who started us off by getting in the work, and my life-long friend Walter Tickler, who organised the unorganisable.

I have been told that people will want to read this book. We shall see! I don't particularly want to see my book on Marylebone Station at a much discounted price because no one wanted to.

K.R.C.

Part One

The Old Man

When Limited Liability Was a Novelty

Some seven men form an Association
  (If possible all peers and baronets),
They start off with a public declaration
  To what extent they mean to pay their debts.
That's called their capital; if they are wary
  They will not quote it at a sum immense.
The figure's immaterial – it may vary
  From eighteen million down to eighteenpence.
          I should put it rather low;
          The good sense of doing so
  Will be evident at once to any debtor.
          When it's left to you to say
          What amount you mean to pay,
  Why, the lower you can put it at the better.

They then proceed to trade with all who'll trust 'em,
  Quite irrespective of their capital
(It's shady, but it's sanctified by custom);
  Bank, Railway, Loan or Panama Canal.
You can't embark on trading too tremendous –
  It's strictly fair and based on common sense –
If you succeed your profits are stupendous –
  And if you fail, pop goes your eighteenpence.
          Make the money-spinner spin!
          For you only stand to win,
  And you'll never with dishonesty be twitted,
          For nobody can know,
          To a million or so,
  To what extent your capital's committed.

If you come to grief and creditors are craving
  (For nothing that is planned by mortal head
Is certain in this Vale of Sorrow – saving
  That one's liability is limited), –
Do you suppose that signifies perdition?
  If so you're but a monetary dunce –
You merely file a Winding-up Petition
  And start another company at once!
          Though a Rothschild you may be
          In your own capacity,

As a company you've come to utter sorrow –
    But the liquidators say
    'Never mind, you needn't pay',
So you start another company tomorrow!

W. S. GILBERT, *Utopia Limited; or, The Flowers of Progress* (1893)
Song by Mr Goldbury, a Company Promoter, afterwards Comptroller of
the Utopian Household, one of the Imported Flowers of Progress

Chapter One

He Challenged the Royal Prerogative

I only became a Chartered Accountant because my father told me to be one. When I left school in 1931 he said: 'You are not particularly bright; I doubt if anyone else would employ you. I have an accountancy business. I'll give you a job. You had better come into it.' I had no option. It was one way of earning a living, and earn a living one had to do! There was not much choice in the thirties. And what a bore an articled clerkship was! I would rather have been planting rubber in Malaya, been an actor, or done some interesting and glamorous job outside London, but unfortunately it was not for me. Work only becomes fun and exciting when you are good at it, and then all jobs become almost the same.

But all work was – and is – horribly boring. So it did not matter what kind of work I did. I believe one should do what one likes *as a hobby*, but never as work. At school they urge you to take up work with which you are sympathetic, with which you can fulfil yourself. Perhaps that is all right for someone who wants to go on the stage or be a painter, but for any other pursuit it is bad advice. Schools should ask their leavers not what they are interested in but what they are good at. The two are seldom the same. If a boy is good at quick thinking and figures, he may hate the idea but he should aim to become an accountant. If he is good at it, he may end up a manager, and then he will have the world at his feet.

A boy is interested in engineering and wants to become a civil engineer. He embarks on a long dreary training and starts at the very bottom of a firm where he plugs away day after day and very nearly dies of boredom. By the time it dawns on him that the work is unbearable he is trapped; he cannot escape and change to something else. Yet he chose to do it. No one else is to blame. When I found myself training to be an accountant, however, and became overwhelmed by the dullness of it all, I said that this was my father's blooming fault. I would never have chosen so unexciting a job as accountancy but, if I *had* to earn a living, which I did, it was as boringly good a way as any. If I had become an engine driver, after doing the Edinburgh to King's Cross run 500 times it would have become intolerably monotonous. In time the wheeling and dealing of a merchant banker, which sounds so exciting, becomes routine tick and bang, and hypnotically tedious.

For me, work began to become less boring as soon as I became reasonably good at it, when people came and asked me to help them. I could then expand and use the skills I had developed to do the kinds of thing I was interested in, the things I wanted to do. Doing work became playing games. The strictly earning-a-living work means leaving the office every day at five sharp because you want to go home and dig the garden. When work becomes fun, a game, the time spent on it is no longer hedged in by 'office hours'. I think I must have inherited this philosophy from my father, who by all accounts was the most thrusting and time-disregarding man of them all.

'One day the Monument will collapse and kill me.' The man who, according to my brother Norman, firmly believed in so unlikely an eventuality and insured himself against it was Oscar Berry, who gave my father his first job – as a fifteen-year-old office boy in 1900. Having to go and work in the shadow of the column which marks the spot where the Great Fire of London started in 1666 was less of a worry to the youthful William Henry Cork. He took a more phlegmatic view of life and took everything in his stride. I do not suppose there was a great deal of forward planning in the fact that he landed up with a firm of Chartered Accountants. Oscar Berry, Froude & Co. were engaged almost exclusively in work which became the speciality of my father, my brother, myself and my son.

Oscar Berry operated in what one might call the lower end of the profession: the retail trade – owner-managers of sweetshops, ironmongers, chemists, greengrocers and the like. For six years young Bill Cork worked in the City, lived at home and contributed to the family income, accumulating a nest-egg against the day when he could ask Maude Alice Nunn, a very clever Hampstead girl who had won an open scholarship to Oxford University, to marry him. Maude had won certificates at school for mathematics, physics, chemistry – and scripture. In 1906 she gave up her scholarship to marry the twenty-one-year-old Bill Cork, who by now had risen to a position of some responsibility in the busy office in Monument Square. They set up house in Finchley where my brother Leslie was born in 1908, Norman in 1910 and myself on 21 August 1913.

Of all the miscellaneous retail clients of Oscar Berry, Froude & Co., those who had had the most failures since the system of deeds for arranging with creditors had been introduced in 1888 were the members of the grocery and provision trades. In the light of the general prosperity which Britain had enjoyed in the first decade of the twentieth century, the number of failures in bankruptcy and by deeds of arrangement among retail traders had fallen from annual figures of 9,000 and 10,000 in the 1890s to 7,874 in 1912. In 1908 there had been 2,239 failed grocers; in 1912, 1,697. The small grocer was having to meet the competition of the Co-operative Movement, which aimed to eliminate the middle man and multiple-shop firms such as the Maypole Dairy, the Home and Colonial Stores, Liptons, Pearks and Cullens. The well-managed grocery shop was able to hold its own, but the incompetent quickly went to the wall.

An ill wind has never blown nobody no good at all, and it was the nature of Oscar Berry's specialisation that the higher the failure rate the more he prospered. A typical client in 1913 was Albert Cunningham of Letchworth, who a year previously had started business (as the late Sir Jack Cohen of Tesco had done) with what was described as 'a hawking round'. Six months later he opened a grocer's shop which took £14 a week at first, rising when times were good to £24, but never made anything but a loss. There was a meeting at Monument House with Cunningham's principal trade creditor in the chair, after which Oscar Berry issued a 'circular' stating that the grocer had liabilities to fifty-four suppliers amounting to £224 and assets of £142. 'No offer of composition was made and it was resolved to leave the estate for me to realise as best I could under a committee of inspection.' No punishment. No committal to the Fleet. It was no crime to have become insolvent. Just a tragedy. So the new spirit of the times decreed.

This was Oscar Berry's bread and butter – a service extended to other retail trades in and around London. In 1913, the year I was born, the handling of the insolvency business of the trade which made the greatest demands on this service, because it had the largest incidence of failure, the grocers and provision merchants, was entrusted to my father.

Precisely how this came about, I am not able to say; but it seems that some time in 1913, perhaps because he was getting on in years and was finding the volume of work overwhelming, Oscar Berry decided to break his firm up and apportion groups of clients within the same retail trade to different partners and senior men on his staff, who then left to form their own firms of insolvency accountants. Presumably these were the people who were already handling these sections of the Oscar Berry activity. Berry did not himself cease working altogether, but for some time at least continued to represent creditors and act as trustee when requested.

It was his plan that the insolvency work of the wholesale grocers

and provisions merchants should be handed over to three of his staff:
Stewart Percy Jackson, Herbert James Paterson and my father.
These three decided to form a partnership for which a draft inden-
ture was printed, a copy of which I have, setting up a firm 'in the
business or profession of Accountants, Valuers and Auctioneers' to
begin on 1 March 1913 under the style S. P. Jackson & Co. Jackson,
who was an auctioneer and valuer, agreed to prepare a balance-sheet
showing the financial position of 'his previous business' (?) and make
any credit balance his capital in the partnership. His salary was to be
£550 a year. My father's salary was to be £450, and Paterson's £250.
Jackson and Cork were each to take two-fifths of the profits, and
Paterson one-fifth. They each insured their lives for £1,000.

S. P. Jackson & Co., however, never came into being, for Stewart
Jackson died before the Articles of Partnership were signed. So, at
twenty-eight, my father went ahead with Herbert Paterson as his sole
partner and changed the firm's name to W. H. Cork & Co. The firm
was named after my father because he was the insolvency expert.
Insolvency depends on a 'personality' known for his expertise and
who is an extrovert and a good speaker. Paterson was a backroom
man and remained so throughout the partnership.

Each of the retail groups who had been clients of Oscar Berry had
their own trade association – the Confectionery Alliance, for
instance. The clients of W. H. Cork & Co. were all members of the
Wholesale Grocers and Provision Merchants Alliance of Eastcheap
Buildings, 19 Eastcheap, EC, and W. H. Cork & Co. were given a
retainer of £500 a year to organise the Alliance's Debt and Enquiry
Department, and relieve them of the responsibilities which failure
always involved. W. H. Cork & Co. were given offices at 19 Eastcheap, from which we only moved in the 1970s.

As in most cities, particular trades tended to collect in one area of
London, often giving their name to the street concerned: Milk
Street, Pudding Lane, Fish Street Hill, Poultry. The spicers,
pepperers and other victuallers who dealt 'in gross' (that is, in large
quantities), and for that reason came to be known as 'grossers' or
'grocers', had for centuries traded in Little Eastcheap which today is
Eastcheap.

My father was qualified but did not obtain that qualification by
examination, although he was later made a member of the London
Association of Accountants, later the Certified Accountants. Success
in the kind of work in which he was engaged depended not on
expertise in accountancy but on *personality* – and he had this in
abundance. He had to fight for his living. He had to make a quick and
lasting impression at meetings of creditors by the way he expressed
himself, by the questions he asked, by having a presence that made

people sit up and take notice. The representatives of creditors who filled the room began the day as equals, but by the end of it, when it came to winding up the estate, one of them had emerged as the dominating character whom the others were happy to appoint as trustee or liquidator. My father managed to be both efficient and popular. In those early days at Eastcheap he earned the enviable reputation of being able to control creditors' meetings. This was the key to insolvency work, whether in the grocery trade or in any other activity.

The typical creditors' meeting ended with the debtor's estate being realised under a deed of assignment with a trustee and a committee of inspection consisting of representatives of the three principal creditors. This was the routine with which my father had become familiar as a member of Oscar Berry's staff, and was now to follow, day in day out, as his own master, with presumably a growing staff of juniors and clerks handling the great amount of paperwork which such a service demanded. As case followed case, he became convinced that what he should aim for in every instance possible was what we call 'reconstruction'. This was an extremely rare approach. Insolvency practitioners of those days wanted a quick turnover above all. Businesses in trouble would be shut up quickly and everything sold by auction.

My father divided insolvency cases into two types: the Dud Business, which no kind of first aid could ever make profitable; and the Good Business, which had run into trouble for some reason. The most serious trouble which a Good Business could encounter was being too successful. If you had a business, he used to say, with a capital of £12,000, you could finance that amount of stock and book debts; but if you were wildly successful, and your turnover went up, the capital required by a little business with a turnover of £30,000 would not finance an exercise with a turnover five times that amount. You could get into financial trouble by success. You could have a sudden setback, lose some money by a burglary or have a fire, but you had a Good Business. All you wanted was time or further capital, or increased and improved management; or preferably all four. Where a little man became too big and got into trouble with his creditors, my father could hold the creditors at bay, get them to accept payment by instalments and then hand the business back to the little man. This was 'reconstruction', which we endeavoured to apply throughout our years as insolvency accountants wherever circumstances made it practicable.

The First World War started eleven months after I was born, and in the four years it took to run its course the climate of opinion and

social attitudes changed at a pace and in a way which made
Edwardian England unrecognisable. The main rôle of accountancy
in the 1920s was straightforward book-keeping and audit. (This
continued to be so until the 1960s.) For an independent audit to
carry weight it had to be signed by a qualified accountant who was a
member of one of the recognised professional institutions. But no
qualification was needed for insolvency work, and for that reason
other accountants tended to regard it as something less than respectable. What my father was doing, however, took him outside the usual
confines of accountancy. By the end of the war his main activity had
become the reorganisation of good concerns which had been badly
managed and had run themselves into the ground. He then sold the
reorganised business, which now belonged to the creditors, to their
benefit. When he found a business was incapable of being built up,
he sold off the assets by auction. Thus inside W. H. Cork & Co. there
grew up a business agency, valuation and auctioneering department.

It was the reputation which my father had won for auctioneering
in the grocery trade that led to W. H. Cork & Co. being appointed by
the Government in 1919 to sell by auction surplus food-supplies
accumulated by the Ministry of Food in stores all over Britain – the
'security reserves' for the civilian population and stocks for the home
forces. To attract buyers the sales were advertised in the different
locations, and then my father toured Britain personally conducting
auctions in corn exchanges and market-halls.

It was a very comprehensive and exhausting exercise but highly
rewarding. When, in February 1922, Sir William Mitchell-Thomson,
Secretary to the Board of Trade, was asked in a Parliamentary
Question the value of the stocks in the hands of the Ministry of Food
including the Wheat and Sugar Commission which had now been
disposed of, he gave a figure of £58 million. W. H. Cork & Co.'s
commission on that lot must have been a tidy sum.

The Government may have been grateful to him for that, though I
doubt whether they were as effusive with their thanks for the change
in case law which was made as a result of hearings in the High Court,
Court of Appeal and House of Lords between 1921 and 1923.

During the war the Food Controller appointed H. J. Webb & Co.
(Smithfield, London) Ltd as an agent for the sale of the frozen
rabbits which the Ministry of Food imported from Australia to meet
the threatened shortage of food in Britain. The company made
contracts for sale on behalf of the Ministry, delivered the rabbits to
the purchasers, and collected the money which it then had to hand
over, less commission and expenses, to the Ministry. On 9 July 1920
the company went into voluntary liquidation and was found to be
insolvent, owing the Ministry of Food (that is, the Government, the

Crown) the sum of £9,689 5s 10d, money received for rabbits sold but never paid over.

My father was appointed liquidator of H. J. Webb & Co. He admitted that the debt due to the Ministry was proven, but alleged it was nonsense to say that, just because it was to a government department, a 'commercial' debt of that kind was a 'Crown debt'. That phrase, he contended, meant money owing as tax. He formally denied that Webb's £9,689 was a Crown debt and argued that, even if it were, the Crown was only entitled to a dividend *pari passu* with all the other creditors.

The Government's legal advisers were appalled, but my father did not give a damn for them, and when the Government took him personally to court as the liquidator to substantiate his assertion he briefed one of the best brains at the Bar, Sir John Simon. The case was heard in the Chancery Division of the High Court before Mr Justice Lawrence in December 1921. The judge ruled in the Government's favour. Webb & Co.'s debt, he said, was a Crown debt; moreover the Food Controller was entitled to priority of payment since the Crown's prerogative right of priority still existed in the case of a company being wound up, though it was extinguished in a case of bankruptcy. He was bound by the decision *in re* Henley & Co. of 1878, which stated that the Crown was not bound by the Companies Act of 1862 and had priority in a winding-up.

Undeterred by this initial setback, my father took the matter to the Court of Appeal where it was heard before Lord Sterndale, Master of the Rolls, and two others. Sir John Simon advised him to admit the £9,689 was a Crown debt, but to claim that the case was in no way governed by the decision *in re* Henley & Co.

It was for Sir Gordon Hewart, a future Lord Chief Justice, acting for the Crown, to raise the matter of the royal prerogative. The highest courts in the land had upheld it, he said. The leading case, *in re* Henley & Co., was one of winding up not bankruptcy. The property had not passed out of the company's possession. The lower court had held that the Crown was still at liberty to pursue its 'extreme rights' against the company's property, and was thus entitled to priority. But, apart from that, under the wider *prerogative* the claim of the Crown must prevail.

Sir John Simon, in reply, agreed with the opinion of a former Master of the Rolls that, where a matter was provided for by statute, the prerogative was merged in that statute. The Court of Appeal agreed with him and allowed the appeal.

So my father's stand had been justified. But of course the Attorney-General was not going to let a decision on so important a matter stay there, and in July 1923 appealed against the upsetting of

Mr Justice Lawrence's judgement to the House of Lords. The
Attorney-General, Sir Douglas Hogg (later the first Lord Hailsham
and Lord Chancellor), and the Solicitor-General, Sir Thomas
Inskip, appeared for the Board of Trade, which had taken over the
responsibilities of the now defunct Ministry of Food and its Food
Controller. Sir Douglas pitched in at once with the insistence that,
since the time of Lord Coke, no one had ever questioned the right of
the Crown to be paid debts to it in priority to debts due to a subject.
Such a prerogative could never be taken away by statute, and in fact
no statute had ever attempted to do this. Sir John Simon claimed
there was nothing in the statute of 1908 to show that the order of
payment should be first specified Crown debts, then unspecified
Crown debts, then subject's debts.

Lord Birkenhead gave it as his opinion that the decision of the
Court of Appeal was right and that the Crown's appeal against it
failed. Lord Atkinson agreed. The expression 'Crown debts' was
unfortunate, inasmuch as it suggested that the sovereign claimed the
right to be paid debts due to him to the exclusion of the rights of his
subjects either for his own use or for the public use. 'Ages ago these
words would probably be considered to apply to taxes or suchlike,
but now, and especially during the war, when the different Departments of Government became more like great trading and industrial
corporations than anything else, it is obvious that it leads to misunderstanding when the trade debts due to these corporations are
sought, by the exercise of the royal prerogative, to be recovered in
priority to those due to subject creditors.'

Lord Shaw of Dunfermline, in a concurring judgement, declared
any 'super-eminent right, whether under the name of prerogative or
otherwise', to have disappeared. The expression 'Crown debts'
suggested that something was being claimed higher than that justice
which was distributed among subjects of the Crown under ordinary
commercial contracts which did not allow for the operation of
preference. 'These questions are enormously important,' he said.
'They will have, unless Parliament itself interposes to clarify the
situation, to be decided one day.' Lords Wrenbury and Carson
concurred, so dismissal of the Crown's appeal against the Court of
Appeal's reversal of the High Court judgement in their favour was
unanimous. Thus that summer of 1923, at the instance of my father,
legal history was made and a far-reaching legal precedent
established. Sixty years later, as chairman of a government inquiry, I
remembered my father's stand in the H. J. Webb case when recommending the abolition of *all* preferential claims. Of course, as usual,
the Crown cheated and changed the law a little to keep some
preferential claims, but mainly only taxes.

Congratulations came in from all quarters. H. J. Webb & Co. were of course by no means relieved of their 'Crown debt', but the judgement ensured that other creditors were not deprived by the Board of Trade extracting from Webb's resources the whole of its debt, leaving only enough to pay other creditors a proportion of what was owed them.

The press welcomed this updating of the concept of the royal prerogative and were effusive in their tributes to the humble subject of the King who, in the steps of Hampden and Wilkes, had refused to be awed by the majesty of the law but, sensing an unfairness and an injustice, had set about giving substance, in terms of the times he lived in, to a concept which was still being applied only because of 'tradition'. A question had been settled in law, stated a long leader in the *Grocer* of 28 July 1923, 'which means a considerable saving to the trade as against any Department of the State which ventures into competition with private firms or companies; and well-deserved congratulations are due to William Henry Cork upon this result of his efforts to secure that if the State competes in commerce and industry, it must compete on level terms'. Something similar happened in my time over the Stern bankruptcy (notorious during the Fringe Bank crisis), not as important but more amusing.

Amongst the creditors in Willi Stern's bankruptcy were the Crown Agents, for approximately £30 million, which there is no doubt that Willi Stern's empire had borrowed from the Crown Agents. During the course of organising the scheme, it suddenly occurred to me to ask what kind of organisation the Crown Agents was, because before I dealt with the Stern case I travelled from Singapore on an aeroplane with a senior member of the Crown Agents, and I had asked him this question. He gave me a long explanation, which said it was not part of the Crown; it was an independent organisation which, like Topsy, had 'just growed'. It therefore occurred to me that it might not be a bank – and, if it was not the Crown, was it an unlicensed moneylender? I thought it was extremely unlikely, because there would be some legislation on the subject, but I decided we ought to consult Counsel, rather than take a risk. We consulted Counsel, and came back with the surprising answer that they did not come under the cover of the banks, and they were unlicensed moneylenders. Therefore they did not have a valid claim. The Moneylenders Act was never intended to apply to people like this, but to stop young people with wealthy families borrowing money and being made bankrupt. Nevertheless, that was the law, so I thought it would be wrong simply to reject the claim. I got in touch with Sir John Cuckney, who was the Chief Crown Agent and explained this to him, and he laughed and said: 'Thanks for pointing it out. It's absolute nonsense.' Subsequently, he was highly indignant on the subject, and the Treasury Solicitors came and pointed out to us that it was the Crown Agents, and therefore they were not unlicensed moneylenders. I said: 'Well, I'm very sorry, but I am advised you are. My suggestion is that you pass legislation – retrospective legislation – to cover this point, because I do not want to reject the claim out of hand, but I am not prepared to be accused afterwards of negligence in accepting a claim that was invalid.' They huffed and puffed, and tried to use all their pressure, but I just said: 'No. Prove to me or go and change the law.' There was considerable pressure exercised on this, but in the end they accepted that they were not exempt, and the final proof came when Parliament passed a new short Act, Crown Agents (Unlicensed Moneylenders) Act. It was no great victory, but it was very amusing at the time.

My father was able to give the time which such diversions occupied in the knowledge that his office would continue to run smoothly under the loyal and efficient supervision of his partner H. J. Paterson. The two of them made a good business team: the personable WHC who impressed audiences with his eloquence and drive, the dogged HJP who excelled as a manager and administrator. But on the personal level there is no use denying they were incompatible. In each other's presence they rowed continuously. But the auctioning of the government food-stocks took my father away from the office for weeks on end, and in any event his main field of operation was outside Eastcheap in different parts of London, in provincial hotels, halls and assembly rooms.

An office staff of a dozen or so grew up under Paterson during the 1920s. Overall administration was in the hands of an employee who imposed an iron discipline on those under him, but failed the employer who gave him his confidence by embezzling the then quite considerable sum of £460. He was not prosecuted or handed over to the police. But to my father, who had come to rely on him implicitly, it was like a slap in the face.

In those days the rare big industrial failures, as I have said, were handled by the big firms of chartered accountants. The Eastcheap firm became involved in smaller-scale everyday occurrences which never made the headlines of the nationals but only the inner pages of the local and trade press: the grocer who could not compete with the non-profit-making cut-price Co-op, which had come to the lower end of the High Street; the ironmonger where co-ordinated control gave way to divided management as the sole proprietor got older and lost his grip; the wine and spirit merchants whose founder had died and his good-for-nothing nitwit of a son with the expensive education, who had never deigned to start at the bottom, quickly ran a once-profitable business into the ground. Inheritance and death caused a large proportion of the failures which fell to W. H. Cork & Co. Though unspectacular and humdrum, they soon constituted a case-history of solid achievement which brought the firm not only publicity but also respectability. The elegant Bill Cork with the easy turn of phrase and commanding presence became a popular figure in the small village that was the City of London.

For the purpose of electing members of the Corporation of London, the City, as any other municipality, is divided into wards. Eastcheap is in Billingsgate ward. Those entitled to vote are the tenants of property. In a non-residential area like the City that means the principals of firms occupying office buildings – partners, not directors of companies. In each ward of the Square Mile these are numerically very small, and everyone knows everyone. Every ward had its voters' club – every ward, that is to say, in the 1920s except Billingsgate ward. The reason was that it was composed of two irreconcilable groups: a so-called Upper Ward of Eastcheap occupied by City businessmen and a Lower Ward, Billingsgate Market, occupied by fish salesmen. Never the twain would meet. Since the ward had no club it had no organised representation. So, grasping the nettle again, the forty-three-year-old Bill Cork set about bringing the two groups together. By 1927, by dint of all the tact and charm he could muster, plus an element of bullying when resistance needed a firm hand, he had formed the Billingsgate Ward Club with himself as Master. He took the chair at the club's first annual dinner in the Fishmongers' Hall on 2 November 1928 flanked by the Lord Mayor, Sir Charles Batho, Sir Herbert Austin the motor manufac-turer, and the Prime Warden of the Fishmongers' Company. Among the diners were his old boss Oscar Berry, his partner H. J. Paterson who was honorary secretary, Oliver Sunderland who was an honor-ary auditor, and my brother Leslie who was studying law. At fifteen, I was not old enough for that kind of thing. I was at Berkhamsted School, which I had joined the Christmas term of the year before.

This put my father on the map so far as the City of London was concerned. Soon the clients of W. H. Cork & Co. included enter-prises who were served by his grocer clients: hotels, restaurants and at least two nightclubs; and from hotel and catering to the infant industry which seemed to hold out so much promise after the formation of the British Broadcasting Company in 1922, the manufacture of wireless sets.

Maudslay Baynes had built up a good business by supplying the big London stores with radio receivers, loudspeakers, headphones and the rest. In 1926 he made an agreement with H. H. Havercroft to let him market his 'Langham (Diamond Clear) Radio' receiver. Baynes undertook to open an account with the Midland Bank and 'to finance production' of the sets. He engaged a Mr Newman as salesman, with whom, however, he soon quarrelled. Langham Radio, a potentially thriving business, was soon in a mess. The relations between Baynes and Newman reached breaking-point. Whatever arrangement he had with Newman, which he believed fell short of partnership, Baynes wanted to terminate it. He had heard of my father's successes in unravelling tangled skeins of this kind and came to Eastcheap to seek advice. What should he do? Accept Newman's resignation? Sell the factory? Inject more capital? Recruit more high-powered management? It was an early example of the kind of exercise with which the firm was to become more and more involved in the years to come – a mixture of human, financial, managerial and technical problems, the solving of which was outside the conventional activities of a run-of-the-mill accountancy firm.

The modern accountant had come a long way from the days when he merely added up the figures. The conclusions he reached from his computations and the advice he based on them made him personally responsible – a fact which was forcibly brought home to the profession when in 1931 one of their number appeared in the dock alongside Lord Kylsant, chairman of the Royal Mail Steam Packet Company. This was H. J. Moreland, senior partner of a large international firm of chartered accountants. The accountancy profession read the daily reports of the Kylsant trial with some trepidation; and, though Moreland was able to go home at the end of it, the fact that so distinguished a member had had to stand in the dock at the Old Bailey accused of fraud underlined, as nothing else had done, the serious nature of their responsibilities and the dire consequences of failing to appreciate it.

If every case of insolvency or bankruptcy in which my father became involved did not end up in court, almost every problem presented to him had its legal aspect. W. H. Cork & Co. was not a combined accountancy and law firm – there was no such thing – but it was the next-best thing. For having his eldest son an industrial lawyer in nearby Finsbury Square – Leslie had become the fourth partner of Oppenheimers at the age of twenty-five in 1933 – he had direct access to a fund of legal knowledge pertaining to the Companies Acts, bankruptcy laws and every legal aspect of insolvency, which enabled him to give his clients a two-pronged service 'all in the family'.

The third prong, the business agency involving the buying and selling of companies, depended to a large extent on advertising which could never be indulged in by a member of the Institute of Chartered

Accountants. So, in order to have all sections of W. H. Cork & Co.'s business covered by his three sons, my father decided that his second son, Norman, should never set out on the path that led to qualification as a Chartered Accountant, which he did not think was as important as getting him into the business quickly – particularly as Norman was an extrovert and certainly had no desire to be a student.

As a young man Norman had ambitions to be a surgeon or a diplomat, but when he was nineteen settled for being drawn into the family business and playing the part in it which his father had cut out for him. He began his career in the time-honoured rôle of general dogsbody sticking on stamps, tying up parcels and running errands traditionally associated with Starting At The Bottom. With the advent of Leslie Lansley as managing clerk, my father had Norman help him to develop the business agency side. So that he knew what he was talking about, Norman spent six months serving tins of peas, bags of flour and packets of tea behind the counter of a Paddington grocery store. It offered more scope than the post room, but he does not look back on the experience with any great affection.

When Dick Mitchell left in 1935 to go it alone, Father took Norman away from Lansley and put him in charge of the insolvency department. He had Started At The Bottom; now he was being Thrown In At The Deep End. He had no experience in insolvency matters, but he had the two Arthurs to turn to: Arthur Bray and Arthur White. The latter had developed into a shrewd and know-ledgeable operator (and was to remain with us until his retirement as chief accountant in 1975). Norman set about learning the insolvency business with characteristic thoroughness, and sought as soon as possible to acquire the technique perfected by his father, of dominating the all-important creditors' meeting.

He has never forgotten the first meeting he attended as a young man of twenty-three in 1935. 'Petrified' is the adjective he uses to describe his state of mind when confronting the meeting of farmers assembled in a church hall in the Welsh hills. After the accountant acting for the dairy who owed a large sum to his client, the new Milk Marketing Board, had read his report, Norman rose nervously to his feet. No sooner had he said that he acted for Milk Marketing Board creditors than a heavily built farmer standing at the back of the hall brandished his stick and shouted: 'I've been waiting for you chaps to come down here. You've buggered up the whole of our milk business.' Whereupon he advanced towards the platform in a manner that threatened physical violence. It was a moment for parley, and with commendable composure Norman calmed the Welshman by insisting that he could not expect miracles from an organisation which had only been in existence a year. 'Look at it this

way,' said Norman. 'If you put a bull in a field of heifers, you won't
have calves the next day.' 'No,' replied the farmer, 'but you might get
a few contented faces.'

The laughter which followed this sally broke the tension, and the
meeting proceeded. It was the first step in the process by which N. B.
Cork assumed the mantle of W. H. Cork in this highly sensitive field.

My father had his finger in every pie, but now that Lansley had lost
Norman to insolvency he became particularly active in the business
agency side. The volume of business-transfer work was now very
considerable. W. H. Cork & Co. sold cheap but potentially good
businesses, which had been spoilt by mismanagement, to go-ahead
operators who could build them up again. The grateful purchaser
invariably opted to entrust the audit work to the firm, but W. H.
Cork & Co. did not have an audit department, so they were turning
away a source of income. My father would recommend the firm who
did his own audit, Messrs Gully, Stephens, Ross & Gregory. But for
him so unsatisfactory an arrangement could not be permanent. His
plan for remedying it centred round myself. I was to become the
member of the family who was the *Chartered* Accountant. So after I
left Berkhamsted in July 1930 with eight School Certificate credits I
began studying for my Institute exams. I sat for the Intermediate in
November 1934 and heard that I had passed the following January. I
became fully qualified in June 1937.

I had married Nina before the war as soon as I became a partner.
We had become engaged as soon as I passed my Intermediate, and
it was agreed that we would be married on my becoming a partner.
I became a partner in January 1937, and we were married on
12 June 1937. Sally was born in June 1944, just before I went
overseas.

And what better firm to be articled to than Gully, Stephens, Ross
& Gregory, which had such close ties with 19 Eastcheap?

Well before I qualified, my father was ready to complete the final
stage of his plan. He had known H. J. Gully for many years, and the
two of them agreed to form a firm of Chartered Accountants to be
called W. H. Cork Gully & Co., with myself when qualified and
Gully as partners, for the purpose of audit work. It had its office in
Broad Street Place. The division of profits was to be a third to Gully,
a third to myself, and a third to my father and Paterson, which meant
they got a sixth each. The new firm by no means took the place of
W. H. Cork & Co., which continued to function as the partnership of
my father and Paterson, with the same management at 19 Eastcheap
which included my brother Norman, Leslie Lansley, Arthur Bray,
Arthur White and the rest.

The actual insolvency work of the firm each year was unpredictable. No one was more aware of this than my father. For so long as things went right, the prizes were very considerable, though far from excessive in view of the specialised expertise required. The fees paid in liquidations, trusteeships and receiverships where the bank had a floating charge were very good. They had to be agreed by a Committee of Inspection of Creditors, but they generally amounted to about $7\frac{1}{2}$ per cent of the assets realised and $7\frac{1}{2}$ per cent of the amount paid to the creditors. Anyone who volunteered to become the receiver of a failed company where the remuneration did not exceed 5 per cent did so in the knowledge that he was personally liable if, in the course of his attempts to put the company back on its feet, things began to go wrong. He considered himself lucky to dispose of a succession of cases without the intervention of the 'unforeseen circumstances' which he knew would play havoc with the calculated risk which he took every time he became involved in another insolvency.

It was bound to happen one day, and it happened to my father in the summer of 1938. How could he have known, when he agreed to become receiver of the Regent Gramophone Company and borrowed money from the bank and arranged credit with suppliers in order to complete and sell the half-finished £100 gramophones still in their factory, that from America would come a combined radio and gramophone which everyone called a 'radiogram' and which put paid to the selling of straightforward gramophones at £10, let alone £100? He was left holding a baby nobody wanted – and he paid dearly for it. I am not sure of the precise figures, but I believe Father had to find something in the region of £50,000 of his own money to pay off the bank loans, the bills of the component manufacturers, the wages of the staff, the rent and the electricity charges. This nearly ruined him. The rainy day against which my mother had stashed away the expensive jewellery which my father had generously bought her in the good days had arrived. The situation was not helped by Paterson choosing this time to threaten dissolving the partnership, and putting a further strain on a relationship which had never been exactly harmonious.

My father faced it bravely and rode the crisis, still driving to his appointments in his Rolls-Royce and still making witty speeches at City banquets as of old. He was certainly in the ascendant in City politics. For long a member of the Worshipful Company of Horners, he became their Renter Warden. In June 1938 he was elected to the Common Council of the City of London for Billingsgate ward in succession to his friend Bracewell Smith, MP, who had just become an alderman. W. H. Cork was the only candidate for the vacancy, and his nomination was unanimously supported by the Ward Club which he had created. He was proposed by Sir Harry Bird, who in doing so reminded members that Mr Cork had been in business in Billingsgate for thirty-nine years.

He was frequently being asked to make up one of the reception committees for visiting royalty and statesmen. In November 1938, for instance, he helped organise the reception and luncheon which the Corporation of London gave to the King of Romania whose country, turned Eastern-bloc republic, I was to visit some forty years later as Lord Mayor of London.

With the Munich Crisis of 1938 giving us advance notice that another armed conflict with Germany seemed inevitable, any plans I might have had for developing the new W. H. Cork Gully & Co. seemed disappointingly irrelevant. I joined the Honourable Artillery Company as a recruit and attended their camp that summer. Father would send the Rolls to collect me for a slap-up meal at home, and when I returned in it to Bulford the sentries thought I was a visiting general and presented arms. I was again training with the HAC when war was declared the following September and was in uniform 'for the duration'. W. H. Cork Gully continued to operate without me of course, but – in a sense luckily – insolvency business fell off. Under wartime conditions it was less easy for companies to go bankrupt. There was little opportunity for over-trading since everything was done on allocation. The Government, through the Ministry of Food, allocated stocks to grocery shops in accordance with the number of customers they had and the volume they had ordered on average in previous years. Allocation was organised by the trade associations, and Herbert Paterson took an active part in this. Apart from this, the Wartime Liabilities Act relieved debtors of their liability to pay until the war was over. There was a limitation on credit, and enforcement procedures were made subject to control.

My father's health deteriorated rapidly in 1940. Cancer was diagnosed, and after a game of golf in the morning – he was a member of the London Society of Golf Captains and a good player – he drove himself to the hospital on Sunday, 15 December for an exploratory operation which was to take place on the Tuesday. He died on the Wednesday morning, 18 December 1940. He was only fifty-five. A memorial service was held at St Margaret Pattens church on 30 December.

The memorial service was held the day after the bombing of London, when a large part of the City was burnt out. I was in York with my regiment, and I came down on the night train to King's Cross. I arrived about midnight and had to sleep in London. There was an air raid. Everybody was underground, so I went to the

Salvation Army home to sleep for the night, and no one was there. I took a bed and slept by myself, rather than go and find somewhere underground. Of course King's Cross was not hit, and I was perfectly safe. The next morning I had to get to Eastcheap, to the memorial service. There were no taxis, no cars, the streets were full of water from hoses; hoses were everywhere, and I could find no means of transport. So I put my tin helmet on, and my gas-mask at alert, and went up to a fire engine which was going into the City and said: 'Are you going into the City? Take me with you.' They thought I was on duty and delivered me to Eastcheap. When I got to St Margaret Pattens, thinking that I was rather clever, I found that all my father's friends had got there and the church was full. That was the attitude of the City of London in 1940, and how little the people were scared of Hitler and his worst bombing efforts.

My father's death left Herbert Paterson in charge at 19 Eastcheap as the sole partner. His share in W. H. Cork Gully & Co. was inherited *pro rata* by Gully, Paterson and myself. Father had no outside assets; all his money was tied up inside W. H. Cork & Co., so there was little he could leave his widow. Indeed, the day he died the firm had a big overdraft in the region of £20,000. After Leslie agreed to indemnify him for his share Paterson entered into a deed of covenant to provide my mother with an annuity.

My mother was a very able person, and a first-class mathematician to boot. She completed the Accountancy Analysis which he found was beyond him. It was used by the firm up to the war and was frequently consulted after it.

My mother, left alone, saved up quite an amount of money. She then started to play the Stock Exchange after the war. My eldest brother, who doubted her ability, being a cautious solicitor, arranged that there should be a limit on the amount she bought and sold. He proved entirely wrong. Her investments were first-class, and she in fact trebled or quadrupled her money, and when she died she left her three sons quite a little sum. But her main contribution to this story was keeping a highly volatile, hail-fellow-well-met, popular extrovert on the right tracks. She was the anchor, he the sail – and the two made a perfect partnership. Indeed, without her constraining influence I doubt if my father would have been able to keep W. H. Cork & Co. going; as Norman has said, the Old Man would have blown it. And then there would be no more story to tell.

Part Two

The New Team

Toujours la Même Chose

No banking system can be invented which will suspend the economical laws under which improvident trading leads to ruin, and the best service that the State can render in this and similar matters is to interfere as little as possible with the operation of those laws.

BERTRAM WODEHOUSE CURRIE, who became
a partner of Glyn Mills Bank in 1864,
in a letter to *The Times* signed
'W' concerning the Baring Crisis
of 1890 when an £18 million fund
was raised to save the Baring Bank

Chapter Two

A Reputation for Being Constructive

During the war I became a lieutenant-colonel, serving mostly in the Central Mediterranean Force, and I ended up running all the catering services at Allied Forces Headquarters, and the Army Catering Corps and all the requisitioned hotels in Italy. I learnt a lot about running businesses.

W. H. Cork & Co. soldiered on throughout the war with no Cork and little insolvency business, other than clearing up the old estates. In an insolvency firm it takes several years to clear up the old estates and therefore there was a coverage of work, but in addition Paterson was appointed to various food trade committees and associations, such as Dried Fruits, and this gave the firm of W. H. Cork & Co. an adequate income during the war. In view of the continued operation of controls and the elimination of competition in the food trade, it seemed likely that on the return of peace the insolvency business would increase and prosper, which in fact it did. With regard to W. H. Cork Gully & Co., on the death of Harry Gully in 1943 I had to make a new partnership agreement with Paterson. I was in the Army at the time, and Paterson sent for me and said: 'Under the arrangements which were originally made, you now own two-thirds of W. H. Cork Gully & Co., and I only own one-third. If you want me to carry on while you are in the Army, then this has got to be reversed, and I will own two-thirds of the company and you will own one-third.' Since I was in the forces, I thought this was extremely unfair, because it was a very small part of the Cork business, and Paterson did not have the skill or the qualifications to run it. It was in fact ticking over, being run by Fred Barger and Eric Harding, but if I wanted a business to come back to I had to agree. Amongst the people I consulted was my eldest brother, Leslie, and Walter Tickler's father. Walter had been articled with me, and we always intended that he should be a partner with me once he was qualified; and so, very reluctantly, I came to this agreement, so when I came back after the war I would only have one-third instead of a two-thirds share. However, I had run the business before the war, and the goodwill was entirely with me. Fred Barger was the manager of the firm while I was away. It was a very, very small business. There was Eric Harding and one girl secretary, and the whole operation was conducted from one room in W. H. Cork & Co.'s office. The turnover was about £2,000 to £3,000 per annum, so that on demob – apart from the fact that I had something to come to and an income – the situation was not very promising.

On returning to the office, life was not very hopeful. I had an income, which in those circumstances was not a bad thing, as a lot of people didn't. I was now a very junior partner to Paterson. Norman had come out of the Army after me and got himself a job as the sales director of a company manufacturing electrical and radio components. I picked up the reins of W. H. Cork Gully & Co., and actually after a few days it seemed like I had never left. I adjusted myself to the City at the age of thirty-three, and the requirements of Civvy Street, in my civvy office and my demob suit, and focused my mind on audit work, in which I was most interested. My salary was £500 per year, and a one-third share of the profits. It was a little lonely coming back. Nobody particularly wanted the returning soldiers. Everybody in the City was settled in. Even the old restaurant, the Falstaff, where I had eaten with my father for many years before the war as an articled clerk, and where all the waitresses used to be dolly girls, was now full of people who had dealt in the food trade during the war, many of whom were suspect and many of whom were not to last for very long. Tables were all taken by regulars; nobody wanted you. It was even difficult to buy a newspaper, because you were not a regular and newspapers were in short supply. Fortunately, I had the name of Cork, and City people remembered the name and remembered me. That helped a lot. I joined the Ward Club, which my father had founded; and, in spite of everybody recommending me not to do it, stood for Common Councilman and was elected. It was very amusing. The Alderman sent for me and said: 'You know, Kenneth, you ought to wait for your turn. We do not have elections in Eastcheap.' I said: 'Well, I thought an election was essential.' He said: 'You'll lose.' I said: 'I know I'll lose.' The Deputy Alderman sent for me and said the same thing. Leslie Lansley, who was my father's managing clerk, now an important person, and secretary of the Ward Club, was standing. As more than one person was standing, there had to be an election. Leslie said: 'You know, Kenneth, you'll be defeated, and you will make yourself look silly. You've registered your note that you want to get it. Wait your time.' I went on to stand, and when Leslie found I was going to stand he then withdrew and I went in unopposed as a very young Common Councilman. In those days, anybody under fifty was rarely elected. Herbert Paterson was very concerned to see that the last Cork was kept very much in his place, but one had to work and keep one's professional relationship as amicable as possible.

It was not, however, to be for long. In September 1947 there was a tragic accident in his house, when his wife unfortunately shot him. This event changed the direction of my life. It was obvious that W. H. Cork & Co. was going to be sold, and so I got in touch with Alan Paterson, Herbert's son, who was an extremely nice man and a lawyer and his father's executor, saying I wanted to buy W. H. Cork & Co. I had very little money, if any. I bought it on the never-never, and put my entire demob pay from the Army into it. Meanwhile, of course, by Paterson dying, I was the sole partner of W. H. Cork Gully & Co., so I brought W. H. Cork & Co. into it and became the sole partner of it and paid Paterson's estate £2,485 1s 8d, which to me at that time was an enormous sum. That settled Cork Gully, and then I had to buy W. H. Cork & Co., which I bought for £4,500 (at the time you could buy quite a good house for about £5,000), less a credit of £2,000 for clearing up the old liquidations. I paid by instalments. I suppose I was technically insolvent. I took over the lease of the offices, and there was I with no business, or very little, owning my father's company and the audit practice of Cork Gully. We made a net profit of £798 in 1945–6 and £1,865 in 1946–7. I was looking for a profit of £2,500 in 1947–8. I invited Norman to come back, as he was the only one who understood insolvency, and he joined us, and my brother Leslie who was a partner of Oppen-heimers, and quite a senior partner, helped us to re-establish the Cork accountancy–law axis of prewar days. I was not very keen to engage in insolvency, about which I knew nothing. I saw my future as a Chartered Accountant lying in audit work, which began to return, and all our old clients came back, and were very, very supportive. Norman came back, and persuaded us to undertake insolvency work, and he would go out and get in the work. As he was not a qualified Chartered Accountant he did not become a partner, but we came to an arrangement where he received a percentage on the work which he brought in, which would have been, and always has been, approximately the same amount of income I was earning as the sole partner. I did not at first intend to become personally involved, for the reasons I have stated, but I determined that if we did insolvency we would do it in the way that Chartered Accountants should, or at least as I thought they should. I had done one or two odd insolvency jobs before the war, and I was clearing up the cases which Paterson had left behind, and then it became necessary to attend a meeting of creditors. I knew very little about it. Norman had not yet joined, so I spoke to him on the telephone. He told me what to do, so I went to the meeting of creditors, which fortunately was in the grocery trade, and stood up and told everybody what I thought ought to be done. I realised that nobody knew anything about it, either, after the six years of no insolvency work being about; because my name was Cork they elected me, and I became an insolvency accountant, about which I knew little or nothing.

I think our great good fortune was that we started with entirely new ideas. The old way of doing insolvency was just to shut up and sell up, and that we were not prepared to do. Norman, of course, at first wanted to do it the old way – it was the way he understood – but I reckoned, and spent my life believing, that business was a national asset, and that we would do far better if we kept the businesses alive and sold them as going concerns. This is the way we worked.

We also decided that there was scope for 'schemes' – schemes, which I will describe later, whereby the advantage we could use was that if you continued a business and sold the business, and did not put it into liquidation, then the previous losses would be a credit to your tax, which of course at that time was very, very high indeed. So we in fact developed a plan. Norman, who had a very ingenious mind, would go out to meetings where everybody was doing it the old way, and promise everybody the earth if we did the job, and what trained my brain was trying to find a way of doing what Norman had promised; and, strangely enough, we succeeded.

Norman clearly had got the message about schemes, and he thought of things which I might never have thought of; but, then, he would never have been able to put them into practice, so it was a very good partnership. The problem was that, as we, the newcomers, came back and started getting the work in, those already in the insolvency world, who in my opinion were not very constructive, suddenly realised that we were walking away with the work. Their method was that all the insolvency practitioners would meet before a meeting of creditors, state the amount of creditors each person was representing, and then the one with the most would go for the job, and later share out his fees with all the other people who had voted for him. This of course was illegal, as was touting for business, and we did not want any part in anything like that. Anyway, it was ridiculous, because if you actually did the work you could not afford to share the profits with anybody else, otherwise you were clearly charging too much or you were making a loss.

Our practice, at first, was almost entirely in the grocery trade, but very quickly what we were doing was getting us into other trades, particularly with Leslie's help, because Leslie's firm was a big firm and was dealing with a number of cases where his clients were creditors of businesses. One of the first insolvency cases which we started and handled on our own was Godfrey Thornfield, a client of Oppenheimers, who became insolvent in 1947. We called the meeting of their creditors, and put our plans to them, which were well received, and we kept the job. We were on our way.

There were still some old jobs left over – very big ones, mainly in the tea trade, where my father had been joint liquidator or receiver with Sir Harold Barton of Barton Mayhew, a very great gentleman. When I came back he said: 'I did this jointly with your father, and I will share the work with you in exactly the same way as I would have done with your father.' He was of enormous help, and he was prepared, as an elderly man and a very senior Chartered Accountant, to take jobs and allow me to be joint with him. All this went well. We did actually have one case when the creditors preferred us to Barton Mayhew, and if I had not stuck to my word we would have had it on our own! I cannot write any record without saying how someone who was a rival in business was so extremely kind to a young person who did not know very much, returning out of the Army and setting up again in practice. Another firm that was extremely helpful was Herbert Smith. When I stuck my neck out over a case, the senior partner pointed it out to me, instead of taking me to the cleaner's, and saved me from having a very red face. They also supported us, and in the end it paid them, too, because throughout our practice we always had an enormous respect for Herbert Smith. As a result, over the years they did a lot of work for Cork Gully.

It was a slow beginning, but after six months' hesitation we were firmly in insolvency, though we practised as Chartered Accountants. At the end of the first full year under my stewardship we had £548 in the bank and we totted up a profit of £2,622 13s 5d. We estimated our goodwill at cost (£2,360). The money needed to buy the company had also been repaid. The work was coming in, and there was promise of much more. Norman was out of the office most of the time attending meetings, and I thought the moment had come to bring someone into the firm who could share the responsibilities (and the liabilities) of an expanding operation and – more important – by purchasing a share in the business provide us with the capital I so sorely lacked.

Walter Tickler had been articled with me at Gully, Stephens, Ross & Gregory before the war but had not had time to sit his finals before joining the Army in 1939. He was now out of the Army and studying for his exams. In the spring of 1948 I made an agreement with him to take him into partnership and give him a third of the capital assets and profits (and shouldering a third of the liabilities) for a payment of £5,000, so long as he qualified as a Chartered Accountant within four years from 31 March 1948. He was still my partner when we amalgamated with Coopers & Lybrand, but unfortunately he died shortly after. Looking back at the letter which I wrote to his father on 30 December 1947 enlisting his support in persuading Walter to sign the agreement, I see I told him I anticipated that Cork Gully 'in three to four years will be as large, if not larger, as when my father ran it before the war'.

As it turned out, this was none too over-optimistic a forecast. In 1951 we took £2,900 in audit fees and £9,000 for insolvency work, making a net profit of £3,700. The next year we doubled our profit at £7,800, fees from insolvency amounting to £22,000. In 1953 our profit was up again to £9,700, four times the £2,600 of 1948.

In the 1950s it was only the insolvency departments of the big Chartered Accountancy firms who got appointed by the banks as receivers. Cork Gully had not yet proved its competence or reliability to undertake these responsibilities, and between 1948 and 1958 we confined ourselves to liquidations and trusteeships. We entered the scene when an insolvent company took steps to place itself into what was known as a 'creditors' voluntary liquidation', at which they appointed an accountant 'liquidator'; or when a private or sole trader – a partnership, for instance – decided it wanted to go out of business, called a meeting of its creditors and agreed to sign a deed of assignment under the Deeds of Arrangement Act 1914. By this he assigned all his assets to a trustee who sold them and after taking his fees distributed the proceeds *pro rata* among the creditors. The rôle of liquidator and trustee is an ancient and honourable one, but now that we had the time and inclination to bring our brains to bear on it as the specialists which we had become we gave the system refinements which in our opinion were to the benefit of all.

We developed schemes for reducing the liabilities of a company in order to preserve and hand it over together with its tax losses. When anyone wanted to buy an ailing concern we arranged for them to acquire its creditors' debts at a discount, so they could take over the company together with its tax losses. Creditors were offered the deal of either awaiting the liquidation process or having an immediate payment and assignment of their debt. By going into liquidation a company would lose much of its goodwill, so we would call an informal meeting of creditors at which we gave a full report of the situation at that date and of the assets available. If, say, it looked as if the company was going to be able to pay 8s in the pound, we would add an extra sum to cover tax losses, making the offer 9s; and then we would urge the prospective buyer to offer all creditors, say, 10s for an immediate assignment of their debts, provided they *all* agreed. If they did agree, the shareholders would transfer their shares to the new owner for a nil consideration, and the business would continue with a limited liability up to the amount it had been agreed to pay the creditors. Our scheme for transferring businesses with their tax losses, and not having to pay creditors in full, proved immensely popular, and was widely copied. Such schemes are no longer in vogue today because of the change in tax laws.

Meetings of creditors were not usually dull miserable affairs and often did not go according to plan. In one case we called a meeting in our offices to give a trader a deed of arrangement which was used a lot in those days. Because debtors' books were often nonexistent or inaccurate, we often got the number of creditors expected to come to the meeting wrong. So if we expected a large number and took a large hall few turned up, and vice versa. We decided in this case that there would be few and called it in the office. Wrong! More and more turned up. We brought more chairs into the room, leaving the staff in the end without any seats in their offices; still more came in, and finally the room was packed, with creditors standing behind the top table and even sitting on it.

The system with deeds was that you gave a report to the creditors then called the debtor in and he was asked questions. If creditors thought he had had bad luck and was not evil, they agreed to the deed; if they thought he had behaved badly, they voted to make him bankrupt and put him out of business.

In this case the story was not good, and when the debtor came in he was very shifty in his answers. He would not admit he had been insolvent for some time. Then I put his balance-sheet in front of him which showed he had been insolvent for about two years. He picked it up, seemed unable to read it; picked his glasses up off the table, and with the balance-sheet and the glasses started to answer more honestly. I then asked him to leave the room while we decided what to do. Much embarrassed, he fought through the crowd to the door and was just going out when a little cockney creditor who had been sitting next to him shouted to him: 'You have pinched my bloody glasses.' Even more embarrassed, he came back, pulled his own glasses out of his pocket to show how anyone could make such a mistake, at which the little creditor said: 'Yes, and if you had borrowed the bloody things two bloody years ago we would not be in the bleeding mess we are today.' At this the meeting dissolved into helpless laughter, and, after he had left the room, unanimously agreed to the deed against the odds and all common sense.

Another innovation which went down well at the time was

inserting an abatement clause when we could not guarantee the
amount the creditors were claiming. The price which constituted the
offer to purchase the company would be based on a fixed amount due
to creditors – say, £200,000. We put a clause into the agreement
stipulating that, if creditors claimed more than, say, £210,000,
payment to them all would be abated. There was always one creditor
of course who would try to get paid in full and threaten to create a row
if he was not. But we made it our practice never to make an
exception, even if the scheme fell through. It was 100 per cent or
nothing. Often we had to resort to asking the principal other
creditors to telephone the blackleg one by one until he was driven
mad and relented.

Gradually we gained a reputation for being constructive, because
we went to great lengths to sell the company and save it from closure.
A company recklessly or dishonestly run deserved its fate, and for
such cases the liquidation process had to run its course. Some other
accountancy firms which were prepared to handle insolvency cases
and employed what they regarded as 'orthodox' methods were
irritated at our taking work away from them by virtue of not keeping
to their 'rules'. These seemed to be that, when a company became
insolvent, it called a meeting of representatives of all those who were
owed money. Before the meeting took place these representatives
told each other how many creditors they acted for, and they then
agreed that at the meeting they would formally appoint as liquidator
the one who acted for the largest sum, *and share his fee among
themselves*. Cork Gully were threatened that, unless we were
prepared to participate in an arrangement of this kind, those who
were would combine against us and make sure we got no more work.

We had no sense of holier-than-thou self-righteousness in refusing
to share the remuneration of a liquidator with others, or indulging in
what was tantamount to bribery of the other representatives to elect
one of them as liquidator. It was simply illegal. Apart from that, if
you were charging the fee appropriate to the job, it made nonsense to
give two-thirds of it away. On the occasions when we were not
appointed liquidator and we were sent our 'share' of the fee, we
returned it.

I admit that returning after six years' absence in the service of
King and country I had no notion of what was 'traditional' and what
was not 'traditional' in these matters. I was an innocent who just
played according to my own lights and considered it common sense
not to 'fix' so important a rôle as liquidator for reasons other than
those which led to the appointment of the person best fitted to benefit
the creditors. This, it seemed to me, was not necessarily the man
representing the creditor who was owed the most. More and more

creditors came to like the way Norman Cork spoke at these meetings without knowing or caring whom he represented, let alone how much he acted for, in the same way as they had been impressed by the performance of my father in the thirties. They came to the very simple conclusion that they *wanted* W. H. Cork Gully as liquidator in preference to anyone else. W. H. Cork Gully were imaginative and innovative, and our refusal to join the gang of old-timers perpetuating the prewar game won the approbation of the modern accountants and solicitors who, as time went on, became the majority at such meetings.

The fixing system came to the attention of the authorities when, by chance, a list of accountants who had shared a liquidator fee on some occasion came into the hands of the Board of Trade. I had a phone call from the Secretary to the Institute, who asked if there was a ring. I said: 'Yes, there is, and it's wrong.' I asked him how he knew we were not in it, which I gathered from his tone of voice he did not, and he said he had phoned me because of the note beside the name of Cork Gully on the list indicating that we had returned the fee! After the Secretary had referred the matter to the Fraud Squad, it became a matter of investigation by the Institute of Chartered Accountants, who ruled accordingly. The practice ended, and a lot of firms had red faces.

Concentration on liquidation in the early years enabled us to appreciate the creditor's point of view and understand his feelings. It was an experience denied those whose first encounter with insolvency was through receivership. When in the mid-fifties we started to do receiverships we always called a meeting of creditors and set up an informal committee to work with the receiver, so they knew what was going on.

What was a receiver? He was invariably a Chartered Accountant (though the law did not say he should be) appointed in most cases by a bank who had lent a large sum of money to a company on the security of its assets (a 'floating charge') and on calling in the debt was told the company could not pay. At the time of the loan the bank received from the company a debenture which gave repayment of the loan priority over any other debts in the event of the company becoming insolvent. It was called the debenture holder, and it had the power to appoint a receiver if the debt was called and not repaid.

The receiver so appointed, as English law prescribed, had dictatorial powers to accomplish one thing and one thing only: to extract from the stricken company by any means it could enough money to pay the 'preferential creditors' as defined by law (Inland Revenue for certain taxes, for instance), the debenture holder, and his own costs. Once he had discharged that duty, he withdrew. He had little legal responsibility to the shareholders or to the 'unsecured' creditors, who had a right, however, to apply to the court to put the company into liquidation if they considered they were not being treated fairly. Thus a company could have a receiver and a liquidator at the same time, but the responsibilities of the former, who had all the assets, took priority. Only after the receiver had satisfied his three claimants could the liquidator apply what remained (if there was anything) to unsecured creditors and shareholders. The liquidator could never interfere in the running of the business or the realisation of its assets. To generalise, a liquidator looked after the interests of the creditors and a receiver was only accountable to the debenture holder who appointed him. It was generally held that they should never be the same person – a view with which I did not entirely agree.

In the case of the more common Creditors' Voluntary Liquidation, insolvency could end there. It might never lead to a bank appointing a receiver, because either no debenture existed or, where it did, the bank was satisfied it would get its money back without a receivership. The term 'official receiver' applied to the official of the Department of Trade and Industry.

Within the framework of receivership set down by the law there was of course considerable room for manoeuvre. The receivership of one man often assumed a very different character from that of another. At Cork Gully we operated in the belief that the people who ran a business knew more about it than a firm of Chartered Accountants such as ourselves. When appointed receiver of a big company, we put in a small staff and located them in a separate room. We made a point of employing the company's management to the maximum. We never moved the directors out of their offices and we kept the chairman wherever practical. We gave our instructions through the company's own management and not by our staff in that little room. So long as they were prepared to co-operate, we wanted to leave them their pride. But we had to exercise strict financial control. In trading we never took credit. If we needed money for buying the goods to sell, we borrowed from the bank at the outset, so we knew the limit of our liability. We notified all suppliers, and goods were bought only against cash or *pro forma*. Not many receivers liked doing that, and tended to take credit in the normal way. But that meant having more people on the spot to watch. Under our method we were not committed until we had signed a cheque. It kept our costs down and achieved better control.

A receiver was personally liable for all the liabilities he undertook. Most suppliers would give a receiver credit personally because he had his firm behind him. This led some receivers to contract out of their personal liability by writing on their invoices they would only be personally liable for the credit incurred in so far as it was covered by the assets of the company. We did not think this was a sensible way of conducting a receivership, and it made receivers very unpopular with suppliers. Though we were individually personally responsible, we were of course indemnified by Cork Gully.

Receivership presented other problems. An active aircraft manufacturer could obtain product insurance to cover anything going wrong with his machine in flight. But if I was the receiver of such a company, and one of their aeroplanes fell out of the sky and demolished the Chase Manhattan Bank, and it was proved that the plane was faulty in manufacture, I would be responsible. It was no longer a corporation which was trading, but an individual with unlimited liability. He was responsible even after the receivership was ended, and he had no assets with which to pay for product insurance. We got over this by forming a new limited liability company and trading in that company's name, so as to return to limited liability for the goods we sold. It was our standard practice as soon as we were appointed receiver to form a new company to carry on the business. But only the undertaking and goodwill were transferred; the assets were left in our name. So when we finally sold the business we could transfer such assets as the purchaser wanted.

This idea of a custom-built 'package' was another practice to originate from Cork Gully. It has since become universal. It is unknown outside Britain. Continental methods of dealing with insolvency did not lend themselves to it. They did not have receivership as we know it. In the United States it was under much stricter control; the receiver was unable to make decisions on his own responsibility as he could do here. The package method has only recently been applied to Scotland where up to a few years ago there were no 'floating charges'.

Of course trading as a liquidator was another matter. Then he still had the benefit of the limited liability of the company of which he was liquidator. It was only the receiver trading as the agent of the company who retained personal liability.

My first insolvency partner was Gerhard (Gerry) Weiss, who joined in 1952 and became a partner in 1954. His family had come to England in the thirties as refugees from the anti-Semitism of Hitler's Germany. I was very impressed by his brain and his apparent willingness and ability to tackle *anything*, and I congratulated myself on persuading him to join me for £100 less a year than he was getting at Peat Marwick. He became irreplaceable as the 'lawyer' of the firm in charge of litigation matters and handling compulsory liquidation. He became the expert on insurance companies.

In 1947, Walter Tickler recommended my recruiting John

Naylor, who became the partner doing investigations. He was a very
fast worker, and this proved one of our most valuable assets. He
would go before a meeting of creditors, produce a readable, acceptable and accurate report extremely quickly. Whereas other firms
would take three months and present a report of 500 pages, John
Naylor produced for Cork Gully a twenty-five-page document with a
reasonably accurate statement of affairs *in three days*. It may not
have contained figures correct to the nearest £5,000, but it could be
read by bank officials *while it was still relevant*. They could make
immediate decisions on the strength of it – such as, for instance, the
all-important matter of whether to appoint a receiver, which had to
be done at once if it was to be effective. This was much liked by the
banks, who were by this time starting to appoint us as receivers.

It helped us, of course, when we were so appointed to have
conducted the original inquiry and written the report, for which we
never charged banks. We never advertised the fact that we made no
charge, and it would have been some time before a bank who
instructed us, and never received a bill, noticed the fact. We felt it
would have been embarrassing for them to have to pay for a report
which recommended no receiver should be appointed, as happened
in 50 per cent of the cases. It would have been particularly difficult
for the bank to charge the company for the inquiry if they were a
valuable customer. We benefited since it was a service to banks which
they greatly appreciated. Where there was doubt about the advis-
ability of appointing a receiver, they knew they only had to call up
Cork Gully and they would have a report before the end of the week.
This led to their wanting to appoint a firm who had done their
homework. Fully primed, we could walk into the head office and
make decisions which were reasonably certain of turning out to be
the right ones *on the first day*. While preparing our report we were of
course considering what to do if we *were* appointed receiver. People
who went in cold generally had to flounder around for a week trying
to hold everyone at bay whilst making up their minds what to do. It is
all very strained in any event, without having to create those kinds of
tension.

Most other firms charged a fee for a report which was very much
longer, more detailed and more accurate than ours *when it arrived*;
but that was long past the decision-making time. There was an
element of risk in doing it the Cork Gully way – of making a mistake,
or producing the wrong answer. I reckoned most audit-trained
accountants felt it was irresponsible to produce a report as quickly as
that. But with the goodwill of the banks, *who knew it had been done
in three days* and were well aware of the extent to which it was By
Guess and By God, it was worth its weight in gold.

We created the format, and it was John Naylor's ability to fill it in quickly and accurately which gave Cork Gully the lead in the insolvency field. Added to this was our insistence on being absolutely blunt at creditors' meetings. Though Cork Gully had been called in by the company, as its representative we would have no hesitation in slating the directors if their actions warranted it. Our fate would be sealed by someone knowing something wrong about the company which we had omitted from the report. Everyone would then rightly look upon the report-makers with suspicion. 'They are on the directors' side,' they would say. The only course was a fully factual report, hiding nothing. As soon as you created a suspicion that you were holding back on some aspect of the operation, it stuck out like a sore thumb.

There were two types of report. The first was to the bank, who were concerned, not about what had gone wrong with the company, but whether it could survive. They wanted information on which to base the decision whether to appoint a receiver. The other was the result of an investigation which looked back in order to discover why a company went wrong, where the directors erred and how things stood at present. It was an inquest, together with a statement of affairs and the prospect of selling the company as a going concern.

When Cork Gully were first called in to help a business, it was always a variant of the same kind of story. You are dealing with completely different kinds of industry – meat, property, cars, radios, textiles – with different markets. Of course, you would never learn everything there was to know about the industry as a whole, but you do pick up a great deal of knowledge very rapidly. Really to learn about how things have been going at a company, you have to look around and certainly not rely on everything you might hear in the boardroom or at head office. There's always someone there – often in the accounts department – who has a complete grasp of what's going on, and what's been going wrong. He's not necessarily the chap in charge, and very often isn't. As soon as this invaluable person is located, you need to use him and his knowledge as much as you can.

A receiver needs to learn about the product and the people involved. He then needs to practise the delicate art of telling people when they're going wrong. You can be quite outrageous here, so long as it's done sympathetically or even with a grin.

I found a main reason for failure of a company was lack of communication on the part of directors sideways among themselves, downwards and upwards to and from their staff. There was a lack of awareness about life in general, of how things and people operate. They so often seemed to live in a closed-circuit world of their own.

They let products get out of date without a thought of replacing them. They so often even failed to see, until it was too late, that they could not make a profit if the volume of sales fell. Over-trading with inadequate profits and cash was as common a cause as any. Sheer incompetence at board level was the basis of almost every failure. Luckily it was rare.

It was only in 1958 when the National Provincial Bank appointed me receiver of Peto-Scott Electrical Instruments Ltd that we were able to practise on a large scale what we had been preaching for so long: that receivership did not necessarily lead to closure. At last we were able to demonstrate our approach, that being a receiver involved a much wider responsibility than merely satisfying the debenture holder by a quick sale of assets and withdrawal. We were able to prove that creditors lost money by a quick shutdown, and that, since one in four of them were likely to be customers of the lending bank, that was not good for customer relations. We showed that employees thrown out of work were likely to goad their unions to attack the bank for acting not only precipitately but also ineffectively. I think we were the first insolvency accountants of our size to make an intention to cure the patient and restore him to health the first consideration of receivership. We knew we were sticking our necks out; we knew how many were ready to tell us 'We told you so!' if we came unstuck. Our convictions gave us courage, however, not to rush foolishly in, but with due deliberation to carry out a well-planned campaign.

It all began with my being kept waiting a whole hour for lunch at the Savoy Grill. My host was Eli Karlin, chairman of the Pena Industries Group which embraced a number of manufacturing activities including the Cambridge Instruments Company, at least one bank (Comcor) and the usual service firms. I had encountered Karlin through involvement in another case. We were putting a 'scheme' through, and he had tried to outbid us. He failed, and a defeat was a new experience for him. When he said he wanted to meet me, I told him I would be glad to do so, but not until the case in which we were both engaged had been settled. That moment came in 1957, and I was looking forward to meeting a man of obvious talent with the traditional 'flair for finance', to whom I now had no obligations, nor he to me. His tardy appearance at the Savoy was due, it appeared, to his having been arrested and charged with fraud. My wait had given me an appetite, but after his humiliating experience at the police station he was in no mood for eating anything other than half a plain omelette, and regretfully I felt unable to embark on the somewhat more elaborate meal I had been planning for myself –

at his expense – during my hour's perusal of the Savoy's fine menu, and in any event I had to pay the bill. That was a social occasion, and it was never to be repeated. But a few months later we renewed commercial relations when the Pena Group crumbled, and with it what was, I suppose, its principal manufacturing interest: Peto-Scott. Karlin had purchased a controlling interest in the television set factory not with cash but with worthless paper – shares in other companies of his group. I was appointed receiver of Peto-Scott on 20 May 1958 and a petition for the compulsory winding-up of the Pena Group was presented on 9 June. Mr Justice Wynne-Parry made a compulsory winding-up order on 15 July, when the company's statement of affairs showed assets of £412,500 and debts of £463,000; if the assets were realised, creditors should get 15*s* in the pound.

The philosophy of the mostly non-British Pena directors was never to use your own money but *always* to borrow from a bank. At their first meeting after the takeover they asked the Peto-Scott directors how big an overdraft they had. When the Englishmen proudly told them they did not have an overdraft, they were told to mend their ways and see they acquired one at once. Peto-Scott was solvent and trading, but had been caught by the technological change of the shrinking cathode tube which made people want to buy 'thin' sets and made 'thick' sets old-fashioned and unsellable. Peto-Scott had a good research and development team but lacked the resources to retool and re-engineer their process to enable them to catch up with this revolution. If they thought their merger with Pena was going to bring them the money to achieve this end, they were quickly disillusioned. Once Pena had borrowed money from the bank on the security of the fixed and trading assets of Peto-Scott – a floating charge as well as a fixed charge – they used it not for the factory at Weybridge but to pump life into other ailing companies in the Pena Group. The borrowed money was switched around the group – a multiplicity of inter-subsidiary transactions which gave a paper impression of solvency, of profitability even. But the lack of substance was evident to anyone who took the trouble to trace the maze of pledging assets, borrowing money, losing it in some remote corner of the Pena Empire.

The bank soon became aware of the bubble nature of the floating charge on which the security of their debenture depended. When they saw that Peto-Scott had lost the use of the money they had lent them, and so the ability to improve their trading position, they decided the time had come to foreclose. Peto-Scott owed money to the Pena Group and was owed money by it. Membership of the group had itself become a liability from which no action of its own could free it. Rescue came through the bank, who demanded an

immediate return of their loan. Within twenty-four hours of Peto-
Scott having to admit that they could not comply, under the powers
given them by their debenture which required no consultation with
or permission from other creditors, employees, shareholders, directors, suppliers, customers or the Government, the bank sent me a
document appointing me receiver of Peto-Scott with complete
control of all its assets and its entire trading operation. The parent
company, Pena, had no assets; these had been in the subsidiaries.
Once they became worthless, which they now were, Eli's group
became a shell. There was nothing left to rescue there; any salvage
operation could only be directed at its subsidiaries.

The next day John Naylor and I drove down to Weybridge.
Unlike liquidation, there is no meeting of creditors to warm things
up; you go in cold. Your confrontation is with the directors. The
circumstances might be such that one did not inform them of one's
coming, but in this case we had telephoned to tell them to expect us
in the morning. And of course the bank had told them they were
putting in a receiver and given them my name.

The factory had closed, and all work had stopped, but the entire
workforce and administrative staff had reported for duty. John and I
climbed the stairs to the offices which overlooked the shop floor and
were ushered into the boardroom.

'Mr Cork?'

One of them had come forward from the group who hung around
the table and introduced himself as the managing director. These
were always moments of tension, but I hoped that by then, after
thirty years, I had developed a way of combining a 'tough' no-
nonsense attitude, which it was essential to establish at the outset,
with an awareness, which I trusted was apparent, of the fraught
sequence of events – the dashed hopes, the regretted miscalculations
and misjudgements, the rows, the heart-searchings, the recrimina-
tions – of which the scene we were now playing was the climax. We
were the first movement of the music they had to face, and we made it
adagio.

That first day at Weybridge there was little for us to do but collect
as much general information as we could to put us in the overall
picture. Our immediate task was to recommend to the bank either to
close the company down without delay or to keep it in being until it
was a sufficiently attractive property for someone to buy. Collecting
the data on which to base such a decision would take longer than a
day, and that in itself was a reprieve. That our meeting was not the
end of the matter was good news to directors for whom this was an
entirely new experience. They had probably reckoned I would be the
bearer of the dread news that Peto-Scott was dead 'as of now', and

that they and all those workpeople and office staff downstairs had lost
their jobs.

I asked John Naylor to spend the next few days making out one of
his lightning reports, and before the week was finished I had spoken
with the bank and told them what we recommended. Our advice was
that the best chance of their getting their money back was to restart
the manufacture of television sets at Weybridge, and to get Peto-
Scott trading again, because we had to borrow the money. They
considered our advice and took it. We told them that to start up again
we would need so many hundred thousand pounds for wages and
salaries, transport and power charges, administrative and marketing
costs in the first month, and probably about the same in each of the
following months. Three months ought to see the company back on
its feet or at least having made sellable the half-finished sets littering
the benches which then only had a scrap value. But we would play it
by ear. It was difficult to say precisely how long it would take. On the
strength of this the bank produced working capital of the amount we
estimated we would need, and let it be known that they backed
whatever action I, as receiver, decided to take. I was personally
accountable for all liabilities beyond the company's assets. My own
house, my car, my yacht could be sold to cover liabilities I incurred,
just as if I was myself a bankrupt. I was young and confident!

There was no question of the new Peto-Scott which came to life
under our sole direction returning to its old habits. The operation
had to be streamlined. But how? In many such cases a choice had to
be made whether to reduce volume, close one of several factories, or
cut out three of the seven 'lines'. At Peto-Scott we merely had to
make up our minds what to do about the thin or fat tubes. We came to
the conclusion that we were only justified in using the bank's money
for components already purchased, or on order, for making sets of
the current design and circuit with thick tubes. As a compromise we
decided to house them in new cases which would give the appearance
of being slimmer and more elegant.

The key department in any electronics firm is its research and
development department, and we made certain that the Peto-Scott
team was not disbanded merely because there was nothing for them
to develop. 'What can we do with ourselves all day?' asked Arthur
Heath, the able boffin who headed the team. Anything you like, I
told him. He phoned me one day and said he would like to come and
see me and discuss what they hoped to develop. I told him I would
rather not know, as long as it was short-term and not expensive. All I
wanted to do was to keep the team together.

After we had sold the business, he came and talked to me, and
said: 'What do you think of the idea of building a car radio set that is

also a portable, so you can take it out and use it in the house or garden, and when you change the car you take it out and put it into the new one?'

'An excellent idea,' I said.

'Good,' he said, 'because that is what you've been developing over the last few months!'

It never caught on, but it did what it was meant to do – it kept the team together.

We had to get rid of surplus fat, and I had no qualms about paying off the hangers-on who had attached themselves to the company at the time of the merger and were drawing unjustifiably large salaries for contributing very little. We had to thin out a few on the shop floor. It was a time before sacking was called 'redundancy', before the operation of cutting down an overgrown workforce had become hedged in by tribunals, compulsory compensation and the rest. We saw that those we had to make redundant were generously treated and we helped them as best we could to obtain re-employment. But in fact only a small number had to go – not more than about 5 per cent. Our revival plan depended as much as anything else on the speed with which we could give the company the healthy look which would attract a buyer, and to that end the more on the job the better. At the top of our dismissal list were the foreign Pena directors who had put themselves on to the Weybridge board and been drawing sizeable salaries for their counsels of incompetency. But we assured their efficient managing director, their chief accountant, personnel and technical directors that they had our confidence, and we trusted the shareholders had theirs. The company subsequently was put into liquidation as well.

Receivership and liquidation added to the tribulations of the directors, but I told them we were in this together. As receiver I had to make sure I made the right decisions and protect myself stage by stage. One false step could bring it down. These may not have seemed words of comfort, but I added that if we came through they would retain their jobs, as would everyone else on the payroll. It was worth taking a few risks for, and making the effort to adjust to unorthodox ways of working. They had to reconcile themselves to abjuring credit. They had to pay for all goods either on or before delivery. Operating on a day-to-day basis like this made customers wonder how long the company would remain in business. Was it worth buying a Peto-Scott television set if in six months maybe there would be no one to repair it? And no spare parts? To such would-be customers we could give no promise. We had to make provision for the possibility that our salvage plan would not succeed, and make agreements with outsiders to maintain a Peto-Scott after-sales service. We had to think of every eventuality and, having done so, press on with supreme confidence. Above all, we must never lose our nerve.

Maintaining the confidence engendered by not closing the company 'at a stroke' was a form of psychological warfare. To have cancelled the stand which the company had already booked at the 1958 Radiolympia would have compounded such rumours as existed that Peto-Scott were going under. So we widely publicised the fact that the company would be there as usual, and saw to it that throughout that summer the factory built up a large stock of television sets, albeit the slightly out-of-date thick-tube models. We reckoned that with luck we ought to be able to sell most of them in view of our low price.

In the event the cheaper Peto-Scott sets on our Radiolympia stand sold like hot cakes. The interest shown in them was enormous – mostly from representatives of the television rental firms who were used to buying sets by the thousand. Our set was just what they wanted for their undemanding renters. It looked attractive in its newly styled case, and the black and white picture was sharp. Who cared that it took up another inch and a half on the shelf? We sold the entire stock.

Directly opposite the Peto-Scott stand was the famed international electronics giant Philips, who watched the business being done by the small manufacturer opposite with growing astonishment. Before the radio show was over a senior representative had crossed the aisle to make contact, and been impressed by what he saw and the people he talked to. Before very long they sent us a formal bid to buy Peto-Scott lock, stock and barrel. I must say so quick and satisfactory an end to the adventure was beyond our wildest expectations. Within six months of our decision to keep the company in business we had sold enough television sets (which otherwise would have been worthless) to contribute a good sum towards the elimination of the debt to the bank, and then, as a result of the radio show, sold the entire company for another sum so that the two together repaid the bank all they had lent the company. Jobs had been saved; suppliers had regained a customer; customers regained an after-sales service and the continued manufacture of the Peto-Scott set by a company of international reputation.

Looking back on it I am not sure it is a gamble I would undertake today. It was extremely risky; but, then, the stake was not only the life of Peto-Scott but also whether there was a future for Cork Gully as a receiver on the lines I and my colleagues had conceived. The Rubicon once crossed meant we never looked back. It was the beginning of the Cork Gully we know today. The big banks viewed

us in a new light, and I would like to think we earned the respect of
even sharp operators such as Eli Karlin, who later made a lucrative
lecture-tour of America on the subject of How To Succeed In
Business!

Chapter Three

Contempt for Savundra

Risk-taking was what we seemed fated to win a reputation for. A short time after Peto-Scott, Cork Gully's ability to handle insolvency cases was confirmed by my being appointed liquidator of the first big British insurance company to become insolvent since the war: British Commercial in September 1959. And I must say it gave me a lot of sleepless nights. The greater part of their business lay in the United States where the attitude to insurance was, and is, very different from ours, particularly to Personal Accident which was British Commercial's speciality. The first reaction of Silas P. Hamburger who trips over the mat in his dentist's surgery and breaks a leg is to engage a lawyer, who charges no fee but takes a percentage of the reward, and recommends suing the dentist for a million dollars. The insurance company with whom the dentist has a Personal Accident policy knows that the cost in lawyer's fees of proving their client is not liable is so great they will settle for $\$\frac{1}{4}$ million, and be thankful. Multiplied several thousand times, this was the nightmare in which British Commercial found themselves playing a leading part. Once caught in it, there was no way of making a profit. They were forced to a standstill, their resources and their patience exhausted. They had to go into liquidation.

But insolvency did not remove the problem, only shifted it to us. We had to decide whether to forget the company's American customers, leave it to them to prove the amounts they were claiming and accept them, and take whatever assets were then left to pay a dividend; or to fight each claim we could not accept one by one in the American courts. I had been made fully aware of what the latter course could cost in terms of hard cash for lawyer's fees, and the risk of claims not being reduced in spite of having engaged lawyers to fight them, who might of course lose. It would be harmful to us as specialists in rescue if we made the decision to fight, succeeded in getting a majority of claims reduced but, having won this pyrrhic victory, incurred legal costs which used up all the assets. In which case there would be nothing for creditors and we would look stupid. We decided to contest all claims. Gerry Weiss then waded in and did battle.

It was a testing time for us. I confess that, as the number of court cases grew into four figures, and thousands of pounds were being paid out every month, I wondered whether there would be any assets left at all. For, apart from the fees which we had to pay our counsel, at the instigation of their counsel British Commercial's American policyholders, knowing the company was insolvent (we paid 30p in the pound eventually), trebled their claims to even things out. However, to our relief, after several anxious months, the outgoings tailed off. British creditors, who had wanted us to settle the American claims without contesting them, could not but agree that our action had brought them a bigger dividend. Through the adroit handling of Gerry Weiss we ended up well on the right side. And I think the long-drawn-out ordeal won admiration for Cork Gully for taking resolute action in a situation which, till then, smaller firms had had neither the inclination nor the guts to tackle. It helped to cement a reputation on which all of us at Eastcheap were determined to build, and made Cork Gully and Gerry Weiss known as the insolvency insurance experts.

So far my knowledge of the problems of business management had come from the occasions when I became temporarily involved in the affairs of a business in a far from normal state of turmoil. I have Dan Prenn to thank for giving me the opportunity to experience what it was like to be in the driving-seat of a healthy company and have to make the kinds of decision which Cork Gully's insolvent clients had to face every day of their working lives.

Dan Prenn was a top-class tennis-player who, in spite of being born a Russian, played for Germany in the Davis Cup. Like so many others, he left Germany in the 1930s to escape Nazi persecution, came to England, was naturalised British and started a manufacturing company called Truvox which made floor polish and loudspeakers. By the 1960s he had built up an electronics group of some size, and was very successful. When another loudspeaker manufacturer, Rola-Celestion, failed, Cork Gully were appointed liquidators. We received two bids to buy the company, one from de Laszlo, the son of the famous portrait-painter, and another, which we accepted, from Dan Prenn. It was a good sale and meant that Rola-Celestion could keep going. When the deal was done and signed I was anxious that Prenn should complete as soon as possible. We needed the money because doubt had been expressed. When I phoned Prenn's office I was told he was in the London Clinic undergoing treatment. So I paid him a visit and asked him when I was going to get my money.

'How can I get you your money? You can see how I am fixed – in bed in a nursing home. If you want your money, you must go and get it.'

'What do you mean?'

'I bank at the Midland and, as I know very well, they are good friends of yours. Would you go and see them and ask them to make the necessary arrangements?'

'It is hardly for the vendor to arrange for the funds; that's the job of the purchaser.'

'If that's the way you want it, you'll have to wait until I get out of here, and that may be some time.'

It was not the way I wanted it, so I agreed to go and see one of the general managers of the Midland Bank whom I knew, and see what I could do. I told him of my unusual errand, and he willingly produced the £$\frac{1}{2}$ million which Dan Prenn owed us, and we had completion.

That was the beginning of a long and friendly acquaintance with Dan Prenn, who from then on began consulting me on every sort of matter, particularly when he contemplated adding to his British Communications Group which was mainly run by Poles. In 1953 a public company, Radio & Television Trust Ltd, which had not been doing very well, came on the market, together with its high-tech subsidiary Airmech which had big Ministry of Defence contracts. Dan made an offer for it which was accepted, and invited me to become the chairman of the now greatly enlarged and reorganised British Communications Corporation. I was glad of the chance of getting myself out of the insolvency accountancy groove and for the first time becoming 'for real' an active chairman of the board of directors of what we hoped would be an important and successful company. To have that experience at so early a stage in my business life was invaluable, and I was very grateful to Dan Prenn for putting it my way. He took over as chairman himself later on, and I became deputy chairman. In 1955 the whole British Communications Corporation/Radio & Television Trust was sold to Racal, and I left the board. But in 1964 Dan asked me to chair a syndicate he had formed to move into the American foundation-garment manufacturer Weingarten Brothers, whose performance had not been very successful. Under our direction Weingarten bought the British subsidiary of the American-owned Maidenform Company, the world's largest brassière manufacturer, founded by Mrs Ida Rosenthal who emigrated to the United States from Russia as a girl of seventeen and was still in charge at the age of seventy-eight. Weingarten shares rose in value from 6s 1½d to 7s 9d, but I must admit we were not able to maintain the growth. Dan kept Rola-Celestion out of the package sold to Racal and he recently asked me to become a director of it. It now makes not only loudspeakers but also pyjamas and underwear for Marks & Spencer.

The Great Pig Caper was one of my more bizarre cases. Some bright spark came up with the idea of 'selling' pigs to people so they would have the profit of their progeny. All the pigs were milling around on a farm, and their ears were tagged so that they could be identified to their owners. The scheme went bust, and we were called in to sort it all out. At the time there were 8,000 pigs (including progeny), and 9,000 angry people asking where their pig was. Not only were there insufficient pigs; they had also developed the habit of chewing each other's ears, so the tags were missing.

It was a real pain. An irate lady turned up one day demanding to collect her pig. We pointed to the field, and said we were not going to investigate the ear of each and every pig, especially as most of the tags were missing. She was not satisfied with this, and came back with the village policeman. He was full of the spirit of the law, and insisted on inspecting the pigs himself to find the right one. We ushered him into the field. His surveillance lasted ten minutes – before he was chased out by an angry sow.

We were also left with the problem of what to do with the pigs. They weren't our assets, and they all needed feeding. So we went to court, and asked if we could sell the pigs off. Unfortunately, we were up before a newly appointed judge, who insisted that all the interested parties (that is, the angry 9,000) should be represented. How ridiculous! It would have taken weeks, and pigs eat enormous amounts. He asked if we could sell some to feed the others whose pigs would we sell? Fortunately, we appealed and were granted permission by a more experienced judge to sell all the pigs and distribute the money. Despite the sad mishap of the roof of the barn collapsing in mid-auction, and the auctioneer falling into a huddle of pigs, we did this. If we had sold only some of the pigs to feed the others, the pigs would have effectively eaten each other in six weeks.

I found it was invaluable to me, as someone dealing with insolvent businesses, also to be involved in running good and profitable ones. Otherwise, one would lose one's enthusiasm.

Apart from this, when people said, 'He's only a liquidator. What does he know about business?' the reply was: 'He is a director of Costains, Ladbrokes, Radio and Television Trust, etc.' Obviously, I chose directorships carefully to avoid conflicts of interest.

I believe also that auditing accountants should have one or two non-executive directorship appointments. If you have not had to make difficult decisions, how can you fairly deal with people who do?

Major accounting firms usually do not agree with this, and do not permit their partners to be directors of companies. I think they are very wrong and that there would be far fewer negligence claims against auditors if they actually had real experience of running businesses.

At that time it was a new world for me, though in these exercises the nature of the product was immaterial. The manufacturing, marketing and financing problems were the same whether it was pharmaceuticals or fashion. But we were back to the food trade we knew so well when in 1964 I was appointed liquidator of Waller & Co. (Food Distributors) of Smithfield Market, a large company in the lamb and beef group of the son of a cattle dealer who tried his hand at empire-building but which went wrong. His companies included a chain of butcher shops and BM Wholesale Meat which was also in liquidation with deficiencies of £50,000. Waller's collapse followed debts running to £250,000: 'the biggest meat market smash since the war', as the *Sunday Times* described it.

For some time they had done very well as jobbers in the market, bringing forward delivery contracts from the original importers. When the prices moved favourably they sold them to those who, unlike themselves, actually wanted the carcasses. In 1960 they cleared £37,000 on a turnover of £5 million. But then things began to deteriorate. In 1963–4 they lost £119,000, and between April and October 1964 another £144,000. Smithfield's cold stores were full to bursting with Waller & Co.'s meat which no one wanted at the asking price. As liquidator I was only legally obliged to accept Waller's forward contracts which showed a profit; I could disclaim the loss-makers as 'onerous'. In that event they might revert to the original importers or even the Australian exporters, both of whom could lose a lot of money if in the mean time the Smithfield price dropped below Waller's figure. Ships carrying 8,000 tons of meat were on their way. In the weeks before they were due to dock, I was besieged by representatives of all the Smithfield official bodies and major traders pleading with me to avoid harming the trade as a whole by flooding the market with ridiculously cheap meat.

The butchers were convinced that we would make a mess of dealing in what they thought was a difficult and highly skilled operation. Also, being market men, they trusted no one outside the market, so the Committee set up by them to deal with us insisted on appointing a watchdog to see we kept our promise to the market. So they appointed Harold Swain, little realising how well we knew each other. His skill and help were invaluable. Harold was a meat and cold store expert, and he was on the same Allied Force H.Q. in Italy and North Africa. We in fact, shared a tent.

The action I did take, with the help of Harold Swain and the Midland Bank, I am glad to say, enabled Smithfield to ride out what all traders considered their worst scare in years.

Waller & Co. were reckless and inexperienced, but far from nefarious. Which could hardly be said of the American gentleman who had the idea of forming a company in the State of Delaware to give members of the United States forces in Europe insurance cover for their private motor cars. Traditional hunting-ground for every get-rich-quick confidence trickster is any operation in which the promoter receives money in advance of having to pay any out: travel, mail-order business, investing in a pig, insurance. Customers hand over their money in good faith and cannot tell whether that has been justified until they take the holiday, receive the parcel with the cut-glass decanter, sample the bacon, or find their claim paid swiftly and fully.

The American promoters of what they called the American Military Insurance Company opened branches in Britain, France and Germany. In charge of the British office was Tony Hunt, later managing director of Vehicle and General Insurance Co. In Germany and France at this time (the 1960s) anyone wanting to start a motor insurance business had first to raise a large sum of money and deposit it as security with the Government. But there was no such condition in Britain for foreign companies. So the men of Delaware were able to set up shop in London merely by 'showing' the Board of Trade they had £50,000. When the premiums started coming in from the Essex and Suffolk airfields, the American promoters shipped the money across the Channel until enough had accumulated to pay the required deposits to the French and German governments, and then began soliciting business from American servicemen and their families in Paris, Bonn, Frankfurt. The three branches of the American Military Insurance Company were soon seen to be in business, but when the claims came in to the London office there was nowhere near enough money to meet them. The Board of Trade stepped in and made an investigation. On their petition the American Military Insurance branch in England was compulsorily wound up, and Cork Gully were appointed liquidators. The two other branches were closed shortly afterwards, and the whole company collapsed. Substantial sums of money appeared to be missing. Gerry Weiss, who handled the case, considered the operation thoroughly fraudulent; but of course with the company being incorporated in the United States there could be no prosecution either in Britain or France or Germany. The claimants lost out, and it is almost impossible to rescue such companies because you cannot continue to insure anything.

There was no doubt, however, about the fraudulent intentions of the man from Ceylon with the criminal record who, when he shifted his activities to Britain, called himself by the shortened version of his name: Savundra.

Emil Savundra had an idea which on paper looked reasonably sound: to set up a motor insurance business and gauge the premium either on the risk which the policyholder represented or the likelihood of risk. In conventional motor insurance where the premium is rated on such considerations as the size and speed of the car and the age of the applicant, and they assess what is the 'average risk', good drivers pay for bad drivers. Savundra proposed offering cover the premium for which would attract the good driver, who paid a small amount, and discourage bad drivers, who would have to pay a big premium. In this way he thought he could cream off the motor insurance business of Britain. He put the information he received from applicants into a computer which in a matter of seconds worked out the premium relative to the risk. Why hadn't someone thought of doing it before?

Because what looked good on paper did not work out on the road. Motorists already insured with an established company stayed put; they had earned no-claim bonuses and wanted to keep the benefits. Those who fell for Savundra's scheme were almost entirely motorists who could not get cover elsewhere because their record showed them to be such bad risks. His complicated and costly system of computing the rate of premium by risk broke down, and he had to fall back on more conventional methods. But with policyholders who were almost exclusively the nation's worst drivers, with rising inflation, increasing cost of repairs, and all the hazards which accompany bad driving Savundra's operation was very soon extremely unprofitable.

Up to this point his rôle was merely that of an unfortunate, if over-optimistic, entrepreneur; it was only in so far as he had no hesitation in seeking to remedy the situation by producing a document designed to assure the Department of Trade that his company had backing of £510,000, when in fact it was insolvent, that he showed himself capable of the criminal action (by no means his first) for which he was convicted at the Old Bailey and sentenced to eight years' imprisonment and fined £50,000. (For a detailed account of Savundra's consistently criminal approach to earning a living, including his deportation from Ghana in 1958 as someone 'not conducive to the public good', his participation in the Costa Rican coffee fraud of 1960, and his association in Britain with fellow-criminal Bobby McKew, who was later convicted of forging American traveller's cheques and was suspected of having printed the forged government bond and share certificates for Savundra, I refer the reader to John Connel and Douglas Sutherland, *Fraud: The Amazing Career of Doctor Savundra* (Hodder & Stoughton, 1979), to whose excellent narrative of the FAM affair I am much indebted in what I have written here.)

The vehicle he created to inflict 'this gigantic swindle' on the British public – to use Judge King-Hamilton's words – had limited liability, and was called the Fire, Auto and Marine Insurance Company Ltd. As a foreigner he saw limited liability as a delightful invention of the Western world which excused people like him from personal risk. As a crook he would only consider it the attitude of a weakling to admit that limited risk assumed unlimited responsibility. It would have been beyond him to realise that to be granted limited liability was a privilege, and that in exercising it an entrepreneur had a debt to society to be excessively honest in every calculation he made. Most of all, such a code insisted that, having led people into a mess, the last thing an honest operator did was walk away and leave them there. Perhaps the most damaging aspect of the Savundra débâcle was not the harm he did to the company's 400,000 policy-holders with their 43,000 outstanding claims, which was bad enough, but what he did to potential overseas customers for British insurance for whom the reputation for honesty and straight dealing of British firms was second to none. For anyone to throw doubt on the reliability of the insurance market in Britain in the way Savundra did was unforgivable. It was this which earned him universal contempt.

But, then, the regulations of the day – or, rather, the lack of them – were much to blame. When Fire, Auto and Marine was registered in February 1963 with an address (three rooms) in Baker Street, anyone could start an insurance business in Britain, as I have indicated, who was able to 'show' capital of at least £50,000. A promoter had no need to obtain a licence from the Department of Trade; there was no vetting of directors to show their trustworthiness or ability, no procedure which might reveal a criminal past. 'Showing' the money was all the law required. There was no stipulation that it should be deposited or invested in gilt-edged securities. The sum could have been borrowed on Monday morning, shown on Monday afternoon, and returned to the lender on Tuesday morning. The £50,000 was the minimum. Anyone who wished to operate on a bigger scale eventually had to show a capital which was 10 per cent of his premium income, though no such solvency margin was necessary during the first two years of trading. It was this, coupled with being a private company exempt from having to send a copy of its accounts to Companies House, which enabled Savundra to operate unprofitably for as long as he did; it was having to provide the Department of Trade with assuring information about its assets at the end of the two years which was his downfall. Up to then he put up a great smokescreen of affluence – and, indeed, afterwards. He was an expert at 'constructive accounting'.

I always remember the day I walked into his ostentatious tasteless office at 'Jacqueline House' (named after his daughter). There, hanging on a blackboard, were sheets of paper on which numbers had been scrawled in huge figures showing costs, expenses, loans and the rest, and at the bottom in the biggest writing of all the word PROFITS and a figure several times underlined of 2 million or whatever it was. But the bubble had already burst. Yet there he was, still trying to impress his managers, and anyone who walked into his den, with an aura of immense wealth. If I had accused him of greed, he would not have felt insulted; he would not have known what I was talking about.

Cork Gully were never concerned with the morals of debtors, however, only with whether they had broken the law or not and with the interests of the creditors who had forced the company into compulsory liquidation. It was a pity that in the Savundra case there had not been an earlier occasion on which someone had asked the questions we were going to ask, and been as insistent on receiving an answer. The two-year period of free-wheeling had finished in February 1965 when Savundra had had to present his balance-sheet, his first audited accounts, to the Board of Trade to prove he had the required solvency margin. He could only muster a margin of £90,000 when his premium income of £2,203,000 demanded £220,000. So he had a 3 per cent Government Savings Bond 1955–65 forged with a face value of £510,000. It was so authentic the auditors accepted it as evidence that the company was solvent. At a second audit in April the place of the Government Savings Bond had been taken by assets valued at £800,000 in the form of a portfolio of shares which again satisfied the Department. But Savundra knew this was only putting off the evil day, and tried to sell FAM to another insurance company, Vehicle and General, whose chairman, however, insisted on seeing this schedule of investments whose value had grown to £900,000. Moreover he asked awkward questions like 'Why have you not shown the interest you have earned from this huge sum?' That was not playing the game – Savundra's game. He broke off negotiations at once. It was the moment, too, to put on an illness act. On his 'recovery', he offered to sell his English associate Stuart Walker his shareholding in FAM for £2,529 on condition he took over his personal debt to FAM of £488,000. Incredibly Walker agreed and, on 22 June 1966, Savundra resigned from the FAM board and flew to Switzerland.

FAM had had a series of chief accountants, and the latest was a very stolid and efficient professional called Cecil Jager. He sensed something crooked, and on 26 June confided his suspicions to another Cecil, the very respectable secretary of the Royal Naval Volunteer Reserve Officers Association whom Savundra had selected to front his organisation as chairman: Cecil Tross Youle. Youle heard what Jager had to say and at once telephoned a barrister friend, Bill Mars-Jones, later a High Court judge, who phoned another barrister, Maurice Finer, who phoned the solicitor David Freeman, who phoned Gerry Weiss, who went at once to Jacqueline House for a talk with Stuart Walker and what he hoped would be disclosure of *all* the facts.

Where, for instance, were these £900,000 worth of securities which, being the capital of an insurance company, were presumably liquid enough to be instantly realisable to meet the running demands with which every insurance operation had to cope? Stuart told him they were held by the Zurich branch of a Liechtenstein 'Anstalt' called the Merchants and Finance Trust which Savundra used as a bank for 'windmilling' FAM premium income into his own pocket (and Walker's) in a way that he hoped it could not be touched by FAM's creditors. Gerry told Walker, who was managing director of MFT, to take a plane to Zurich that afternoon and bring the securities back to London. When Gerry saw Walker the next day he found him empty-handed. He had been unable to take them away with him as they were tied up in a ten-year loan – a time deposit. They were in any case the property of MFT not of FAM. Walker then produced a letter signed by Paul Hagenbach, the Swiss lawyer who had set MFT up for Savundra, saying he was instructed by his client MFT to assert that they could not agree to FAM's request to make available any funds against fixed-deposit arrangements made with MFT's London place of business.

This of course set Jager checking up on the share certificates, of whose numbers FAM's directors had a note. There were no such numbers on the various companies' registers. They were forgeries.

Gerry attended the FAM board meeting of 4 July and declared the company insolvent, and told the directors that there were certain irregularities in the investment portfolio. The company then went into liquidation. If it had not done so, the Board of Trade would have been bound to impose compulsory winding up. I was appointed liquidator. When Gerry Weiss told the 450 staff over the office intercom what had happened they went berserk. They threw the typewriters out of the window, wrecked the coffee machines, pulled the drawers out of the desks and wrenched the papers from the filing-cabinets. Gerry found Tross Youle drinking a lonely glass of champagne in the boardroom. He suggested the chairman put his glass down and take the winding-up petition to the Law Courts before they closed. Cecil Jager made a report to the Fraud Squad, and Stuart Walker caught another plane to Zurich to consult Hagenbach and Savundra who had retreated to a nursing home, a favourite ploy which fooled only himself.

Gerry Weiss began his investigation at once. The Fraud Squad had had no reply to their letter to the Chief of Police in Liechtenstein asking for information on MFT and the missing securities. So Gerry also took a plane to Zurich. But Hagenbach said he had no knowledge of what went on; he merely signed whatever was put in front of him. Though his Zurich office was a registered office of MFT, he had no idea who owned it. So on – by taxi – to Liechtenstein and the village of Vaduz, which is its administrative capital. Gerry told the driver to take him to police headquarters, where he confided to an astonished chief of police that his mission involved inciting another to breach the secrecy of a bank account, which was a criminal offence in Liechtenstein. The chief then delved into a pile of paper on his desk two feet thick, and from the bottom extracted the letter from the Fraud Squad. What a coincidence Mr Weiss should come to Vaduz on the very day when he had planned to act on the request of his police colleagues in London! If Mr Weiss would be so good as to accompany one of his officers, they could go and get the required information together.

So Gerry's tiring journey had done the trick. He succeeded in getting one of MFT's directors to show him the agreements by which £380,000 was tied up in a twenty-year loan to Savundra, a £220,000 loan to Walker, and £400,000 to individuals and enterprises in England. But none of the bits of paper, fine examples no doubt of the printer's art, purporting to be share certificates of BP, GKN, Shell and the rest. They had 'disappeared'.

Gerry held the winding-up meeting of FAM on 24 July. He showed a deficit of £3 million of which £300,000 was owed in claims to 43,000 policyholders. There was little we could do for them, and it was little compensation that, on 6 March 1968, Walker and Savundra were convicted of plotting to defraud them by misappropriating premiums, falsifying the 1965 and 1966 balance-sheets; and, Savundra alone, of uttering forged share certificates. The 'doctor', said Judge King-Hamilton at the end of the forty-two-day trial, had used all the techniques of the confidence trickster. The MFT 'bank' was completely bogus. He had been utterly ruthless and unscrupulous.

We obtained a judgement against Savundra on behalf of MFT for £400,000; and when Emil appealed on the grounds that his loan agreement with MFT gave him twenty years to pay Lord Denning said it was not worth the paper it was written on. The House of Lords likewise rejected his version of what had happened.

The bubble of his phoney affluence took three years to prick. Bankruptcy proceedings of the convicted swindler took all of that time. What had he to lose? At his public examination in April 1969 he refused to take the oath, and again and again he stalled on the grounds of his feigned 'ill health'. He served only six years six months of his sentence and was out in October 1974. He died in 1976.

Gerry Weiss failed to find the missing premium income; the windmills had apparently blown it away only too successfully, except for £15,000 worth of securities he located in a bank in Geneva. It took eleven years to sort it all out. It was not until June 1977 that we were able to announce that, if we could trace them, we should be able to give the 300,000 FAM policyholders who were still owed money 30p for every pound they claimed. That was Savundra's real crime, stealing £70 from the man whose accident had cost him £100. That was the penalty paid by those who had every reason to believe him an honest trader. But of course it was on that trust that he was trading.

An eleven-year-old address-list made it impractical to write 300,000 letters, so we obtained the permission of the High Court to advertise in newspapers appealing to FAM policyholders with unpaid claims to write to us. We reckoned this saved creditors £350,000. All in all Cork Gully, through the hard work of Gerry Weiss, managed to rescue £1 million for FAM's creditors. Why had not someone taken action against Savundra earlier? It was a question everyone was asking. The libel laws were probably responsible for the press being reluctant to expose his record. As *The Economist* wrote at the time, 'Was it the tradition in British newspaper offices which said don't print a word, he's got a good lawyer?' He traded on that, too.

Fire, Auto and Marine was only one of many motor insurance firms to go bust between 1966 and 1972. Some 750,000 motorists were affected. We only became involved – or, rather, half-involved – with one other, Vehicle and General, which compared with FAM was very much more genuine an operation. Before the meeting of creditors the Department of Trade had appointed as special manager a partner of Coopers & Lybrand, Paul Shewell, who had carried out the investigation. Some of the insurance companies who were creditors of V & G and many other creditors, however, asked that we should be the liquidator. There was a vote, and the creditors resolved that Coopers and Cork Gully should be joint liquidators. I was the joint liquidator, but Gerry Weiss did most of the work.

The collapse of V & G in 1971 was due not to a human but to an electronic failing. The management followed Savundra's enterprising example and installed a computer to calculate their profits, ratios and reward risks. It was obvious that at first the machine was being highly inaccurate. The chairman, realising it was producing the wrong answer, told everyone to ignore it. But then the programmers and the rest became more expert, and the computer began giving the correct answer, which was that V & G was going to the wall fast. Unfortunately, the management were unaware, or unwilling to acknowledge, that the computer was now working properly and continued to take no notice of it.

They had a number of trading companies as subsidiaries, one of which bought investment trusts. In the course of liquidating V & G, Paul Shewell and I had to put a value on the assets of this company, First Finsbury Trust. The management of an investment trust handles many millions of pounds for a very small element of profit indeed against equally small expenses. With this as our criterion we valued it very low. But there were some others who saw ownership of an investment trust as a way of making money which I might describe as not exactly legal but not too illegal then. For them, the value of the investment trust was in its buying power. They could buy a large number of Alpha Beta shares, say, at 105p and then put their investment trust funds into Alpha Beta, when – surprise, surprise – the share price of Alpha Beta would rise and they would sell them at 205p. Thus, to secure an investment trust could be an easy and swift way of making a profit personally.

Just after V & G went into liquidation I was in the South of France, and I received a telephone call from someone there who said he wanted to buy one of their assets, First Finsbury.

When I got in touch with him in Cannes – I think it was Cannes – it turned out to be Tom Whyte of Triumph Investment Trust, and he asked me over to lunch with my wife at St-Tropez, which was halfway between us, at the very expensive restaurant just by the harbour wall. I arrived at 12.30, the time suggested, and waited and waited with my wife, drinking the odd cocktail to stop being too bored, and also thrown out, although they confirmed that Mr Whyte had in fact booked lunch. I was just giving up all hope after about an hour and a quarter, and deciding that I would have to buy my own lunch and have it in expensive peace with Nina, when Tom Whyte came in. He apologised for his late arrival, but he had started in his yacht, and the weather had got too bad outside the Estoral and he had turned back and come by car. I could not understand it, because the

weather was not that bad, and the kinds of yacht which millionaires
have are not worried about a small force 4 or 5 wind off the Estoral. I
subsequently found that it was only a small open motor-boat, which
gives some idea of the kind of people we were involved with!

Over the langoustine he intimated that he was prepared to pay a
sum eight times the amount Shewell and I had agreed between
ourselves was the amount we would ask. Could I use my influence to
see that he got it? I telephoned Paul, who was as mystified as I was at
this extraordinary offer. We both agreed the man was out of his
mind. But who were we to stand in the way of V & G's creditors
benefiting in any way, however strange?

We sold First Finsbury for a very high price. This became one of
the sales which created a future buying price for all investment
trusts. The price of investment trusts became a multiple of the total
funds, not a multiple of the income. From then on everyone realised
that investment trusts were very valuable to those who wanted to use
them as a buying power for making money, the income from which
did not justify so high a value.

This was the exercise which landed Sir Denys Lowson in so much
trouble. He was a director of a large number of companies all of
which had a stake in the same investment trusts, all given a quotation
on the Stock Exchange in relation to their income. He saw the price
he could get collectively, and realised that if he could get control of an
investment trust he could make money. He turned to his co-directors
and said, for instance, 'These shares are quoted at 50p. I will buy
them from you at 75p.' When he had bought himself a controlling
interest in all these companies, and thus in the original investment
trusts, he hoped to sell the shares for eight or ten times the sum he
paid for them. He had cashed in on a huge scale, because he had
bought the shares for only a percentage of their value, although much
greater than the market value. The insider-trading laws of today have
stopped much of this.

The criticism of Denys Lowson was that he did not disclose to his
fellow-directors that if they amalgamated their share holdings collectively they would be worth £8 million instead of £800,000. His
justification for acting the way he did was that he took the risk of
buying them in, and they were all willing sellers. They did well out of
it. If he had not found a buyer, he would have been landed with them
and suffered a considerable loss.

The standards of what a director can and cannot do have changed
since then. The obituary in *The Times* of 11 September 1975, after
the sixty-nine-year-old ex-Lord Mayor of London had died three
hours before summons could be served on him for conspiracy to

defraud shareholders, was unsparing in its condemnation of Lowson's tactics.

As Lord Mayor of London he showed a flair for publicity. In his personal affairs he shunned such exposures. His empire was a tangle of cross shareholdings, based on some 100 trading and industrial companies throughout the world, owned and controlled at the end through 14 often inter-related investment trusts.

Last year, following exposure in the *Investors Chronicle*, inspectors appointed by the Secretary of State for Trade and Industry accused Sir Denys of grave mismanagement of companies in his control. They concluded that his motive was 'to obtain very substantial gain for himself and his family'. These charges arose out of an episode in 1972 when Sir Denys bought shares from the National Group, which he controlled, for about 62p each, selling them again within a few months for £8.67 each. It was estimated that this personal transaction netted Sir Denys a profit of some £5m. The inspectors' interim report charged him with putting personal gain before his duty to the companies of which he was a director and their shareholders.

Sir Denys admitted error and undertook to make substantial repayments. His counsel attributed his mistake to age, ill health, obstinacy and secretiveness rather than to any intent to deceive. The inspectors rejected this defence, concluding that throughout his evidence to them he had demonstrated 'a firm grasp of the points at issue'.

To be fair to Sir Denys, this sort of thing had been normal procedure before the war and was only slowly being considered immoral.

The charge against his associate Thomas Daniel Mullins was, on the application of the Director of Public Prosecutions, withdrawn. He and Lowson were charged with dishonestly buying shares from companies in the Lowson group in 1972 at deliberately low prices knowing they could be sold afterwards at much higher ones. It was a conspiracy to defraud shareholders in his own companies. It was dubbed 'insider dealing'; and from being an accepted practice and the hallmark of the sharp operator with the flair for finance it has become widely condemned – but is unfortunately sometimes still practised.

Chapter Four

Sympathy with Bloom and Handley Page

Insurance owes its existence to risk, though of course insurers have problems and responsibilities of a very different nature from those of industrialists. Vehicle and General collapsed because its managers made incorrect calculations of the risk, with the result that the premiums over all were unable to meet liabilities and claims. There was no conspiracy here, just bad judgement. The directors' only mistake was to continue trading when the red light was already shining brightly and should have brought them to a halt – or at least warned them to slow down. They would never be allowed to make such a mistake today as a result of Vehicle and General and others. The Department of Trade monitors all insurance company balance-sheets and accounts. Government actuaries scrutinise the figures, and the moment the calculation of the liabilities and assets fails to meet a standard the Department not only turns on the red light but also brings down the barrier to stop them taking any more premiums. And once a small insurance company has to do that it is never likely to trade again. In the insurance field the Government has seen fit to 'interfere'. The new insolvency laws now endeavour to deal with this situation.

Anyone who has had to face the situation that his business can be saved from collapse only by conjuring up from Lord knows where a six-figure sum can surely be forgiven for postponing the actual act of throwing in the towel to the last possible moment. I never found John Bloom a particularly attractive character, but with all the bad advice he had to suffer and his inability to see it as such I could not but have a certain amount of sympathy for him – which was far from the case with Emil Savundra.

As its name implies, Rolls Razor Ltd was founded in 1927 to manufacture razors, and it continued to do this in its factory at Cricklewood until the 1950s. In 1954 the sale of Rolls razors slackened off, and in July 1958 it decided to diversify by entering the

washing-machine business and marketing one called the 'Foamatic'.
It was a model, however, which failed to please the public, and
between 1954 and 1959 the company lost something in the region of
£300,000. The directors contemplated putting it into voluntary
liquidation. Then, in November 1959, out of the blue came an offer
from a firm called Equity and Share Company (London) Ltd to
acquire their entire issue of 3 million 1s shares (£150,000). They
gladly accepted it. Behind the deal was John Bloom, who the year
before had begun earning a living by buying and selling washing
machines of various makes. He did very well, and by May 1958 had a
team of salesmen selling sixty machines a week. For his trading he
formed the Electromatic Washing Machine Company Ltd. Later
that summer he found a small manufacturer in Holland making a
cheap twin-tub machine, which he imported in vast numbers and
sold in Britain for 49 guineas when the average price at the time was
nearer 100 guineas. In September an advertisement he put in the
Daily Mirror brought a flood of enquiries. He arranged hire purchase
facilities with a finance company, and by the following September he
was selling 400 machines a week. He could sell even more, but he was
taking the Dutch factory's total capacity as it was.

How to get more machines and, even more important, how to
finance getting more? Electromatic was only a private limited company. He was told he must 'go public' or, better still, acquire an
existing public limited company with a 'quote' and with factory space
in which he could make his own machines. He had a look around,
heard about the difficulties of Rolls Razor and their Foamatic, and
put in his bid for acquisition through Equity and Share. He sold
Rolls Razor the assets of Electromatic in return for the 3 million Rolls
Razor 1s units. Under this agreement, Rolls Razor Ltd agreed to
produce for Electromatic all the washing machines Bloom's company
could sell for a period of five years at cost plus 10 per cent. Bloom was
made managing director of Rolls Razor in March 1960, and given
complete control of the Cricklewood factory. And then, having got
everything set up, a group of the old Rolls Razor staff, for reasons I
have never been able to fathom, broke away and formed their own
company selling washing machines to compete with the new Rolls
Razor.

Overnight John Bloom found himself with far from sufficient
stocks to meet the demands generated by his press advertising
campaign. Cricklewood had to cut corners to turn out machines in
the quantities and in the time required, with the result that quality
fell off, and the Rolls Razor washing machine acquired a reputation
for shoddiness and breakdowns which caused sales to fall off. By the
end of 1960, Rolls Razor had lost £232,000 in the changeover from

razors to washing machines. In July 1961, Bloom and Richard
Reader Harris, MP, who had been appointed chairman, decided to
diversify the operation by forming a joint company with Sir Charles
Colston to sell a Rolls-Colston dishwashing machine.

At the beginning of 1960 the Stock Exchange had suspended
dealings in Rolls Razor shares, which still had no quotation two years
later. But in May 1962 it was allowed to offer 500,000 ordinary 1*s*
shares at a minimum price of 20*s* each through Kleinwort Benson. So
Rolls Razor, no longer making razors, had certainly come up in the
world. Confident in the future, the directors of the company gave
John Bloom a seven-year contract as managing director from 1
January 1962 at a salary of £15,000 a year, and the use of a Rolls-
Royce motor car. A major step was taken in March 1963 when
production was moved from Cricklewood to the Swansea works of
Pressed Steel, with whom Rolls Razor made an agreement for the
purchase of washing machines at a low contract price. They also
agreed to sell Prestcold refrigerators through a company they formed
calls Rolls-Prestcold Ltd, making use of Bloom's network of sales
reps. During 1962, Sir Isaac Wolfson's General Guarantee Corporation agreed to provide hire purchase facilities up to £10 million on a
revolving credit basis.

It seemed he had successfully overcome the setback of the secession
of old Rolls Razor employees and was poised for even greater
profitability. Sales of all products in the group rose impressively. By
the end of 1962, Bloom reckoned he had disposed of 100,000 units.
Turnover in 1962 amounted to £6,900,000 and doubled to
£14,700,000 in 1963, but only owing to costly sales promotion
campaigns which, coupled with a heavy rise in overheads, reduced
profit margins very considerably. In spite of double the turnover, the
net profit after taxation in 1963 was only £394,000 compared with
£383,000 in 1962.

One way of reducing long-term costs was seen to be expanding
laterally and, in January 1963, Bloom acquired the equity share
capital of Bylock Electrical Ltd, manufacturers of the fractional h.p.
motors used in so many of his products, and hard to get. Bylock also
made vacuum cleaners and other domestic appliances which fitted
his overall marketing plan. To share his newfound wealth with the
family Bloom appointed two of his brothers-in-law directors of Rolls
Razor.

But the scale of the company's operation was something foreign to
Bylock's experience so far, and they were swamped with orders
which they could only fulfil – the old story – by sacrificing quality.
Bloom's high-powered marketing was killing the operation on the
shop floor. Record sales only produced a serious stock shortage.

Neither Pressed Steel nor Bylock could cope with the demand. And when Bloom heard that housewives were clamouring for 'automatic' washing machines he had his production engineers work out plans for a Rolls Razor 'automatic'. But it was not going to be as easy as that. Came the summer of 1964, and still no Rolls Razor Automatic. Moreover Bloom was no longer alone in the cheap washing machine market; many competitors had appeared and were undercutting him. The flow of enquiries fell off throughout 1963, and frantic measures were taken to stimulate sales, such as offering free or low-priced holidays to every purchaser and giving trading stamps. He actually bought his own trading stamp company – the Golden Eagle from Sir Isaac Wolfson, putting his own head on the things – and a half-interest in another. He formed Rolls Tours Ltd to handle Continental holidays; Rolls Rentals Ltd to promote the rental of television sets; and Rolls Photographic Ltd to sell home movie kits and still cameras.

This feverish activity at the beginning of 1964, for which most of the paperwork was never properly executed and minutes rarely acted on in the way intended, created a complete state of confusion. Directors were unaware of many of the transactions. Chairman Reader Harris and six directors resigned. But the trouble lay deeper than that. The company had been suffering from a severe liquidity problem for several months. In the spring of 1964 it resorted to short-term borrowing. Patrick Hutber was appointed 'financial co-ordinator' on 14 May, a position with no clearly defined duties. Hutber was a financial journalist who joined the *Financial Times* in 1957 and from 1961 took over the 'Lex' column. He wrote the 'Questor' column in the *Daily Telegraph* as a freelance and from 1966 to 1980 was City editor of the *Sunday Telegraph*. He died after a car accident in 1980 aged fifty-one. Hutber obviously had the confidence of the board, who were apparently unable or unwilling to study the books for themselves. For they placed great weight on Hutber's forecast that the trading profit for the three months to 31 March 1964 would probably be £125,000, and the year's total £500,000. When he told them that cash would be needed at once, Bloom said he would try to raise £300,000.

I am sure Hutber had good reason, but personally I cannot see how he felt able to give them this advice in the light of Rolls Razor's accounts showing a loss of £179,000 in the first five months of 1964 – a figure which in our opinion should have been put very much higher. The basis of costing was, to say the least, somewhat inaccurate. The accumulation of twenty-six weekly accounts to 30 June 1964 showed the company had made a net profit of £38,106, whereas in fact trading losses exceeded a quarter of a million. It is difficult to see therefore how the directors could have ascertained anything resembling a true picture of the company's hazardous position by listening to the cheery analysis which their financial co-ordinator gave them that afternoon of 21 May.

The board met a week later, after which John Bloom, Patrick Hutber and another director, Aaron Wright, went to Kleinwort Benson, the company's bankers, for a frank discussion. Apparently Kleinworts agreed to provide £250,000 if Sir Isaac Wolfson came up with a similar sum, but neither of these, if they were ever formally made, materialised.

The following summer Patrick Hutber was replaced – or perhaps joined? – by one Claude Miller who was given the title of 'financial adviser' at a fee of £25,000 (payable in advance) for five years. No mention of this appointment seems to have appeared in any minute, but Miller was certainly sent a cheque for his first year's remuneration before assuming his onerous task. So there was money somewhere. And then it all seemed to acquire the nature of a game of Monopoly, when in May the board approved a dividend of 120 per cent for 1963 which was going to cost them £209,719.

They came down to earth on 3 July when John Bloom told them that to make Rolls Razor financially sound they would need an immediate injection of £1,750,000. He had tried and failed to get underwriting facilities for an issue of this size. One of the directors, Jack Jacobs, said if Bloom could not obtain permanent finance to the required amount the board must recommend the appointment of a liquidator. When they met three days later, John Bloom was still unprepared to admit that Rolls Razor was insolvent, though a proper examination of his books would have told him he could draw no other conclusion. He clung to the hope that perhaps the trading figures of the first five months of 1964 (Hutber's version) would enable them to raise a convertible loan of £1,500,000 by giving underwriters £600,000, the balance to be offered to shareholders. He somehow produced the £209,000 to pay the dividend due on 24 July, which he understood was his part of the finalisation of the financial arrangement he was making with Sir Isaac Wolfson. Confident that he would ride the storm, he then (on 11 June) took a plane to Bulgaria to make holiday arrangements in that country for Rolls Tours Ltd and stayed on his yacht. Incredibly, with the fate of the company hanging in the balance, he did not see fit to return to England for the board meeting of 17 July. If he had done, he would have heard Claude Miller earning his fee by telling the directors what had been hidden from them for so long, that Rolls Razor was insolvent. The company, he said, should be wound up voluntarily immediately. No further cheques should be issued except for wages, salaries and preferential claims.

Faced with reality, the board with a chairman but no managing director felt obliged to take his advice, and issued a statement to the press and the Stock Exchange there and then. Miller had seen Sir Isaac Wolfson again before the meeting and been told of the chairman of Great Universal Stores's desire to come to Bloom's rescue, but only after the position had been further clarified. Miller told him the position was now crystal clear: unless Rolls Razor was shored up by his or someone else's money *that afternoon*, it would collapse.

I suppose news must have reached John Bloom at Sofia of the reports in the British press of the decision taken in faraway Cricklewood. When he returned to England, and met his colleagues on 20 July, he had no alternative but to give his consent to it. That same day the directors of Rolls Razor sent round a letter to 19 Eastcheap instructing Cork Gully to carry out an independent investigation into the company's activities, and to prepare a detailed report and Statement of Affairs for submission to a meeting of shareholders and creditors which had been called for 27 August. At the same time an inquiry was instituted by inspectors appointed by the Board of Trade. One of the inspectors was Henry Benson (later Lord Benson). This was the first time we had worked together. I was most impressed by his energy and thoroughness in the way the investigation was carried out.

John Naylor did another of his intensive and quick exercises in which he pinpointed the trouble by stating in his report: 'Throughout the whole of our investigation . . . the lack of accurate information and the inadequacy of the Accounts Section of the company, was to a great deal responsible for the failure of the directors to realise the true situation and take adequate steps to remedy this.' The board minutes during the final weeks of trading showed quite clearly, he wrote, 'that during this crucial period the directors were never in possession of accurate and up-to-date financial information on which to assess the position, and that monies raised in the last two or three months were measures taken under considerable pressure, and without full knowledge of the facts'.

Our Statement of Affairs showed a total deficiency of more than £4 million. There were 1,200 unsecured creditors. The one with the largest claim was Pressed Steel with £400,000. Press advertising had continued right up to the week before liquidation, and a lot of money had yet to be paid to the advertising agent. Tallent Engineering Ltd, who had made an agreement in February 1964 to manufacture 4,500 washing machines a week for Rolls Razor over a five-year period, claimed £866,000 for breach of contract. General Guarantee Corporation were owed £200,000; Barclays Bank were owed the £209,000 they had lent Bloom to pay the 1963 dividend. The company had an overdraft of £455,000 at Barclays, who had the Cricklewood factory as security, however, valued at £427,000. As far as preferential creditors were concerned, the company owed Customs and Excise £287,000 in purchase tax, and some £210,000 to the Inland Revenue for profits tax. There was a sum of just over £9 million representing contingent liabilities arising on hire purchase finance with nine separate houses; but with retention money held against such liabilities the outstanding amount was nearer £500,000.

The company had a lease of a fifth-floor flat at Aldford House, Park Lane, with three bedrooms, two bathrooms and three other rooms, which John Bloom himself occupied. A new five-year lease had been obtained at £1,350 that very year of 1964. In addition, on 14 May, when a glance at the books would have told them the company's precarious state, the directors entered into an agreement to take a lease of two more flats in Park Lane 'as a residence for Mr Bloom' to whom 80 per cent of the cost would be charged personally. It was not yet ready for occupation by the time the company went into liquidation. These flats were part of the company's assets, which included of course their factories, fleet of 1,040 vehicles (many on hire), machinery, the completed washing machines, refrigerators and other 'stock'. Assets totalled some £772,000.

The case of Rolls Razor and the reasons it was unsuccessful were typical of many which followed and met the same fate, including of course Laker, who tried to break the monopoly of the major world carriers in a lucrative market across the Atlantic. It came about in this way. John Bloom found that the big people in the white goods trade, that is, washing machines, washing-up machines, refrigerators, etc., were charging an enormous price over the cost of the articles they manufactured, and this made the machines luxury items for the wealthy only.

John Bloom saw that there was a great market for a cheap reliable machine. He then found a Dutch firm which manufactured twin-tub washing machines, then the acceptable product, bought them, and marketed them at what was probably under half the price of those being marketed by the English manufacturers. For the first time, the housewife could afford the luxury of a washing machine, and John Bloom became almost a folk-hero. The machines were advertised direct in the daily press, and sold by mail order. They went like hot cakes but, the monopoly having been broken, the big manufacturers realised that they could no longer go on as they had in the past, and they started manufacturing and selling a much cheaper machine, cutting the price, which they could well afford to do.

At the same time, the public began to demand more exotic machines which did everything – washing, drying, the lot! John Bloom then decided to manufacture in Britain, and that is why he bought Rolls Razor, and made contracts with other English manufacturers to make washing machines for him. Meanwhile, with a price-cut by big manufacturers, and the retailers fighting against direct selling, there was no further need for John Bloom and his cheap equipment, and as he did not have the financial facilities to fight back, he was in fact put out of business.

To try to recoup his fortunes, he had gone into other kinds of business, such as cameras, electrical goods. You name it, he tried to sell it! He also gave enormous further discounts and prizes for those who bought the machines – all of which ideas were copied later – but he could not do this at a profit. Meanwhile the company was showing the same rate of gross profit on paper, which they were not making, because that was what Bloom told the accountants to do. He lived in a fool's paradise, and lost the battle with the big manufacturers. It is a tragic fact that, once someone comes in and breaks a monopoly, having done it there is no further use for him.

An extensive direct-selling campaign of this sort, building up as it did to a turnover approaching £15 million, needed to have a very strong financial base of its own, rather than having to be continually looking to 'finance houses' for money. If the directors insisted on playing it that way, they should have made sure they had proper cash forecasts and raised money when they were trading successfully.

They were naturally compelled to switch to automatic machines when the market dictated, but the change-over was very badly handled. Delay in introducing them meant that when sales of twin-tub models fell there were not enough of the successors to maintain a follow-through. The red light came with the falling-off in sales in the third week in April 1964 – from 18,600 units in March to 13,800 in April. In May they only sold 8,800, in June 6,800. Production was geared to 5,000 *a week*.

Consumerism played a notable part in the decline and fall of Rolls Razor. Several million housewives noting the criticism of the company on the television programme 'Choice' cannot have been entirely a coincidence. Also, the twin-tub machine of a competitor was criticised in the April edition of the Consumers Association magazine *Which?*, and as a result the manufacturer disposed of large quantities at reduced prices. They were sold in the High Street for 39 guineas when Bloom's price was 59 guineas. Another direct-selling competitor was offering a fully automatic machine at 49 guineas.

The main reason, however, was that concentration on sales and production obscured the financial issues. If, early on, Bloom had disposed of the Cricklewood factory and offices for £400,000 and moved to smaller premises and reduced overheads, he could have cut back to allow for less twin-tub production pending the introduction of the fully automatic machine. Unfortunately, when all was set fair he had made long-term contracts with outside manufacturers like Tallent to take large numbers of machines every week, and if he had had to reduce orders too suddenly and too drastically he might have been faced with claims for breach of contract.

We thought the directors' decision to seek liquidation the right one, and I said as much to the 250 shareholders who attended the meeting at the Kingsway Hall on 27 August. John Naylor, the author of the report, was at my side. The largest shareholder of Rolls Razor of course was John Bloom himself with 500,000, now worth half a million pennies. The Jon cartoon that day in the *Daily Mail* showed a mother giving her boy a penny to go shopping with, and the little chap protesting that all he could buy with a penny was a Rolls Razor share. As managing director, Bloom sat beside us on the platform. A posse of his salesmen outside the hall had jeered him as he entered. But inside the audience of shareholders were by no means all howling for his blood. Indeed, when asked to vote from the floor in support of the directors' resolution to liquidate, seventy-four were against and only seventy-two for. A proxy vote, however, showed an overwhelming support for the resolution.

With no longer the will or the personal fortune to make a gesture of the kind that had characterised the beginning of the venture, for the once-dynamic 'tycoon' with the little beard who had made the headlines with his wild parties patronised by the stars of showbiz it was the end. And once more Cork Gully were invited to make it as painless as possible. I was appointed liquidator, and by May 1981 after long-drawn-out proceedings we had managed to make a return to the unsecured creditors of 11.98p in the pound.

John Bloom went to America, and in 1972 opened a chain of 'Merrie England' restaurants around Los Angeles. In March 1979 he was in the news again when he was given a suspended sentence of one year for pirating the film *Star Wars* by making and selling copies of it he had made on videotape.

The Bloom case raised the question of how a company should be valued. When Bloom sold Electromatic to Rolls Razor it was no longer the practice to value a company by its assets. What a company was worth, when it came to selling it, was a matter of multiplication of profits. So if Bloom could augment Electromatic's profits he could demand more Rolls Razor shares for it than, to put it mildly, was reasonable. John Bloom invented a new kind of fraud. He had to get, and keep his quote on the Stock Exchange, and he needed financial capital both for himself and his company. Therefore there had to be disclosed to the Stock Exchange the facts about his company, to justify the price. In those days, and still to a certain extent, the value of a company is based on a multiplication of its profits. John Bloom's profits in these opening stages, were reasonably small. What did he do? He formed a new company, a very small company, with practically no share capital, which he owned personally. Then he charged the greatest expenses to that company. For instance, purchase tax, advertising, and items like that. They were invoiced to this small, quite empty little company which he owned. The result was that when the profits were disclosed in the manufacturing company they were magnified enormously; in fact the market price increased by ten times the amount that he had paid himself. Then, when the operation was over, he sold sufficient of his shares at the advanced price to put the money into his own little company to pay for the expenses which had been paid on behalf of the manufacturing company! A very profitable transaction, although of course quite illegal. For this he was prosecuted later on for fraud.

What he had thought of, which nobody else until that time had thought of, was actually paying, and putting money into the company, as a means of fraud! Until then, people had mainly thought of only taking it out. The result was that when the case went to trial they realised the difficulty of proving to a jury that it was fraudulent to pay expenses on behalf of a company and not a generous gesture to the shareholders!

The result of this was that a deal was done during the trial. Bloom pleaded guilty, and was only fined a reasonably small amount of money. To my mind that was very hard on John Bloom's army of creditors. If he had committed a fraud or some other wrong, then the creditors were owed money by the debtors. To fine the guilty party, to suit the Government, reduced the fund from which the creditors would be paid. If there is to be a prosecution in such cases, and the man in the dock is found guilty or pleads guilty, it should not end up with a fine but with either no sentence at all or a custodial one. Otherwise the creditors are bailing out someone who has caused them wrong. Even today, some courts fine directors for fraud, which means merely that the creditors who have been defrauded have the privilege of paying the fine, as the fine is always taken first.

Sir Frederick Handley Page's company, which he founded in 1908 only six years after the Wright Brothers demonstrated that powered

flight was possible and could be commercial, for many years *was* the
British aircraft industry. His name became a household word. He
presided over his company's affairs for fifty-four years until his death
in 1962. He began making aeroplanes at Barking, moved to Cricklewood in 1912 and acquired the works and aerodrome at Radlett in the
1930s. Up to the end of the Second World War, Handley Page made
a succession of famous big aircraft with government subsidy, civil
machines like the Hengist for Imperial Airways, military planes like
the Halifax and Victory bombers. After the war it produced the Dart
Herald, but there were no big sales. In spite of this Sir Frederick
refused to be swept into the round of Government-based mergers
which ended up as British Aerospace, and chose to remain
independent. It cost the company dearly, but I might well have made
the same decision at the time.

In the early 1960s, Handley Page realised there was little hope of
maintaining a stable aviation business based on government support
and began to investigate the possibility of diversification. The first
venture was in the field of electrical and oil-filled radiators; a
production unit was set up at Cricklewood. A number of subsidiaries
were bought, but none of them proved profitable. In fact the policy
was little less than disastrous, and the company lost at least £100,000.
In 1965 the directors decided to re-examine the possibility of further
exploiting the company's traditional background in aviation
expertise. The company was now on its own and could not look for
government support. A private venture, they said, would have to
abandon the large aircraft which had been the Handley Page tradition and enter the general aviation field. In 1966 the board decided to
build a mini-airliner of some 12,500 lb weight, attractive to executive
and commuter airline operators. It was to be an inter-airport feeder
plane and was also for the military market. They called it the
'Jetstream', because it was not a jet! They planned to make these
fifteen-seaters on a vast scale and sell them all over the world. Some
£12 million was invested in research and development, but the
project took very much longer and cost very much more than
estimated. Delays in development, due to changes in specification
for the Mk 1 and the Mk 3M, cost the company about £3 million. A
contract with the American government was cancelled. But, apart
from that, the projected cost of the Jetstream operation was very
wide of the mark, and the need for successive rights issues at such
short intervals showed that costs of development had become much
greater than originally envisaged. In 1967 they issued £1,120,000 of
8 per cent loan stock to raise additional capital. The organisation of
the company was top-heavy, and an over-ambitious production
programme adversely affected the levels of stock and work in

progress. The turnover which had been £12,255,000 in 1963 fell to £5,966,000 in 1961.

This case has led to a rule, indelibly fixed in my mind. You cannot develop something which you cannot write off against other profits. Handley Page at this time had no other business, and the only way they could find money to develop the aeroplane was either by rights issues, share issues, or borrowing from the bank. No one should ever, once they have started in business, develop something which they cannot finance, where there is no other business to pay for the cost of development.

By the beginning of 1968 only thirty Jetstream machines had been completed at Radlett, and two of them were very unfortunate. One was bought by British Steel, and crashed on landing when it was delivered to the chairman. Fortunately for everybody concerned, including me, who had finished off the aircraft, the crash was held to be due to pilot error. The other had been sold to a German airline, and that crashed when the chairman and his family were making a journey to Switzerland, and – fortunately again – the crash was due to failure of the turbo mica engines with which they were powered, and the company was not held responsible.

The company had succeeded in appointing the K. R. Craven Corporation of St Louis as their American distributor, who had formed the International Jetstream Corporation for the purpose. But all the time the company's resources were being drained by over-long research and development, and no substantial income was being earned by the sale of aircraft. In 1968 development expenditure amounted to £5,543,000. In June 1969 there was an injection of £2,500,000 to meet an acute cash crisis. But to no avail. Barclays saw Handley Page's overdraft climbing to £7 million and thought the time had come to call a halt. On 7 August they appointed me receiver. We presented a Statement of Affairs to an informal meeting of creditors on 16 December.

In the spring of that year there had been many comings and goings to and from the Handley Page board, and on the date of my appointment five of the several directors had only been in office for a few weeks, and they included J. E. V. Tyzack, the chairman, and T. D. Robertson, the managing director. This new board had been appointed with a view to examining the company's affairs and taking steps to restore the company's position. But their appointment came too late, and they could only agree with the bank's decision to put in a receiver. The day after I took over, John Tyzack told the press that the main reason for the crash was the fact that a substantial part of the £12 million spent on research and development for the Jetstream 'must be considered unproductive and should therefore be written

off'. The knowledge that an improved version of the Jetstream was
due out shortly of course inhibited sales of the Mark 1. Now that
Handley Page's troubles were filling the newspapers and television
news programmes, suppliers were reluctant to extend credit. I and
Robertson met shop stewards and the officials of ten trade unions
representing Handley Page's 4,000 workers who wanted us to appeal
to the Government to rescue the company by raising more capital.
They sent a telegram to Tony Benn, the Technology Minister. The
Government was reluctant to save a company which had spurned its
invitation to merge with the others. The best hope of salvation came
from across the Atlantic. The International Jetstream Corporation
proposed forming a new company to be called Handley Page Aircraft
Ltd, backed by £5 million sterling, which would pick up what
remained of Handley Page Ltd and start all over again. But just after
K. R. Craven, the Missouri banker behind IJC, signed he was taken
seriously ill and returned to the States. The second company was
registered, but Mr Craven was not in a position to produce the sum
expected. So the company went into receivership and the assets
returned to America under our charge.

My job was to keep Handley Page Ltd running with a view to
selling it – the basic Cork Gully conception of receivership. But
within a few days it was obvious that in the light of the cash-flow
position the amount of time I had to run the business with a view to
sale was very limited. Even with the most stringent economies and
restricting purchases to the minimum, expenditure was running at a
level of about £150,000 a week. Against this, anticipated income was
extremely small. I only managed to keep the firm going until
December by insisting during the negotiations with International
Jetstream that they purchased further aircraft. They agreed to buy
five, which brought in some £650,000. If I had not been able to make
this deal, I would have had to close Handley Page within weeks. In
that event, to have realised the assets on more or less break-up value
would have resulted in a shortfall even on the Barclays Bank
debenture, and given no return to unsecured creditors. A main
difficulty was that Handley Page had a very substantial amount of
work in progress on the Jetstream project, and even further
expenditure was needed to bring the aircraft up to specification. One
could not expect a would-be purchaser of the assets to pay a large
sum for aircraft with many problems still to be solved. I suggested
that the assets should be sold to Handley Page Aircraft Ltd for a
small initial payment together with the opportunity to develop and
produce the Jetstream. If they succeeded, they could pass back a
royalty to the receiver of Handley Page Ltd to settle outstanding
claims on that company. I further proposed that the K. R. Craven

Corporation, parent of IJC, should lend Handley Page Aircraft Ltd £4 million in instalments before December 1969, and this they agreed to. The new company would buy the old company's assets, but its freehold property, plant and machinery would remain the property of the receiver to whom the new company would pay an annual rental of £310,000. It would become wholly theirs, however, when the old company's full debt of £14 million had been eliminated. Craven would acquire the shares of the new company at the price of £100. Craven would ultimately acquire control of Handley Page Ltd, but at the same time give a 10 per cent holding to existing share-holders who would not otherwise have received anything for them.

That was the plan I put forward on 16 December 1969, but within a few months a receiver had been appointed for Handley Page Aircraft Ltd, too: R. N. D. Langdon. So the situation arose that Receiver Langdon owed Receiver Cork £13 million in liabilities and had to pay me rent. In the end we were not the ones who had to close the business. It ran for some time under the new scheme and new directors. But when Craven's heart attack was found to be serious the American bankers withdrew their financial support from him, and the planned necessary finances stopped coming over to the new company. Handley Page might have continued to produce aircraft if bad luck had not intervened. Craven had his own business and was in a position to use the aircraft and create sales in America. The British government refused to buy the planes for their own military purposes in spite of my pleading. But we did sell the rights and plans to Scottish Aviation, who continued to build Jetstreams which the British government did buy eventually. If they had only done that when we wanted them to, a great British company might have been saved.

When I was trying to sell the company to Craven and the new company, I could not get the British government to agree to give them the contract which they had for converting the V Bombers, which were being converted to refuelling aircraft. This was a lucrative contract, which would have enabled the new company to finance the continuation of the development of the plane. So in the end, so as to put them in an impossible position, I sold the company to the Craven Corporation, with a stipulation in it he would only complete if he got the V Bomber contract. The Government, therefore, was left with the decision as to whether they allowed the company to go into bankruptcy, with a loss to British aviation, or give them the contract. They capitulated and gave them the contract.

It was the first time I ever blackmailed the British government, and I think the last!

About two or three years after the Jetstream had been transferred to Scottish Aviation, the Government then bought the Jetstream plane for the Royal Air Force. It is tragic how often government shilly-shallying ruins a business – or it was in those days.

My experience with Handley Page and the niceties of the aircraft industry stood me in good stead when in January 1971 the Secretary of State for the Department of the Environment appointed me receiver of Ashford-based Skyways Coach Air, 50 per cent of whose share capital was owned by the state-owned Transport Holding Company, who were owed about £1 million on outstanding debentures. John Peyton, the Transport Industries minister, was not prepared to commit further public funds to shoring up Skyways, which he had come to consider a high-risk venture. The company was put on the market, but there were no bidders. I went down to Ashford on 20 January to take over the company's affairs, but I heard that the news of my appointment had never reached staff at their London office where not unnaturally there was alarm and despondency. However, I was able to assure everybody that my arrival did not spell the doom customarily associated with that event, and that the company would not necessarily be wound up. I told them I was aware of the valuable contribution which Skyways had made to the expansion of low-fare air travel in Britain, and that I might be able to devise a scheme which would enable the company to resume its inexpensive London–Paris service (Victoria to Hythe by bus; Hythe to Calais by plane; Calais to Paris by bus) as soon as possible. This had been withdrawn on 20 January. But I am afraid when I became fully acquainted with the situation I realised it could only be a clearing-up operation. It was what I call 'a legitimate failure'. There was just not enough income to make it pay, and never would be. John Peyton was right. It was high-risk, and its continued trading would no longer be justified. I managed to sell the airfield to a property speculator who was prepared to wait until the market improved and resold it at a considerably higher price than he paid for it. I was criticised for not obtaining a better price, but at the time I was selling no one wanted it.

A more successful exercise from our point of view, also in the field of aviation, was our handling of the light aeroplane manufacturer Beagle Aircraft of Shoreham in Sussex, whose chairman was the experienced Peter Masefield, once head of Long-Term Planning at the old Ministry of Civil Aviation (where Lord Nathan, a fellow-partner of Leslie's at Oppenheimers, was for a time the minister in the Labour government) and boss of civil servant Edward Heath before he resigned to go into politics. Beagle was formed in 1961 with a 100 per cent government stake, to which a further £6 million was added to help it out of the financial trouble it encountered in its early days. The Government was convinced there was a big market for British light aircraft, and I think they were right. The 'Beagle Pup' which was their main offering was seen as a challenge to the mass-produced, very much cheaper American 'Cessna' plane. In order initially to compete with this machine the Pup, which cost £8,000 to build, was offered for £5,000. The plan was to have as many as possible flying in different parts of the world and, once established, to raise the selling price, and/or have enough on the production line to lower the manufacturing price. They also made a strengthened, tougher military version of the Pup which they hoped the world's air forces would buy as preliminary trainers: the 'Beagle Bulldog'. It was not much of a recommendation to foreign buyers that, to Masefield's disappointment, the British government placed no orders with their wholly owned company for Bulldogs for the RAF. Though better at aerobatics, the Beagle machines could not compete with the Cessna range. The Swedish government liked them, however, and contracted to buy a number of Bulldogs at £8,500 each. But inflation had increased the manufacturing price, too, and to make a profit the Swedes should have been charged at least £12,000. So inevitably Beagle Aircraft ran out of money, and the Government was not prepared to invest any more taxpayers' money to save it from collapse. Though the Government owned the company, it was not a 'nationalised' undertaking like, for instance, the National Coal Board, but a limited liability company of which it happened to own the shares, all or part of which it could sell at any time it liked. Creditors who thought that, the Government being the owner, they would be paid in full without further question were disappointed. They had to reconcile themselves to having the percentage of what they were owed determined by a receiver, just as if it had been any commercial enterprise. John Naylor and I went through the usual routine of a receiver, with our usual confidence that we would be able to continue the manufacture of Pups and Bulldogs and within a few months be able to sell the business for a sum which would give the creditors good dividends. In April 1970, George Miles of Miles Aviation and Transport offered to take it off our hands for £800,000, but I told him it was not enough.

The reason it was not enough was that they had a very good engineering business, a certain amount of which they did for Rolls-Royce. That was the one lucrative part of the business. It was very well run. The aircraft business we would have been pleased to get rid of to anybody who would carry it on. There was one interesting point, and this was before Rolls-Royce went into financial difficulties. One of the reasons Rolls-Royce got into difficulty was that they were arrogantly taking enormous credit from all their suppliers. When I got there, I found that Rolls-Royce owed several months' back invoices, where they had received the goods but not paid for them. I got in touch with Rolls-Royce and said I wanted payment at the end of one month. They said: 'We're Rolls-Royce. We pay when we think it appropriate. If you want our business, then you will accept these terms.' I said: 'I'm a receiver. I don't accept these terms. If you want the goods to continue without a break in your supply-line, you will pay in a month, or I will stop it.' They said: 'Well, we'll put you out of business.' I said: 'It's not me you will put out of business – it's yourselves!' They paid up.

This, of course, was their great trouble. They had taken everything, so when they were in difficulty nobody was prepared to give them further time. Even in those days, large firms bullied small firms into financing them. Totally unjust!

The importance of keeping production going was underlined by the existence of the uncompleted Swedish contract, on which they had already made a deposit. I had to cope with indignant Swedish Air Force officers who could not understand how the British government could allow its own 'nationalised' aircraft factory to stop production. Surely the Government would never stop producing coal from its 'nationalised' coal mines? Pointing out the difference between Beagle and the NCB to foreigners strained my powers of explication to the limit. As things stood at that moment, I said, there was no chance they would get their Bulldogs in spite of the contract; they just had to take their place in the queue of unsecured creditors. I told the Government that they could not get away with it. They sympathised with my predicament and agreed they either had to compensate the Swedes or arrange to have their aircraft manufactured elsewhere. Obviously the latter was preferable, but where? What about Scottish Aviation? suggested the Department of the Environment. This was a manufacturer with maintenance and repair works near Glasgow, a subsidiary of a Scottish shipbuilding company and receiving a government subsidy. So I opened negotiations with Scottish Aviation on the lines that they would take over our stock and complete the Swedish contract, with the Government paying them the cost of manufacture. As it happened, Scottish Aviation were already making some of the parts of the Bulldog, and they contracted to take over Beagle production with their own Scottish labour and with technicians sent up from Shoreham. I agreed on the sum they would charge the Government for making each plane, but soon after I had done this there was a change of management at Scottish Aviation, and the new team complained to the Government that this was inadequate. Would they instruct Cork to raise it? Officials of the Department of the Environment felt obliged to ask me whether I thought I was being fair, and I answered a contract was a contract. Unless they gave me a direct instruction, I was against changing the figure accepted by the former management. My relations with Scottish Aviation became strained, to say the least. What possible motive could I have for digging in, they said, when I had the Government's authority to change the amount? Words like 'bloody-minded' and 'pig-headed' were implied if not actually bandied. I told them, as unemotionally as I knew how, that they were wrong about my brief from the Government. The Department had given me authority to change the price if I thought such a step was justified. I did not think it was justified. Scottish Aviation were obliged to put production of the Swedish order for Bulldogs under way, and for the sum their former management had agreed with me in writing. The Swedes were overjoyed. There was never any question of course of the purchase price being altered; it remained the one contracted for with the Shoreham firm. Any other course would have been fraud on the creditors.

Every time the Swedes came to see me, they were absolutely furious that the British government would rat on them when they were in trouble for buying British aircraft instead of Sabre, and it was very difficult for them to explain back to their government that they had invested in a company which had gone broke. Each meeting was very tricky. At the time, there was the Boat Show, and I was looking round the boats, which are one of my hobbies, when I saw a group of these Swedish officers and civil servants looking through the window of a big catamaran. They all waved and said 'wait' and came out. They were extremely nice – very cheerful and very friendly. I thought: Oh, gosh, that's all right. They're coming to see me this afternoon, and we'll have an easy meeting. Quite the contrary. When they were on official business, they specialised in being as difficult as possible! When we arranged things, however, they did become friends.

While I was trying to continue the manufacture of the Pups at Shoreham, Tony Benn, whose baby it was, was the Minister involved, and I talked quite a lot to him. In spite of what anybody might say, he was an extraordinarily loyal person to work for. When I told him I was carrying on the business, he said he would stand by me. Unlike quite a number of politicians, he put that in writing. When I was criticised for carrying on, he took his share of the responsibility. He later agreed that, if we got into a contract with another firm, he would in fact continue the sponsorship and aid to the company, and I went with him to see the Treasury, who turned him down absolutely flat – rather rudely, I thought. Whatever criticism you may have of Tony Benn – and I do not agree with his politics – he was an absolute gentleman to work for, and you felt that he would stand by you through thick and thin.

Other air forces of the world came to like Beagles and Bulldogs, and Scottish Aviation went on to make a very good thing out of the manufacture of both planes. The Beagle Aircraft operation at Shoreham as such died – it went into voluntary liquidation after receivership – but its new lease of life in Scotland was a conspicuous success, and the taxpayer's money invested in the initial project was completely justified.

It is amusing to note how Government-controlled companies at that time organised the price of the goods they were going to sell. No one could work out the cost of building the Pup, particularly as it was a new venture and had a learner curve. So they took the price of the Cessna, which was mass-produced but not nearly so solid or well built, or with such manoeuvrability, and sold the plane at the same price as the Cessna. The loss on each plane sold was of course fantastic.

Chapter Five

Not in the National Interest to Save Lyon

Like Beagle and Handley Page, Tulketh had a single product: cloth. This Midlands textile group – owned, if I remember rightly, by a Czech – specialised in what they called 'ladies and gents suitings'. A number of individual cloth-mills had been acquired over a period, building up into a sizeable group. But, unlike the aircraft firms, Tulketh acquired a second string to bolster its income, something very far removed from weaving: insurance. Tacking on a service to a manufacturing activity did nothing to prevent Tulketh from becoming insolvent, however. A combination of circumstances, including bad luck but mainly the inability to sell its products or make them for a price that would bring a profit, forced them into liquidation. And the insurance company designed to make them buoyant became instead a dead weight which pulled them even further down. The bank with the debenture put me in as receiver: I was in Germany at the time, read about my appointment in the papers and took the first plane home. The Department of Trade had already served a notice on the insurance company subsidiary to stop trading.

Other insurance companies announced their readiness to mount a rescue operation, and Phoenix Insurance was asked to do it. But how much was it worth? I had no idea. Premium rates had just been revised, but they had not had time to take effect. I was not willing to sell until I had a better appreciation of just how valuable the company was. It embraced both motor and life business, and the latter was certainly valuable. Phoenix, who were a reluctant buyer, said as I had to close the firm why did I not transfer the shares to them at a peppercorn. I had no intention of handing over something for nothing, however. I told Phoenix I would sell them the company on a formula. The ultimate price would be a multiplication of the profit which our actuaries and two accountants calculated the company was likely to make over an agreed period on prospective business at the new premium rate. I could not keep the company going, as I would have liked to have done, since the Department of Trade had stopped it taking on new premiums. Phoenix accepted my formula. Years later, it was claimed that we had sold the business for nothing, which of course we had not. You cannot value something making a vast loss merely because you put up the premiums, and we had no idea whether the amounts by which the premiums had been put up were the right premiums. Motor insurance at that time was in a very bad way. However, if there had been profits, the formula would have worked, but no one was able to convince Phoenix, and Phoenix were confident that the company still had in-built losses and was worth nothing.

As regards the textile side, we managed to sell all the individual cloth-mills separately as going concerns. Tulketh had a big loss carried forward, and this was taken over by others who tried to collect money for the insurance company from Phoenix under our formula. But they never managed to come to any agreement with Phoenix. They alleged claims were still coming in for higher amounts than allowed for in the formula. But that soon ceased to be our concern. Our involvement ended with devising the formula and having it accepted. We realised all Tulketh's assets and paid their creditors 100p in the pound.

One of the difficulties of being an insolvency accountant is that the press like to call you an 'undertaker', and state that you are only interested in shutting things up, so that people are frightened when the banks get you to go in.

The truth is quite the contrary. We spent a lot of our time – in fact nearly all our time – trying to rescue companies, and few of the companies which came into our hands, or at least the big ones which the senior partners dealt with, were other than sold as going concerns. Thus we transferred businesses from bad management to good management, and this was the reason why we were very successful in attracting new work. To be able to get credibility for this, I believe that one should be directors of going companies, good companies, so that when the banks say they are sending in one of the partners in Cork Gully, and people lift up their hands in horror, they can say, 'Well, he's a director of Costains,' or this, that or the other.

So I welcomed opportunities to go on the boards of healthy growing companies, like Dan Prenn's British Communications Corporation, of which I was chairman for a time, and which was extremely successful in making most of the communication equipment for the Tank Corps and the other mobile units of the British army.

In 1965 I assisted in the promotion of Plantation Holdings, which was mainly a rubber company, and the group's profits doubled to £506,000 in 1968, and in 1969 they were £695,000. We realised money in the rubber estates and invested it in Britain in engineering and electronic businesses, so that when ultimately the company was taken over by the Malays, as it was bound to be in the end, we had a viable business in Britain.

There was another thing I did which was very interesting. I have always felt that a constructive merchant bank would be a challenging thing to do, and Willie Whitelaw asked me to become chairman of the Merchant Bank in Northern Ireland – the Northern Ireland Finance Corporation, where I took on the chairmanship from Charles Villiers. Operating in Northern Ireland was far more difficult than in England. Half my board was Catholic and the other half Protestant, and they got on extremely well, except occasionally some spark would set them all off. I found a way to deal with this. Usually it happened in the morning, so I said, 'Well, this matter is adjourned until after lunch,' at which they immediately all turned on me to complain of arbitrariness, to which I replied: 'You're both bloody impossible in the morning, but when you have had a drink at lunchtime you will be all right.' They would then grin, knowing it was true, and after lunch the matter would go through without any further trouble.

The job of the Northern Ireland Finance Corporation was to promote new business, and try to maintain and rescue such businesses as were already in Ireland. The difficulty at first was that we were only able to make loans, and not put in equity capital. The Government and some of the papers out there could not understand why we did not put money into companies, but if companies are having difficulty – and the rate of loan interest was very high at that time, 18 or 19 per cent – the loan was the kiss of death. What we wanted was equity capital. In the early part we were not allowed to put in equity capital, but only loans. Later on when permission was given to put in equity capital, then you could move and be very much more constructive.

That I was able to be active in so many other spheres outside Eastcheap Buildings (we moved to Guildhall House in 1975) was due to the highly qualified and energetic partners we had been lucky enough to attract to the firm who shouldered the vast amount of insolvency work which poured into Cork Gully, with the aid of the large and efficient administrative staff which now filled twenty times the three rooms in which Walter, Norman and I had started when we returned from the war. To our managerial team we had been able to attract some of the best brains in the profession, men of the calibre for instance of Danish-born Edmund Hanson. The tripartite operation of myself, brother Norman and Walter Tickler, with the backing of Gerry Weiss and John Naylor, became four-pronged when Michael Jordan joined Cork Gully on a merger basis and his clientele, mostly in the building trade, were amalgamated with ours.

We linked with Alan Fabes and Arthur Chapman of North Chapman & Co. Other banks besides Barclays and National Provincial entrusted us with receiverships, and by the 1970s, though the big firms of Chartered Accountants still had their big insolvency *departments*, I think it fair to say that Cork Gully had more or less a monopoly of the major insolvency and rescue work. We became so conceited that we felt deprived if any major case went to another firm.

The addition to the managerial team which naturally gave me the greatest pleasure was that of my son Roger, who after passing his CA finals joined the firm in 1969. I was trying to run down the amount of work I personally did, and it was satisfying to see the third generation coming into the business.

Life was never entirely smooth for Roger, because obviously a son coming into the father's business finds it very difficult. People could feel that he is unfairly promoted, but Roger was extremely hardworking and he did very well. He was starting to do major work. However, one of the snags, which turned out in the end to be an advantage, was when Mr Registrar Berkeley ruled in 1973 that in view of his junior age and status in the profession he would not approve his appointment as liquidator in Icknield Development who were compulsorily wound up on the petition of First Finsbury Trust Ltd.

For more than thirty years it had been a rule of practice in the Companies Court not to appoint an accountant of less than five years' standing as liquidator, and Roger's appointment was a challenge to this 'rule', which of course was only a tradition and had no force. Creditors went to the High Court and challenged Berkeley's ruling. Roger's name had after all been put forward by Moore Stephens, to whom he had been articled and who were the auditors of First Finsbury. At the meeting the only creditors entitled to vote, First Finsbury and the Inland Revenue, had both voted for Roger.

In his judgement Mr Justice Plowman said there had never been any doubt about Roger's integrity or professional competence. But he was very junior in his profession. Liquidation work was specialised and carried heavy responsibilities. A liquidator in a compulsory liquidation was an officer of the court. Various powers and duties imposed on the court itself were delegated to him by virtue of the Companies Act 1948. The court ought not as a general rule to

Not in the National Interest to Save Lyon

appoint a junior and inexperienced accountant to the position. It was a good working rule, but the court had overall discretion.

Ought an exception to be made in the present case? On the one hand, to do so might create the false impression that Mr Cork was being singled out for favourable treatment because he was the son of his father. On the other hand I have had evidence which the Registrar did not have of the impressive and intensive experience which Mr Cork has had since he joined his present firm [Cork Gully] in relation to bankruptcies, voluntary liquidation, receiverships and trusteeships of deeds of arrangement, many of them involving considerable sums of money.

He was satisfied that Roger had had sufficient experience in insolvency matters in the past three years to match the average Chartered Accountant's experience of those matters over a considerably longer period, and he proposed to appoint him strictly on his own merits liquidator of Icknield Development. Roger was twenty-five. I am sure his grandfather would have been pleased. I certainly was. After all, his grandfather had not been much older when he started the firm.

It was good not only for Roger and Cork Gully, but for insolvency accountancy as a whole. Mr Justice Plowman's judgement helped to put the seal of respectability even more firmly on this much frowned on activity. A further step in the same direction was the Institute of Chartered Accountants in 1972 inaugurating its first course of instruction in liquidations and receiverships.

As it turned out, it was fortuitous that a younger and more tolerant man than I had to face the situation which developed in the course of the IPD case. I doubt if I would have handled it with the same cool as Roger did.

IPD were manufacturers of central heating plant – castings, radiator ribs and the rest. Their works were on the Kirkby Industrial Estate at Huyton, Liverpool, in Sir Harold Wilson's constituency. Like Tulketh, their management had opted for diversification and chosen the making of fruit juices; like Tulketh, this, too, had failed to save them from insolvency. Barclays Bank appointed me, but Roger Cork did the work.

It was for him to execute the usual Cork Gully stratagem of continuing trading with a view to a sale. But the men of Kirkby thought little of that. When Roger went to the factory he found they had downed tools and called a strike, a common habit when receivers are appointed. While he was sitting in his car, a gang of them came up behind, lifted up the back wheels and humped the car with him in it out of the factory gates. He took it in good part. The incident made him more determined than ever to win their confidence and persuade them to end the strike. He succeeded, and the factory came to life again. But his efforts to find a buyer met with less success. When we had all but despaired, the employees came forward with a plan to acquire the business themselves, and run it as a workers' co-operative. Roger got Harold Wilson's Labour administration to give us taxpayers' money to repay the Barclays loan; Tony Benn gave the co-operative support in other ways. The new owners/shareholders dismissed the old management whom they considered had let them down. They ran IPD with some success for at least three years. With no buyer in view, we could not have afforded to keep the company going much longer, and would have had to close the works eventually. However 'shutdown' is not a word which Kirkby workers recognise. We would undoubtedly have been faced with a sit-in. In that event Roger would have been lucky to have escaped with a mere car-humping. He extricated himself from the IPD exercise, however, with little damage and much credit.

There is an amusing side to this. Roger had, slightly arrogantly, argued with the Government and insisted on the terms at which he would sell it, and what he required for financing it. The Government were slightly irritated at a young man dictating to them. One day I was having lunch at 10 Downing Street with Harold Wilson and one or two other people, and Harold Wilson said: 'We have just consented to Roger Cork's rather arrogant conditions for refinancing a company. Who is he? Is he your uncle?'

I said: 'No, he is my son.'

'Well,' said Harold, 'he is even more arrogant than you are!'

Harold Wilson and that side of the then government were extremely helpful. Although the Conservatives were against, and rightly so, supporting bad companies, it was very sensible of the Wilson government to allow receivers who were getting new people in to have finance in very difficult times, thus saving businesses. After all, once a business has gone, it has gone for ever. I do not think on any occasion where they gave us money, or lent us money, we did not in fact pay it all back. It was very disappointing later on to find that under the party which I supported this sort of thing was more difficult. However, as far as Cork Gully was concerned, it was a happy if unusual outcome.

Many people have criticised Harold Wilson as being devious, and I must say I thought so until I met him. I found, if anything, he was extremely honest and extremely naïve. The difficulty was that if you were a friend he believed anything you said. Very many times one said something outrageous, and Harold would accept it as gospel. Where he was devious was that he convinced his left-wing Members of Parliament and ministers that he was a left-winger, when in point of fact he was very right-wing. While he was Prime Minister, there was very little reduction in the forces; he kept our nuclear deterrent, and with Healey as one of the best Secretaries of State for Defence the security of Britain was maintained. For this he has never had credit, and people still believe that he was devious, left-wing and a bad Prime Minister. I am not sure financially he was a good Prime Minister, but certainly his heart was in the right place.

The IPD case demonstrated more than any other the rôle of communication in running any business. As I told Rodney Lord, who came to interview me for the *Daily Telegraph* at that time, it is a myth that someone labelled 'a worker' does not understand what managing a company entails. He understands the financial realities of a company just like anybody else if it is put to him in plain language. I do not believe that if a workforce is given sensible and simple figures they will make demands for wages the company cannot afford. But they must be genuine figures and be given in good times as well as bad, otherwise workpeople tend not to believe them. Too often the people on the shop floor find themselves unable to trust what the people in the office say because of the nonsense language in which they say it. By the nature of the phraseology they *must* be hiding something! They cannot be coming clean, otherwise they would say what they have to say in clear, and not the code understandable only to those who have the codebook – the 'economists'. I never understood how 'confrontation' came to be a dirty word. It should be the rule of industrial relations *every day*.

I am convinced that five times out of ten the answer to saving a business is communication. Unfortunately, some managements cannot communicate with themselves, let alone with the workforce. I told Lord I thought co-operatives could have a chance of success but it depended on what they were manufacturing. The trouble with the average co-operative is the marketability of the product. It is difficult to trade without risk capital because you do not have to pay on risk capital (that is, share capital, not loans) unless you are successful. Management is required in a co-operative just as in any other business. But, if a co-operative can employ management of the necessary ability and pay interest on the entire capital put up by the Government, there is no reason why it should not work. It does not seem to me to make sense for the Government to advance cash to support management in any company which has already demonstrably failed. If it subsidises a bad company, it may subsequently be obliged to subsidise a good company in the same trade. The best way Government can help a company in receivership will often be to provide a temporary grant to enable the business to continue operating for longer, and give the receiver more time to sell it as a going concern. It may also be worthwhile to support a prospective buyer.

Nobody will buy a business where they think the labour problems are difficult, so a successful sit-in can probably only end in a co-operative. We always explain to them that to sell a business it must be a *going* concern, not stopping and going. If this means a reduction in labour, the workforce has to choose between keeping two-thirds of the workers employed and selling the business, or keeping everyone, not sell the business and in the end having to close it. Which is better?

This of course is the kind of question which the paid trade union leader with his career at stake, and a wife and family to support, is very reluctant to put to his members who, faced with the sacking of a third of their number, would round on him with the counter-question: What do you think we pay you for – to condone sacking? Even more reluctant are they to face the question: is it better to have a job at a wage, and under conditions less than you would have liked, than no job at all?

Simple figures and simple language are needed. It is the jargon and the 'clever' writing that people think they ought to be impressed by, and pretend to take in, which prolong these disputes. To many, simple arithmetic and argument are beneath their dignity. Most cases are basically very simple, however. Take a company with £40 million turnover. Wages cost it £15 million, raw materials £15 million, bits and pieces in the factory £3 million, adding up to £33 million. That gives the company a gross profit of £7 million. Advertising costs £2½ million, factory overheads another £2½ million, shop overheads £3 million, financing costs £2 million in interests on loans and dividends. That adds up to £10 million. Anyone can understand that when it is written down on a single bit of paper. You do not have to be either a wrangler or a computer to get the message that that company ends up the year with minus £3 million.

To make the company go forward instead of backwards you either have to increase the £40 million turnover so you can earn £3 million extra gross profit; or, if you can only manage a turnover of £40 million, you either have to make the goods for less or knock something off your overheads. If you cannot do either, then you have a dud business and it ought to be shut.

Those who in the 1970s saw insolvency closing in on them knew that well-tried practices and well-trained practitioners would ensure that the ordeal which lay ahead, though distressing, would be fair both to them and their creditors. Moreover the procedures which the profession and the legislators had evolved enabled those whose fall was sudden and unexpected to be taken care of at once. Immediate action was concerted to prevent a bad situation deteriorating even further.

When, in June 1973, Consolidated Tin Smelters Ltd withdrew the financial support on which their subsidiary Williams Harvey & Co., the largest tin smelter in Europe, was entirely dependent, the directors had no alternative but to call an extraordinary general meeting at short notice and appoint a liquidator able to obtain the temporary finance for maintaining its continuous manufacturing process. Their Mellanear Works at Kirkby in Harold Wilson's Huyton constituency in the North-East operated twenty-four hours a day seven days a week; once the furnaces went out it would take considerable time and money to start them up again. The announcement of my appointment as liquidator pointed out that they had acted swiftly 'as it was thought dangerous to risk any interruption in that process due to possible uncertainties during the interim period between calling meetings by normal notice and the holding of such meetings'.

The company obtained its tin ore concentrates from Cornwall and Bolivia under arrangements which might have given rise to serious problems, and the directors thought a liquidator able to speak authoritatively would be better-placed to deal with them than they. The company's principal asset was its large stock of raw materials, which were valueless unless processed; thus the importance to creditors of keeping the plant operating. Martin Iredale worked with me, and our first job, therefore, was to ensure that smelting never stopped; but I had to make it clear that I was not necessarily adopting all the contracts entered into with Williams Harvey. Any supplier who had delivered goods since my appointment on 8 June, but ordered before that date, had to give me details so that we could establish that they were still required. If we decided they were, we would pay in cash or on a *pro forma* invoice. Any products sold and delivered by Williams Harvey since my appointment had to be paid for in full, and could not be set off against the company's debts. In the mean time we set about drawing up a Statement of Affairs for the meeting of creditors for 6 July – rather, assisting the directors of Williams Harvey to do so.

Many of their employees believed that the failure of the company was a political plot to put them out of business with the collusion of their competitors Rio Tinto Zinc who were after their Bolivian ore contracts. When in July they learnt that the possible purchaser of Williams Harvey was the Rio Tinto Zinc subsidiary Capper Pass of Hull, they not only gained the support of the shop stewards at

Liverpool Docks to black the ore but also picketed the warehouses containing the finished tin. We had the greatest difficulty in making the men see that if they did not give me the tin to sell I could not pay them. They went on to black, as far as they could, not only the tin in the Williams Harvey warehouses but also the tin in everyone else's. This made the price of tin escalate. When the significance and truth of what I was telling them finally dawned on them, they allowed me to send people into their warehouses to collect the tin for the market, but kept the pickets on those of their competitors. Not unnaturally, this time it was the other smelting companies who accused me of plotting. I had cunningly contrived to keep them out of the market-place, they said, while Williams Harvey, of which I was receiver, was at liberty to exploit it as the sole suppliers. I had no say in the trade union's tactics, but I can see that when the effect of them was to raise the price of tin and Williams Harvey was the only firm in a position to benefit from it it looked to many as if the wily Kenneth Cork had masterminded the whole operation. In fact it was just an extraordinary stroke of luck. For while the picketing lasted the receivers were able to run the Kirkby works at a good profit, and it put the price of tin up permanently, which was good for the industry.

What they would have been right in laying at our door was the astute enlistment of the dust on the factory floor in the profit-making process. The Bolivians always sent the firm larger quantities of tin ore than they could cope with, so to catch up with the stream of material which was continually being delivered to their gates they had to use it up as quickly as possible. In the process a considerable proportion of the ore got blown into the air and settled as dust on the factory floor, on the ducting, on the rafters – everywhere. So we had all this 'waste' collected up and converted into tin which we then sold at the market price – which had only cost us the cost of the processing. Harold Wilson was fond of saying that I was the only person he knew who had made money out of a company's dust. And that was not the only waste we turned to our advantage. We scraped a large amount of finished tin off the insides of furnaces and chimneys, which we also sold. We also got financial support from the British government under the Industry Act in the interests of maintaining employment – and I must say that was handsome of them. For only a short time earlier they had given Williams Harvey a grant of £1½ million to diversify into other non-ferrous metals; but the plant which was built with the money, the most up-to-date in Europe, had been standing idle ever since for lack of funds and for a variety of other reasons. But that is another story. We found a buyer (Rio Tinto Zinc) for the smelting plant at Kirkby who was ready to keep it going, and in doing so earned the undying gratitude and respect of the Right Honourable Member for Huyton, Harold Wilson, Prime Minister and First Lord of the Treasury. Now Lord Wilson and a good friend!

Ronald Lyon was an unusual property-dealer and tycoon. First of all, he did in fact create things; and everybody, including his creditors, liked him. He had the familiar luxury home in Sunningdale, flat in Knightsbridge, villa in Majorca, hundred-ton yacht on the Riviera and another ordered from an Amsterdam shipyard for £3 million, two Rolls-Royces, one Jaguar, and a collection of valuable paintings valued at £2 million.

He was the son of an Essex builder; he was hiring out loudspeakers at the age of sixteen, started manufacturing garden sheds and was a millionaire before he was thirty. In spite of this record, the twenty-three banks to whom he owed money refused to give him temporary financial support of £8.5 million, which he claimed would save him from collapse. 'What?' they said. 'On top of ninety-four million pounds?' 'Yes.' But they had heard it all before.

The Treasury was equally unsympathetic. When they turned him down Lyon was quoted as saying: 'They really said they were not convinced it was in the national interest to save me.' His group owed £101 million in all. Only £6½ million of this, however, was due to unsecured creditors.

We saw it as our job to protect the property market with which the banks were so heavily involved. A meeting of representatives of all the banks concerned in the Ronald Lyon case was called at Keyser Ullman's office for me to outline to them our scheme – holding on to the property and selling it in a controlled way – and to get their assent to it. The trouble was that none of them came with authority to bind their banks to the action I suggested. When Mike Jordan and I had finished our presentation, there was a general nodding of heads.

'OK,' I said. 'Can I take it that you accept that we carry out this scheme for the orderly realisation of the assets, with the banks giving time for it to happen? Those in favour?'

No one raised a hand.

'Those against?'

No one raised a hand. It was a disaster.

We had to get agreement to the scheme that afternoon, or the property market would take another dive. We had to take a big gamble, one of the biggest in my life, so I said as jauntily as I knew how: 'Now let me put it formally to the vote. Is anyone voting *against* the proposal?'

I looked round the motionless meeting, and then at Mike Jordan.

'The proposal is therefore carried.'

It was the only occasion, said Mike, when he had known a negative vote being taken as a vote of approval. There is some advantage in having a meeting at which no one has the authority to vote.

There was one company that the Government did consider it in the national interest, however, not to abandon: Brentford Nylons. It felt it had a duty to prevent the loss of some 3,000 jobs in the factories and in the retail shops from which the company sold its large range of nylon sheets, blankets and clothing.

Brentford Nylons was started by an Armenian, Kaye Metrebian, in 1959 with £75 and two secondhand sewing machines. By 1976 he had a turnover of £30 million and was employing 1,600 people. Sales were stimulated by a series of riveting television advertisements in which the disc jockey Alan Freeman proclaimed a Bargain of the Week. After a time the credibility of the advertising came into doubt. The volume of sales fell as the cost of advertising rose. Metrebian had a stroke and he had to hand over to his brother-in-law. A point came when they could not meet their liabilities. They owed Barclays Bank £8 million and other creditors a further £7 million. Their assets were worth £14 million, but only so long as Brentford Nylons was a going concern. Continued trading, however, could only have added to their liabilities.

In February 1976, Barclays appointed John Naylor and me receivers and managers. Confident that we would soon find a buyer, we carried on trading. But we had failed to reckon with the stance taken by their Dutch nylon-yarn wholesalers on the question of retention of title, which at that time was a new thing, and it threatened to put a spoke in our wheel of unforeseen proportions. The question was whether ownership of goods passed from the seller to the purchaser at the moment of delivery even when the purchaser had not yet paid for them; or whether the seller retained ownership (title) until he had received payment, even though they had been delivered. The Dutchmen who had not been paid for much of the yarn which Brentford Nylons had bought from them, and were a major creditor of the insolvent company, held to the latter view. As receivers of the company, Cork Gully possessed £5 million worth of the stock – of goods, that is, made from the nylon which the Dutch were claiming under retention of title.

If we had sold this stock and it had afterwards been shown that it belonged to the Dutchmen, I would have been guilty of misfeasance. To make sure I did not do so, they applied in the English courts for an injunction to stop us as receivers selling 'their' property. If we had accepted the retention-of-title argument, which had still to be tested in the courts, we would have had nothing to sell, and we would have had to close the whole business and all the shops. So we decided to fight their injunction. But, the night before the application was due to be heard and we were to oppose it, it came to me that there was another and more subtle way of resolving the issue – and to our advantage. Fighting the application was going to be a long and costly business, and during it we would have no chance of disposing of the stock. On arrival at the law courts next morning I went over to our group and told them we were not going to fight the application after all. In that case we are finished, they said. On the contrary, I said, if an injunction forces us to stop selling the stock and then their claim that the stock is theirs under the retention-of-title law is found to be bad, then they have smashed Brentford Nylons without reason. The damages they would have to pay for closing the factory and killing the business would be enormous. My plan, I said, was to instruct our counsel to point this out to the judge and say we would accept the injunction and take the risk of things turning out as I believed they might. Since foreigners were not subject to British law, the receivers of Brentford Nylons would want an indemnity of up to £5 million in the event of closure of the works. Furthermore, if Brentford Nylons did not go on trading and giving the Dutch the orders for the nylon on which their profit depended, their factory, too, would have to close. The Dutch took the point, thought the risk of proceeding too high and withdrew their application for an injunction. We agreed to pay them something in the region of £$\frac{1}{2}$ million for the nylon they had delivered and not been paid for, and this released £5 million of stock which might well be their property.

Only after we had done that could we be certain of keeping the factories going after we had used up all the yarn which had been paid for. Our next task was to sell the company. Our theory was that the most likely buyer would have connections with Africa to which they could sell the factories' surplus goods. Unilever? Lonrho?

Both of these expressed interest but made no offer. We kept going as well as we could, but when our overdraft topped the £3 million mark it became rather nerve-racking. Potential buyers knew we were having a tough time; by holding out they thought they would get it more cheaply. Sales dropped; stocks would not shift. The factories were pouring out new goods, but the Brentford Nylons shops in the High Street had no room for them. So we decided to clear the old stocks by holding the first genuine 'receiver's sale' – our first on television – in each of the sixty-four Brentford Nylons retail outlets. We offered 30 per cent reductions. With the prospect of Brentford Nylons closing for good, housewives thronged the counters and bought whatever they could lay hands on. In two weeks we had sold £4 million worth of nylon underwear, pillow-cases, sheets and other goods. There was no longer any obligation for a potential purchaser of the company to pay for the old stock. It had disappeared, and been replaced with new.

With their minds on a possible 3,000 unemployed if the Brentford Nylons factories in Northumberland, Durham and Greenock had to close, the Department of Trade was persuaded to lend Lonrho £5 million, and we got Barclays to allow them an overdraft of a further £5 million. (New responsibilities regarding the number of workers it was proposed to make redundant as a result of a liquidation or receivership were given to liquidators and receivers by the Employment Protection Act 1975. The Department of Employment demanded notification of proposed redundancies on the first day of liquidation. It issued 'occupational guidance' to liquidators in a booklet entitled *Employees' Rights on the Insolvency of Employers*.) Within six months of the receivership we had sold Brentford Nylons to David Whitehead & Sons, a wholly owned subsidiary of Lonrho, for £9,800,000. Trading had never stopped; the factories had never closed. With the business theirs, free of all liabilities, Lonrho then formed a new company to run it. Our only mistake was to make a profit during our period of trading. We had to pay back the money we had borrowed from the Department of Trade. By the terms of the loan, we could have kept it if we had never shown a profit.

Lonrho rejected the fifty-two-year-old Kaye Metrebian's offer to act as consultant to the new company, and put a padlock on the door of his penthouse suite at the top of Brentford Nylons head-office tower beside the M4, which upset his twenty-year-old son Damon, who decided to sign on for National Assistance. The family continued to live, however, in their mansion in Palace Gardens, Kensington – the only ex-millionaire in Millionaire's Row? At least the company had not been broken up, and the workforce kept their jobs.

Tiny Rowland always claimed we had sold him a pup, but at that time he needed British profit, as most of his income came from abroad. He later made a great success of the company, as he usually did in the end with most of his projects.

Chapter Six

All Stern's Eggs in One Basket

The first of the fringe banks to get into trouble was Cedar Holdings, and it so happened that I was called upon to help them out of it.

It was early in 1974. I was at Barclays Bank head office one afternoon and had just started making a report to one of their senior committees chaired by a regional general manager when the latter was handed a message to say that Tim Bevan, chairman of 'Domestic', wanted me to go to the Bank of England immediately. I asked the chairman if I should go. He just said that if Tim Bevan wants you, then you go!

Barclays merchant bank had floated Cedar Holdings when it went public but were not its bankers. For that reason they felt that whatever trouble it had got itself into was no concern of theirs. But there was Tim Bevan at Threadneedle Street, along with some thirty others – representatives of Cedar Holdings's bankers, their merchant bank Samuel Montagu, the various financial institutions involved and their advisers – who had been called to a meeting by the Governor to prevent a run on the bank after the quote for Cedar Holdings had been withdrawn, which would be the next move. The message was that none present was expected to leave until the rescue had been agreed. Downstairs were the directors of Cedar Holdings, who were told to stay there until the Governor's meeting had decided what action was required of them.

Curiously enough, each of the four City institutions involved had representatives on the board of Cedar Holdings. The directors had caused the crisis by borrowing on the money market a very large amount of instantly repayable money and investing it in property. When trouble loomed, however, it was not recalled; just not renewed. So, though it had these assets in the form of property, Cedar Holdings could neither have met its liabilities nor paid out its depositors. It was therefore technically bankrupt.

While the representatives of the institutions and banks debated
how best to save Cedar Holdings, Tim Bevan and I kept quiet. It was
not our problem. Eventually they came up with a rescue package
whereby money would be pumped into the company and the
directors would be relieved of its control – one of the first so-called
'Lifeboat Cases'. They sent one of their number downstairs to give
the waiting Cedar directors the glad news. After some time he
returned to the room looking both miserable and astonished, and
announced that the directors of the company would have nothing to
do with the rescue scheme. Consternation and disbelief. It had never
occurred to any of these top brass that the directors they were
offering to rescue would reject their helping hand. But why were
they all looking at me? Who knew better how to deal with debtors and
bankrupt companies, said someone, than Kenneth Cork? Would I go
down and knock some sense into them? I looked at Tim Bevan; after
all, the only reason for my being there was to advise *him*. He
shrugged his shoulders as if to say: 'Why not?' And down I went, and
found the directors were very unhappy.

They could not understand why they had been left downstairs
while the four directors upon whom they had relied, the institutional
directors, were upstairs with the top brass, and felt they were in a
kind of debtors' prison downstairs. I pointed out to them that they
had no option but to agree to a scheme, because if the Quote was
cancelled in the morning, as it was going to be, then there would be a
run on the bank and the company would go into liquidation. With a
scheme, something could be saved and, what was more, the company
could be saved.

I said I agreed that the proposals upstairs were unreasonable and
that they should be revised. There was a grudging acceptance, and
they seemed to have some faith in the one person who had no other
interest than being helpful, and who had bothered to come down and
explain the situation to them. I went upstairs and said that the
directors would be reasonable, provided a fairer scheme was
proposed.

Something had to be drafted at once to which we had to get the
signatures of the Cedar directors committing them to play their part
in our plan. Once again they all looked at me, and I asked Tim Bevan
if he had any objection to my working for the 'other side' when I was
there as his adviser. He smiled and said he had no objection if that
was the only way they would get home that night. So I jotted down a
simple 'heads of agreement' statement giving a general outline of our
rescue package. A principal feature of it was that the institutions who
were shareholders would have to buy in the property at current
valuation as if the crisis were not happening. Upstairs they agreed

the revised proposals, and I again went downstairs.

The Cedar director who was their chief accountant had once been with Cooper Brothers. He at once cottoned on to what we were trying to do, and before any of his fellow-directors could start remonstrating anew he told them in no uncertain manner that the time had come for them to stand up and be counted. Without this very decisive lead it would have gone on even longer and we would all have been in Threadneedle Street when dawn broke. As it was, they gave their written assent, however reluctantly, to an arrangement by which Barclays put up £20 million with a prior charge on Cedar's assets. The institutions agreed to buy Cedar's property, which they reckoned would realise £25 million, and to put up a first tranche of that sum. The cost to the directors was having to sign away their power and letting other people run the company.

I brought back the document with all the directors' signatures on it to the meeting upstairs and they congratulated me on breaking the deadlock. But, asked someone, what happens to the bank tomorrow? Who would be in control in place of the board who had just been deprived of their powers, and oversee the execution of the plan? Again, it was taken for granted that it would be me. In for a penny, in for a pound. I could hardly turn back now. But it was with very little enthusiasm that next morning I got up early and went along to Cedar Holdings premises. I was now *de facto* chairman, managing director of this wounded fringe bank, with a committee of representatives of the financial institutions.

I found myself in this unwelcome situation because, though the Tory government had released credit, no manufacturing or commercial business wanted it. The only people who did were the property developers, but when they went to their banks for money they were turned down. All banks at this time fought shy of lending money to property men whom they regarded as an unacceptable risk. There were so many 'developing' land, and the only way they could pay interest was with the money they received from selling the property at a profit after their development of it had added to its value. But there was never enough genuine *income* for interest. So the property developers asked the fringe banks, all of them quoted companies and of some substance, to lend them the money to pay the interest. They *were* prepared to take the risk. Fringe banks had insufficient money of their own which they could lend, so they borrowed it from the clearing banks, who reckoned a loan to a reputable fringe bank was all right. So the money came from the clearing banks after all, though indirectly. That was how the Fringe Bank Crisis arose.

The people who started dealing with property at first made big

profits. They borrowed money to buy land and develop it for
eventual sale to the insurance companies and pension funds. But
they failed to notice that these customers had put a limit on the
proportion of their funds they were prepared to allocate to property.
Fund managers decided to invest a certain percentage and no more.
For a time there was a shortage of property; as soon as it was cleared
up the developers started buying as heavily as before, and then found
there was no one to sell it to. The insurance companies and pension
funds had fulfilled their property quota and were investing
elsewhere. With no buyers and no income, the property men were
unable to pay the interest on the huge sums they had borrowed to buy
the land in the first place. The same thing has happened since in
Hong Kong and Singapore, and may well happen in Australia and
New Zealand where bankers are coming in with more money on offer
than the countries need for trading. In Britain the Bank of England
told the banks to stop financing the purchasers of land. When we
started our rescue operations no one had enough actual cash to buy
developed property, so there was no property market. If the
developers had not been so greedy, they would have worked out the
ultimate market. But they surged ever onwards without pausing to
heed the fact, which the smallest amount of commercial intelligence
would have told them, that the total buying power of the pension
funds and insurance companies was only a third of the amount of
property being developed. So they were riding for a calculated
disaster. Among the riders was Guardian Properties whom we dealt
with, but in the lead was the forty-year-old Americo-Hungarian with
the London base, Willi Stern, whose property group at one time had
assets of £200 million. He helped his father-in-law Osias Freshwater
to build the Freshwater Group into the biggest residential property
operation in London. He obtained the regular three-year rent
reviews to which he was entitled under the 1965 Rent Act, and each
time remortgaged the property for higher rents. He borrowed to the
limit to maximise the profits to which he could see no end. Such was
his confidence in his own ability to keep them flowing that he
eschewed the protection of limited liability. He was convinced he
was a genius whose Flair for Finance could never let him down.
Moreover he successfully convinced others to share that opinion.
Whenever he was asked by a bank if it was agreeable that he should
give his personal guarantee, he always said yes. He also secured
substantial debts against the personal guarantee of his wife (a mother
of six). The very opposite of the Savundra-style schemer who salted
away secret reserves, he openly laid all he had on the table. He also
hoped his creditors would rate his record to date as an asset. But of
course once you have personally guaranteed the first 5 million it is

pointless to go on. The only security he had was his own group. His personal assets amounted to some £7,500. If his business was insolvent, his 'guarantee' was shares in an insolvent company.

His agreement to give a personal guarantee in so confident a manner had such a hypnotic effect, however, that few thought twice about accepting it. With so much at stake, the man *can't* be bluffing. Property values were on the up escalator, rising ever higher. It seemed that nothing could stop them escalating till the crack of doom. No matter Willi's group reaching the point when it had to find £30 million a year in interest on his loans, when his total rental income was only £11 million. The selling of more property would meet the shortfall. Or would it? Well, only so long as there was property to sell and there were people ready to lend. The Crown Agents seemed willing enough to throw in a few more millions, but then they themselves got into difficulties. In May 1974 the Stern Group owed £170 million to thirty-three financial institutions with no means to pay it back. 'Britain's Biggest Property Bust.'

What to do? Call in Cork Gully and try to have a moratorium. Our first concern was to avoid a collapse, which would help to bring down the property market. But the very scale of this collapse demanded special handling. Our first step was to call a meeting of the creditor bankers, mostly fringe banks. Here, we said, is £200 million worth of property. If it is thrown on the market and the clearing banks are not allowed to lend money to prospective buyers, there is no price at which it is saleable. If a property worth £2 million does not sell and has to be reduced to £500,000, actuaries and auditors will look at the insurance companies and pension funds, and find they are not achieving the safety margin. Companies will fall like dominoes.

Having got them to accept our version of the consequence of throwing Stern's property on the market *en masse*, we persuaded them that the realisation of Stern's assets could only be carried out by an orderly Scheme of Arrangement, which we then explained to them. Afterwards we outlined the plan to the Bank of England, who also gave it their support and agreed that it should be voluntary.

These meetings are always tricky. Most of the creditors are extremely worried about their own situation, being owed millions of pounds, and Willi Stern was meant to be taking the chair at the meeting, with me beside him, to put over the scheme and talk people into agreeing to it. Suddenly, Willi went out, and did not come back, so creditors were furious that their principal debtor had disappeared. He could not be found, and when he finally turned up – by which time most of the things had been agreed – he said he had been out to try to arrange some additional money, so that the meeting would be unnecessary! Of all the difficult meetings I have ever had, this was the only time that I found that the man I was trying to find a scheme for had disappeared.

The basis of our scheme was that the banks should finance the finishing of the development on all properties they had mortgaged and retain a charge on them. A hole in the ground had no value, and there were many such holes. It was part of the Stern Method to buy old buildings and knock them down with a view to 'developing' the site, even though there was as yet no planning permission – or perhaps *because* there was no planning permission. He had got the land cheap for that reason. Civil servants giving a hole in the ground planning permission is what adds to its value of course, and gives the developer his easy profit. For me this taking money out of the community to no good purpose and swapping it for sewing machines, television sets and motor cars made in Germany and Japan is stealing. You have taken away community assets and put back nothing in return. I could never get Willi to agree with me!

With the Bank of England having put a temporary stop on the clearing banks lending money for property development in an attempt to divert it into industry, once they saw the way the property world was going, no one could buy property. Under our scheme the property would be held until times changed and the property again became valuable.

The scheme provided that finished properties should not be put on the market in the normal way by advertising at a price, but by making it known through agents that they were for sale without a price being quoted. We invited anyone interested to make an offer and we would tell them if it was acceptable. We were widely criticised for this by estate agents and chartered surveyors. That's not the way to sell property, they said. You have to put a price on it. What they did not understand was that not putting a price on it was the very essence of the scheme. We were convinced that as soon as the market was held we would be able to realise the property in a year's time, say, at twice the current depressed price.

Property and financial correspondents in the press attacked the Cork Barrier, assuming wrongly that the banks were being bullied into the scheme against their better judgement. The only people to be bullied into it, if that is the phrase, were some American bankers whose advisers realised that if I held 98 per cent of the market they had a good chance of selling their 2 per cent at a reasonable price. Some did in fact sell several properties and thought they had been very clever. But the Bank of England was insistent that if they chose to operate in Britain they must play by our rules. They blew hot and cold for a time, but they toed the line in the end. Many American banks were sensible enough to appreciate the potentially explosive situation in which they found themselves and played ball from the start.

Our scheme for the Stern Group went through, with me as the administrator and Gerry Weiss doing the work, and had most of the results we predicted. Realisations in the second year were twice the price of the first year. But of course, if you have a piece of property for sale in which everyone is interested, the moment you have an offer you get others, because the first offer has put a value on it. If you then make a sale at whatever price, it is inevitable that the purchaser will sell it for a higher price later on.

What is the 'right' price of a piece of property? This was not something which Cork Gully were qualified or willing to say. We put every transaction through a reputable Chartered Surveyor from whom we received a written statement that in their opinion the price at which the property was being offered by the liquidator was the 'right' price. The bank which had mortgaged the property also had to agree the price. Many outsiders – mostly the press – were at pains to demonstrate that Cork Gully had sold at a 'wrong' price on the Stern properties. Many were people who were buying in to resell for a quick profit. It was of course in the interests of such people to make others think that the stupid liquidator had sold the property at a wrongly low price, and that the price at which they had resold it was the 'right' price. It was a ploy to cover the making of money out of something to which they had added nothing, which the climate of opinion was beginning to frown on. In wartime it is called 'profiteering' and far from respectable. If in the first place, they said, the liquidator had asked the price they were asking the second time round, there would have been no need for them to intervene. Specious nonsense. Stern's property was never worth the £200 millon he valued it at, which was why he became insolvent. We sold very little of it the first year, but after two and a half years we had sold everything that was saleable for between £100 million and £120 million.

We could not sell whole blocks of residential flats occupied by tenants with protected leases. The only way to realise this part of the group was to break up the block and sell each flat to the sitting tenant. Tenants thought that by clubbing together they could acquire the block, and their respective flats, more cheaply. However 60 per cent, say, would agree to buy, but then those with protected leases were happy to stay as they were. In many cases, too, the amount of money they could all scrape together was far wide of the value of the property. Putting up £50,000 for a block worth £2 million got us nowhere. This, too, led to criticism of Cork Gully on the same matter of the 'right' price. When we rejected offers which were

unaccompanied by the appropriate money we were accused of selling
them to friends of Stern who did have the money. In fact here, too,
we acted all along on the advice of Chartered Surveyors. It was not
Cork Gully who were doing the selling. We had a price veto and we
could hold up the sale for three months if we thought the price was
wrong, which we could never do if the experts said the offer was a fair
price. We had tender sales and wrote out conditions of sale, one of
which was that the buyer had to produce a certificate from the bank
to say he had the money. Whenever any aggrieved member of the
public or writer in the press accused us of underhand action over the
selling of Stern's residential property, I used to telephone Detective
Superintendent Keith Taylor of the City of London Fraud Squad
whom I got to know quite well. I would tell him that allegations had
been made that my people were conniving with others to sell flats at
'wrong' prices, so what about the Fraud Squad investigating us? We
would put all our books at their disposal and let them reach what
conclusions they could, and notify our accusers. We were satisfied
we were whiter than white.

In the House of Commons on 28 March 1977, Mrs Judith Hart,
Minister for Overseas Development in the Labour government, told
Dennis Skinner, the Labour Member for Bolsover, that she had
taken a close look at our scheme for the orderly running down of
Stern's business, and she could assure him there was no fiddle. Cork
Gully's voluntary plan did not preclude the Crown Agents, who were
owed £40 million, from taking bankruptcy proceedings 'if they wish
and if that would serve their – *and the country's* – best interests' (my
italics).

The fiddle which we were meant to have perpetrated was that we
had not taken tenders properly; and that we had sold property
cheaply to people we knew. All tender sales were in fact handled in
solicitors' offices, not at Cork Gully, with a representative of the
Chartered Surveyor present.

Our task was the one to which we had been devoted day in day out
with almost monotonous smoothness for the last thirty years. But, as
I have said, the very size of Willi's empire posed problems which
demanded an approach which was far from routine. For instance, we
decided for very good reasons that he should not be made a bankrupt,
as the First National Bank of Chicago wanted. This stance also won
us considerable criticism. To conduct business, the boards of these
companies had to have a quorum. Remove Willi Stern as a bankrupt,
and we would never have found a replacement. No one wants to be a
director of an insolvent company. So until we made arrangements for
the clearing banks to indemnify anyone who volunteered to take on
the job of a director of one of Stern's companies we could not let the

chairman be made a bankrupt. Apart from that, we needed him there. No one knew more about the Stern Group than its creator, and its dismantling would be that much more difficult without him. I arranged that he should pay two-thirds of his annual income over £20,000 to a creditors' trustee with a limit of £500,000. I put him on the payroll of Cork Gully at £1,000 a year, to enable him to pay his bills.

We spent £250,000 on establishing our scheme, and once that was accomplished it was less important to keep Stern out of bankruptcy. On the petition of merchant banker Keyser Ullman who were owed £20,500,000 he was declared bankrupt in June 1978 with total debts of £104,400,000, and assets of £10,070. I still hold it was a mistake to do this. He was only made bankrupt for guarantees. In the end I think it will be shown that, though he borrowed money rashly, he was thoroughly honest about his own affairs.

Our failure to prevent the bankrupting of Willi Stern at that time was of minor importance, however, compared with our success in preventing, through our Scheme of Arrangement, such a ripple of insolvency that another £1,000 million worth of property would almost certainly have come on to the market after his crash. I am not exaggerating when I say that it would have destroyed many pension schemes, might well have brought down some of the clearing banks and certainly an insurance company or two whose properties would have had to be revalued in the light of the property being sold. That would seriously have affected the margins of solvency.

After considerable battles Stern was discharged from bankruptcy in 1983, and that is the position today (1988). The whole sum (£142 million) is lost. The reason I felt he had possibly been more harshly treated than he deserved was that when other property companies became insolvent their directors were protected by limited liability, and they were criticised for walking away from their debts leaving others to hold the baby – the creditors. But Willi guaranteed the borrowings of his company personally. But owing to the problems he had created by his reckless borrowing on the value of the property, which subsequently fell, the size of his bankruptcy, of his debts, caused so much public excitement that he came in for very much more criticism than directors who had not stood personally behind the debts of their companies. Giving a guarantee and pledging the shares in his own company in support of it was indeed a curious thing to do – and it was even more curious that the lenders accepted the arrangement. For if the debt – the guarantee, that is – was called in the company was patently insolvent and the shares valueless. But few would believe that the man dubbed 'Britain's biggest private land-lord' would allow matters to go so far without something up his sleeve which he would pull out at the last moment and put everything right. But, as Mr Justice Walton said in giving Willi his discharge in April 1983, 'It was – and I mean this in no pejorative sense – largely a confidence trick. Mr Stern was supposed to be a man of immense wealth who did not have all his eggs in one basket. Unfortunately, as it turned out, Mr Stern *did* have all his eggs in one basket.'

'As the banks have discovered to their cost,' commented Stephen Aris in the *Sunday Times*, 'those eggs that remained were rotten. . . . Stern did not deliberately deceive; by his manner he merely fostered the impression that he was an immensely rich man, and some banks, incredible as it may seem, did not trouble to enquire further.'

The property boom was the prop of the Fordham Insurance Company, which Willi Stern bought and renamed Nation Life. He invested policyholders' money not only in gilts and high local-authority stocks but also in speculative property bonds, to enable the man with small savings to benefit from the property boom – so long as it lasted. When the Property Crash came in 1974, Nation Life crashed with it. The government insolvency margin laid down by statute had vanished. One of its investments was the ill-fated Bournemouth Town Centre Plan. It was compulsorily wound up, and Cork Gully were appointed liquidators. Gerry Weiss handled the case. It was certainly the most worrying spin-off of the Stern collapse, though eventually creditors were paid 65 per cent. The Government were criticised for not rescuing Nation Life. They had compensated those who had lost holidays as a result of the failure of Court Line and, said the critics, surely the loss of savings in life insurance deserved equal or more generous treatment?

We found that the legal position, once an insurance company went into liquidation, was that 'separate' funds – high income geared to gilts, and property which was a risk bond – were not separate in law, and had to be lumped together. So anyone who had invested his savings in what he thought was a guaranteed return from matched short-dated gilts found he had to pick up the loss on the Bournemouth Town Centre Plan. As a result of the Nation Life débâcle, the Government introduced the Policyholders Protection Act of 1975 which gave policyholders of an insolvent insurance company 90 per cent protection by statute. Compensation was paid out of a fund created by a levy imposed on the insurance industry. Now life savings are protected as well as holidays.

It was liquidators not policyholders, however, who needed the protection of the law when, in the *Law Society Gazette*, the Law's own organisation attacked Cork Gully's rôle as liquidator and other major accountancy firms for a motor insurance company which had crashed. In a big important action where the original insurance company had reinsured, we had sued the reinsurers under their contracts for the surplus. This was common practice among all liquidators. The reinsurers rejected our claim on the grounds that they only paid out to recover the money paid by the original insurer. We told them this was stuff and nonsense. They had a commitment, we said, and if a company went into liquidation the acceptance of the claim was what triggered it. Our opponents refused to accept this.

The article in the *Law Society Gazette* held that our case against the reinsurers was a very bad one. Moreover, claimed the writer, the risk we took by bringing the action as liquidators was cushioned by the fact that the creditors were bearing the cost of it. If we lost, we would not be out of pocket; if we won, we would receive a large percentage fee. But any articled clerk, sneered the writer, would know that our case was a bad one.

When your solicitors, who were members of the Law Society, and the counsel they briefed advised you and your creditors' committee that your case was a good one and well worth pursuing, and you came across an article like the one in the *Gazette*, libelling you in your profession, it was a serious matter. If we had lost the action against the reinsurers, no one would have believed we ever had a good case. So, after discussion with other liquidators, we served the Law Society with a writ for libel. They immediately took fright and printed a so-called apology in the next issue regretting publication but claiming it was written in good faith. To me that was perpetuating the libel. My colleagues the other liquidators were for accepting the 'apology' and taking no further action. I could not believe it had been written in good faith, however, and declared that it was still our intention to take the issue to court. Someone from the Law Society telephoned me and asked me what I wanted – which I took to mean how much money I would settle for. What I wanted, I told the caller, was for the chairman, vice-chairman and director of the Law Society to come and see me in my office.

'What for?'

'I will tell them that when they get here.'

Duly settled in my room in front of me, they once more asked me what I wanted to settle the matter. I looked them straight in the eye and said that if I had found I had wronged another professional in my official publication the first thing I would have done would have been to telephone him at once and say how sorry I was, and how I would do everything in my power to make amends. Second, I said, I would have agreed the apology I intended to print with the people I had libelled, and not insert an arbitrary notice drafted by myself stating that the article had been written in good faith. If, I told them, they were prepared to publish an unqualified apology and, as gentlemen, say they were sorry, then the answer to their question 'What do you want?' was nothing but that. It was obviously a great relief to them, and they thereupon confided to me that their embarrassment had been compounded by the fact that one of them had been on the liquidators' committee which had authorised our suing the re-insurers. They also revealed that the article had been written by the dismissed manager of one of the firms of lawyers engaged in the case.

They also gave as an excuse for letting the article be printed that the president lived in Wales and was cut off by snow that Christmas, so he could not get to his office to read the *Gazette* before it was published, as was his custom. I wonder how well that would have gone down in court. Not many people have issued a writ against the Law Society.

If banks – or, rather, bankers – could misjudge a situation as grossly as so many of them did over the Willi Stern affair, was there something wrong with Britain's private banking system? Was there reason for thinking they would have been more likely or more concerned to read the danger signals before it was too late if, say, they had been state-controlled? In so far as Britain had a coherent financial 'system', did the country's banks, insurance companies and pension funds serve the community and encourage new investment in a way best suited to the circumstances of the 1970s? If there was a system, how many people understood it?

I for one certainly had little detailed knowledge of it, and seized on the opportunity of becoming more closely acquainted by accepting the invitation which I received from James Callaghan, the Prime Minister, to serve on the committee he appointed in January 1977 'to review the functioning of the financial institutions in the United Kingdom'. I hoped I would be able to contribute something from my particular corner, and at the same time come to a fuller appreciation of what made the City tick – knowledge which hopefully I could pass on to others concerned like myself in the government of the City who seemed to be even more ignorant than myself.

In 1976 I was a new sheriff; and at a meeting called to consider rumours that the Greater London Council were planning to 'take over' the City I was surprised to hear the Town Clerk expressing his unfamiliarity with what went on in his domain, and assuming that the rest of us were equally in the dark.

'Who do we have', he said, looking round the table, 'who really knows the City, its people and its workings?'

I must say I had assumed the very opposite – that the other sheriffs and the aldermen would be bound to know City people much better than I did. But I was wrong. And I saw in my membership of the Prime Minister's committee, and the knowledge I would acquire from taking part in its deliberations, the opportunity for me to try to bring about a closer relationship between those who ran the City's financial institutions and those who governed it. When in 1978 I became Lord Mayor, therefore, I was in a position to share my knowledge with the people to whom the Town Clerk had been referring and try to 'educate' them in a way few other Lord Mayors had thought necessary or desirable.

Chairman of the committee was Sir Harold Wilson, who had resigned as Prime Minister in March 1976. On his appointment, he declared that he and his fellow committee members would conduct 'the most thoroughgoing probe there has ever been into the workings of the City'. There were seventeen of us – trade union leaders, academics, journalists, bankers and businessmen – but of course no one from the Stock Exchange Council or the merchant banks. They were the people we were going to investigate.

I had known Harold Wilson from the days when I was brought in to handle the affairs of Tulketh and IPD who were in his constituency in Huyton. We developed mutual respect, and indeed friendship. In the years that followed I think he came to appreciate the efforts I was always prepared to make on behalf of companies in receivership or liquidation; and he told James Callaghan he would chair the committee provided Kenneth Cork was a member of it. He knew he could trust me, and he also knew that as senior partner of Cork Gully I was reasonably familiar with the City and its people. For my part I felt here was something with which I could be of genuine assistance and I would enjoy doing. And in so important an investigation I also felt I was well equipped to see that, after a thorough study of the evidence which was brought before us, we made undeniably *fair* recommendations.

I was well aware that behind the decision to appoint the committee was the considerable pressure being exerted on the Labour Prime Minister to nationalise the banks and insurance companies – which, however, the Labour government were unwilling to do. Once a party get into office, whatever they may have said in the hustings, they always find practical difficulties to do that sort of thing. They had said the banks were refusing to lend money, and it would be better for the country if they did. Glib statements of that kind were no substitute for precise knowledge of the motives behind the actions of City banks and insurance companies in the particular circumstances of the day, and serious examination of the case that the City and the nation would be better served if they were nationalised. Socialist ministers and prime ministers had always been suspicious of 'the

City' without any solid reason for their suspicion. It was an intuitive stock response with little foundation other than inherited socialist dogma, and I felt I was well placed to act as the medium by which the clouds of suspicion, mostly of an emotional nature, could be dispelled from the minds of both 'sides'. Maybe I could help both of them to revise their attitudes as a result of becoming acquainted with what actually happens, and ceasing to rely on assumptions with little basis other than political bias and prejudice.

To this end, I brought the two 'sides' together by arranging a series of lunches in the Aldermen's Court Room in Guildhall in which leading members of the City could meet Sir Harold Wilson, who could take the opportunity to put over the fact that he was going to conduct a fair inquiry with very reputable people from both the trade unions and the City. The lunches also enabled him to get to know the people who were going to give evidence, before they did so, at a social occasion. By meeting the Labour leader about whom they would also have had politically biased assumptions, they were assured that they were going to have a fair crack of the whip. At these lunches it was just Sir Harold and myself and half a dozen guests. I had the full support of the Lord Mayor, Sir Murray Fox, who agreed to my suggestion that the City Corporation should provide committee rooms in which the Harold Wilson Committee could meet. The first session of the committee was held in a room provided by the Treasury, but the rest were in Guildhall where all facilities were provided by the City Corporation. So leading representatives of the City's financial institutions came to their own City to give their evidence, in the premises of their own Corporation, where they felt more at home than in an unpleasant little office at the other end of Whitehall as had originally been intended. It was a good example to the Labour government that the City Corporation was helpful and constructive. When they understood what I was attempting to do, the Corporation welcomed the arrangement; and those who came before us to give evidence were happier to do so in a neutral place in the City than in a government office.

Having Len Murray and Clive Jenkins propping up the bar in the Guildhall Club was no bad thing. Every session at noon and half-past five drinks were taken into the Committee Room which so far as they were concerned were 'free' but had in fact been paid for by me. And for us, the City, having people from the banks, the Treasury, civil servants and the rest turning up to give evidence was enormous prestige. They had to tell us how they functioned and to answer our questions. Each 'witness' had submitted a written paper which explained and justified the way his organisation worked at the present time. For us on the committee this meant reading through

volume upon volume of evidence, which physically was very exact-
ing but for me at any rate was a very illuminating exercise. I learnt for
the first time how Government Debt was financed; how the banks
refinanced their money when they had surpluses or shortages; how
Treasury Bills were taken up, and what rules they followed in doing
so. For me it was invaluable education in matters of which I thought
I had knowledge but really had not. And it made me realise how few
of my fellow-members of the Common Council who ruled the City
had other than a limited idea of its financial institutions. They knew
their own patch, but not the overall scene.

Because of this, many of them – and others of course – blamed the
banks for business doing badly. They complained that the banks
were keeping people short and went on about the difficulties of
obtaining a loan. This was a lot of nonsense. There was plenty of
money to lend. But bankers would not lend it unless they could be
assured it would serve a useful purpose. There was a current belief
among some politicians that provided you had assets you were
'entitled' to borrow money from a bank. They believed that because
they did not know how banks worked. A bank could lend someone
money on the security of their premises or business, but the
borrower could then fritter it away, which left him in an even worse
state financially. Banks wanted to see that the money they lent would
be used to make a profitable business and not a financial disaster. The
evidence we heard from the bankers made it clear to us on what terms
they were prepared to lend money. This was sufficient, for me at any
rate, to rebut the claims of those who came before us that they could
not borrow money and that the banks were being unreasonably
'difficult'. Those who made the bland assertion that banks were no
longer lending money were quite obviously those who on no account
should have been given a loan.

An informal inquiry was held by various people who interviewed
people who had not been granted banking facilities. They did not ask
those that were satisfied. The evidence produced purported to show
that the banks were not supporting the country. When this was
produced with a great flourish I just said that if you conducted a poll
at Wormwood Scrubs I doubt if you would get an enthusiastic vote in
support of the police!

It was fascinating to hear straight from the Governor of the Bank
of England, in answer to a query from trade union leader Clive
Jenkins, how the Bank advised the government of the day in regard
to financial policy and what influence they had on it.

'Where do you get advice?' asked Clive Jenkins.

'From my senior management,' replied Sir Gordon Richardson,
'who then consult discount houses and clearing banks, if appropri-

ate. My rôle as I see it is to represent the City's views to the Government and the Treasury.'

'Did you not consult the trade unions?'

'No, I did not do that.'

'Surely you should invite the views of the trade unions on such matters?'

'No. That is for the political people to do.'

'How so?'

'Let me ask you a question, Mr Jenkins. Do you consult management before you call a strike?'

It was the only time I have ever seen Clive Jenkins short of words.

(This is my recollection of how it went, and is not from the official report of the evidence.)

Having read the papers and listened to the oral evidence, all of us, trade union members included, recommended unanimously that it would serve no useful purpose to nationalise the banks and insurance companies. This was the fair conclusion we drew from what we read and heard. On the other hand, what was also evident was that almost all people's savings went into insurance companies and pension funds. They invested a certain amount in property but mostly they put their money into investments quoted on the Stock Exchange – all the big firms. Collectively the insurance companies and the pension funds had a controlling interest in most British companies. Inflation was running very high at the time, and many wondered whether in view of the ageing population the pension funds would be able to meet their commitments – to give the pensioners on their lists their due pensions when the time came. If they found they could not, then they would have to ask the Government for help. In that event the Government might well say they would take on their commitments but would of necessity have to take over their assets. So at one stroke, without any Act of Parliament, the Government would *de facto* have nationalised the country's major businesses.

'When I nationalised various public institutions,' ruminated Harold Wilson in considering the significance of this possible turn of events, 'I had to fight it through Parliament. A future government could do it at the stroke of a pen.'

This worried us on the committee because if the controlling shareholders became pension fund managers, and if the company got into financial difficulty, what ability would they have to use their power to instal new management and sort the company out? The fear that that might happen was greatly reduced in 1979 with the election of a Conservative government dedicated to cutting inflation down to size. Even so, I suspect that even in 1988 collectively the insurance companies and pension funds, although diverse, have a *de facto* controlling interest in most major British public companies. But with this big shareholding it behoves the insurance societies and pension fund trusts to take a bigger interest in the companies they have invested in. They can only do it together, not individually. If a company starts doing badly, a big institution would find it very difficult to sell its shares because that would cause a run on the company. The investor would find it impossible to withdraw. Indeed, it would have a *duty* to stay with its investment and sort its business out.

Before the report was published in June 1980, the Harold Wilson Committee had had fifty-five meetings, spread over three years, but halfway through November 1978 I was elected the 651st Lord Mayor of the Square Mile, which was earning at that time £1.7 billion per year net in foreign exchange, simply by hard work and expertise in exporting its brains, which very cleverly it still retained. Today this figure is greatly increased. Even then it was a very large part of the national income. It was, and still is, the principal insurance, financial and shipping centre of the world, and there was I, part of a team investigating whether its institutions were serving the country as they should. Of course they were. The City is a great part of England, and we are extremely fortunate that it is able to be so. Partly the reason is historical. There is a joke that God was an Englishman, and he placed London in the centre of the time zone, so they could talk to one side of the world in the morning, and the other side in the evening, both sides finding it difficult to talk to themselves during the working day.

The other reason was that London was designed to run an empire, and as it ran the empire the markets were in London, so London was the arbitrator of prices throughout the world, and had its institutions which had grown specially for that purpose. It was an advantage that certainly no other European country could match.

It was a good thing to have an inquiry. First of all, when I became Lord Mayor I was able to know as much, if not more, about how the whole of the financial City worked than any of my predecessors. Also, there is considerable mystique and misunderstanding of the City, and a good report would be able to explain what the City does and, if anything was wrong, would criticise it. This should give confidence to people who up to now had been ignorant of the functions of the City. It enabled me as Lord Mayor to bring both the City commercial and financial and the City corporate together.

I take off my hat to Harold Wilson about that committee. The object officially was to decide whether the banks and insurance companies should be nationalised. I believe Callaghan had set this up, because he was under pressure and did not in the least want to do it. But Harold Wilson, who was a master of the art of getting people together, managed to persuade all the diverse sections of that committee, the academics, the journalists, the trade unions and the representatives of the financial City itself, unanimously to decide that it would be daft to nationalise the banks and the insurance companies.

It is a curious thing that later on, when there was an election, and the Labour Party were advocating further nationalisation of the City, the Tories never used the result of Harold Wilson's report.

I hoped with my membership of the Wilson Committee, and my mayoralty, I would be able to change the widespread belief in less informed circles that D. Morier Evans, in *The City; or The Philosophy of London Business* (1845), was wrong. He said: 'Of the general fact that the chief aim of the city man – whether he be banker, merchant, broker or speculator – is to raise and amass wealth there is no doubt . . . for in all walks of life, whenever conversation turns upon the subject, this appears to be well known and admitted.'

Part Three

To the Mansion House

Chapter Seven

Closing the Corporation–City Gap

The unique experience begins on Michaelmas Day, 29 September, the day of reckoning for all who aspire to becoming Lord Mayor of London. In 1978 it was a Friday. To make sure the person chosen is fit to fill 'a civic office of national and international, indeed legendary, fame and repute, free of all political association', candidates have successfully to complete a long apprenticeship. Ever since 1385 anyone wanting to be Lord Mayor of London has had to serve as sheriff 'so that he may be tried as to his governance [i.e., ability to govern] and bounty [i.e., his ability to pay for much of what he does out of his own pocket]'. The liverymen of the City – the members of the various City livery companies – elected me one of the Queen's Sheriffs for the year 1975–6. If you have not served in that office, you cannot become Lord Mayor. Since 1435 a Lord Mayor has also to have been elected by the voters of a ward as its alderman, and before they can do that he has to be a freeman of the City and a Justice of the Peace. I had been a Common Councillor for Billingsgate ward since 1950, and in 1970 elected alderman by the voters of Tower ward. I had previously decided that I would not become an alderman of the City and be in line for Lord Mayor – first, because I did not think I had time for it, but mainly because one very surprised alderman became Lord Mayor a year before he expected and had to carry out a programme for his year designed for someone else.

At one time the aldermen sitting in conclave were the council by which the City of London was governed. In the eighteenth century, however, this Court of Aldermen invited 'commoners' from the wards to join them in their deliberations, after which the aldermen–commoner municipal authority became known as the Court of Common Council. This numbered 240 as late as 1826, but in 1973 it was reduced to 130 with a quorum of 40, of whom the Lord Mayor had to be one with at least two aldermen. The Court of Aldermen continued to have a separate existence without commoners as a

'House of Lords', so to speak, and apart from appointing the City Recorder and other officials had jurisdiction over the livery companies.

I had fulfilled the requirements for election as Lord Mayor of London, as had others. But one never feels home and dry. Every 29 September a number of equally qualified aldermen formally offer themselves for election, and the liverymen of the City companies assemble in Guildhall to choose. By a show of hands they usually choose the senior two to submit for scrutiny by the Court of Aldermen who then elect one of them to be Lord Mayor. It all happens in the one day. I remember on one occasion in the 1930s when the senior alderman's name was called the livery shouted 'Never!', to the horror of the Court of Aldermen.

I woke early that morning – at 4 a.m., to be precise – to consider what to do, and to plan what I would say in the speeches I was going to have to make in the next twelve hours. I confided to my diary:

> Decided to say almost nothing at Court of Aldermen and stick to the written script at Guildhall, also short. Also decided to say nothing about myself but only gently to get on to my theme: 'Today the City is a great place; England is the greatest country, the Livery Companies the cream of it and the best electorate.' Don't apologise for the election by the Livery – praise it.

At the church service with which the proceedings began the Lord Mayor's chaplain gave a fine sermon in which he attempted a light-hearted reference to a little doubt about the 'Ladbroke's odds' on the outcome of the election without knowing presumably that I had been a director of that company. Or did he? In any case it was a great joke at a point in the day's events when I sorely needed it.

It seemed that all eyes were on me as we processed into Guildhall. My wife Nina and my daughter Sally were in the gallery next to the Lady Mayoress, not quite sure what to do with themselves if the Livery said 'Never!' to my claim. To my relief there was a reasonably loud 'All!', so *that* was settled. I had jumped the first hurdle, and off we went to wait upon the Court of Aldermen. 'Pretty quickly out of suspense,' I told my diary. We returned to Guildhall, and I made a short speech on the lines I had thought out in bed. It seemed to hit the right note. It was moving to hear the cheers at the end of it. The strain and uncertainty were over. I was able to face the photographers outside in a reasonable state of relaxation. All that remained was to make a speech to my friends at the Mansion House where Sir Peter Vanneck, the current Lord Mayor, produced a very welcome tankard of champagne. I decided not to give the speech I had prepared to this little gathering but merely to chat to them. I think I went on a bit too long – that Moët, I suppose – but it seemed to go down well. There was a wonderful family feeling about the occasion, everyone drinking to my year as Lord Mayor being a success. My secretary, Mrs Winifred Garner, sent me a carnation – a very sweet thought. There was a lunch, and then back to Cork Gully and a two-hour session with the press.

Stage 2 took place on 11 October – going to the House of Lords in an official car to meet the Lord Chancellor, who informs you of the Queen's approval of the election. I had no idea what I was supposed to do, but it was explained to me by Brooke Johnson, one of the two household officers, on the way in the car. As instructed, on entering the Princes Chamber I left my hat with the Beadle so there was no chance of my dropping it while holding the loving cup. There was a kind speech by Sir James Miskin, the Recorder, and an even kinder one by the Lord Chancellor, Lord Elwyn-Jones, whom I had known for many years. It was all very informal and friendly. That afternoon Downing Street announced my knighthood – the traditional Grand Cross of the Order of the British Empire (GBE) – and the next morning, articulate but rather tired and adjusting myself as well as I could to being called Sir Kenneth, I faced my first television camera as Lord Mayor elect. It was with difficulty that I restrained myself from being provoked by the aggressive interviewer. A week later I went to Shell House for television training and learnt how to smile and give the appearance of geniality from start to finish. At the end of October I got my own back by taking eight BBC television men out on the Solent in my power cruiser *Gander* in a thick sea-mist when visibility was only fifty yards and we could only move on radar. I think they were all very frightened. I enjoyed watching their faces as we roared into nothing, the big ships' foghorns monotonously sounding in their ears; but, truly professional, they kept filming throughout it all. Perhaps I was over-compensating for my earlier baptism of fire. Much of it, I knew, would land up on the cutting-room floor, but when I saw the edited programme on 15 November I thought they – and I – had done a jolly good job.

Stage 3 took place, as always, on the Friday before the second Saturday of November (10 November in 1978). It was the day of the Silent Change when the outgoing Lord Mayor surrenders his emblems of office to his successor inside the Court of Aldermen.

On great occasions in your life, there is always something that goes wrong. What happens on the actual day is that you go over to the Mansion House about eleven o'clock, chat with the retiring Lord Mayor and have a glass of champagne with him; and then, clad in morning dress, you have a lunch which is paid for half by the outgoing Lord Mayor and half by the incoming Lord Mayor. Traditionally, a very simple meal, because the old Lord Mayor is supposed to have run out of money. It is the day for the menu to be an amusing joke on your name and his name, and he proposes your health, and you propose his. Then you go to the Silent Change.

I had sent my morning suit over the day before, and when I came to change before the lunch it could not be found. The Mansion House staff said it had never arrived! Well, I knew it had arrived, because I had brought it myself and had placed it in the Sheriffs' room. Fortunately the lunch is carried out with the Lord Mayor wearing a gown, so no one could see that I was not wearing a morning suit. Happily, during lunch the lost morning suit was found; amusingly, it had been put in the former Lady Mayoress's wardrobe, and they only discovered it when they started moving her clothes out.

After lunch, you go on to the Guildhall for the Silent Change, which always seems to me in a way rather cruel. Not a word is spoken, and all the City treasures, theoretically in the possession and ownership of the Lord Mayor for his year, are brought in one by one by various officers of the Corporation, who bow to the old Lord Mayor, who then touches them, and then they bow to the new Lord Mayor, who touches them, and then they go out. It is a solemn and ceremonial stripping of all the former Lord Mayor's assets, and finally he goes out, without his hat, and you put the hat on, and you are Lord Mayor and he is not! After that, you both go to the Mansion House and you give the outgoing Lord Mayor tea on the silver service in the Boudoir, where up to now it had been his private room. Then he goes to an emotional farewell downstairs by the staff, and you are left in charge.

We accomplished the dumbshow ceremony without any mistakes, and after tea was over and the past Lord Mayor had departed I went over the programme for the next day's procession to the Royal Courts of Justice in the Strand where before judges I was to promise faithfully to perform my duties. I drafted a letter to the Queen thanking her for the loan of her 1757 coach and six horses and other royal carriages in which I and my entourage were to be conveyed.

The system for electing Lord Mayors is obviously illogical and open to attack, but it works. No other method would keep undesirable people out. If you tried to make sense of it, it would collapse, and in any case it would be very difficult to make it logical.

I had already had a rehearsal of the show, which was carried out very early in the morning. This proved quite interesting. First of all, a police car came and called for me at the flat in Queen's Quay in the

My first visit to the Mansion House

At Minshull, July, 1934

Maude Cork, my mother

Nina at the time of our engagement

"WELL, NO, I DIDN'T ACTUALLY GET MY MONEY BACK."

"But I can't buy anything for a penny, Mum—except a Rolls Razor share."

'It seems a De Lorean does about 25 miles to the million pounds.'

Question of a likeness

WHEN Sir Kenneth Cork announced the arrangements for his Lord Mayor's procession on Saturday week —3,500 yards, the longest yet—I was handed a folder bearing a caricature of the incumbent-elect in the bottom right hand corner.

According to the Guildhall, Sir Kenneth once wrote a letter to someone in the City who was unable to read the signature and returned it to

No authoritarian

the sender. Thereupon, Sir Kenneth drew a self-portrait for easier identification and sent it back again.

But the new Lord Mayor has a different story. Apparently " someone drew a cartoon of me for the Lord Mayor's Show programme and it looked nothing like me at all," he said. " So I did this on the corner of a piece of note-paper. Bull-headed, weak-chinned and without any authority—that's me."

Daily Mirror (opposite above)
Daily Mail, 28 Aug, 1964 (far left)
Daily Mail, 22 Oct, 1982 (left)
The Sunday Times, 1 Feb, 1976 (top)
The Times, 19 Feb, 1974 (above)
Daily Telegraph, 2 Nov, 1978 (right)

David Poole portrait

You get some surprises at the Mansion House

On resigning as Chairman of the Royal Shakespeare Theatre

My boat is called Rum Run, *because when I'm aboard a rum from Martinique is served every day at 12 o'clock. When I explained this to the Press, United Rum, the UK importer of Jamaican rum, got very upset that I was advertising French rum. So they asked me to pose in front of their car RUM 1, gave me a case of their product to try, and asked me to make a nice comment about it. So, of course, I did.*

With HM The Queen, our Patron, at the Royal Shakespeare Company

'Bankruptcy begone,' by Sir Kenneth Cork

Daily Mail June 10th 1982.

The RSC rings up a box-office bonanza

Evening Standard October 20th 1987.

De Lorean: how Cork put the stopper in

Sunday Telegraph February 21st 1982.

'God's gift to the receivers' that's Benn, says accountant

Daily Express August 6th 1975.

City at about five o'clock in the morning – giving rise, no doubt, to the belief by the other residents that I was being arrested. We were then taken and put in the Lord Mayor's coach, and 'Jim'll Fix It' had arranged that a little girl who wanted to ride in the Lord Mayor's coach should also come on the rehearsal. We had this very nice little girl with us, and we rode the course in the real coach. I was going to be wired for sound, so that I could give outside St Paul's a greeting to the citizens of London, which would be broadcast on the radio. I asked where the message should be given, and I was told: 'About the blue sandbox just before you get to St Paul's.' This seemed quite simple. However, on the actual day, and on the actual ride, what nobody had thought of was that there were about a thousand people lining that part of the road, and the sandbox was completely obscured. It is very difficult to recognise points when the street is crowded with people, so I said my little piece three times, in the hope that one would be at the right place, and on the final one I finished it and said to the household officer who was with me in the coach, 'Hope that's all right, because I am not going to say it again,' and that was of course the one which came out!

Incidentally, we arranged for the little girl to ride in front of the whole show in a taxi, which was part of the procession, with the Master of the Parade, and she thoroughly enjoyed it, and came to lunch at the Mansion House afterwards. However, on the actual day I woke up with a sore throat and a streaming cold, wondering what on earth I was going to do for the big set piece of the Lord Mayor's Show in which I had to play the lead. There could be no understudy if I was *hors de combat*. A dose of the antibiotics beside my bed did the trick, and waking six hours later I felt reasonable.

> Downstairs for a briefing. Then over to Guildhall for the Presentations, including a beautiful silver plate from Tower Ward Club, and lovely medals from the Royal Shakespeare Company of which I was chairman. Then for drinks and to the Lord Mayor's Show.

I had the longest ever procession for the Lord Mayor's Show which featured several six-foot corks flanking a monster bottle of champagne. Roger, my son, took two of them home afterwards. I never sat down inside the coach once but stood waving from the window all the way. I had always been very disturbed that the Armistice Day custom of stopping everything at eleven o'clock had been discontinued after the Second World War, and I determined that if ever I got into a position to bring it back I would try to do something about it. By luck the chance came when I was Lord

Mayor. For by sheer coincidence the head of the Lord Mayor's procession was due to pass the Mansion House at precisely eleven o'clock sixty years exactly after the first Armistice Day, and when the guns were fired from the Tower of London to make the beginning of the two minutes' silence there was a complete stoppage of everything in sight. The huge crowd below me as I looked down on them from the balcony of the Mansion House stood absolutely still in total silence – not even a child whimpered. It was just as it used to be. Trumpeters played the Last Post and Reveille, the silence was broken and the traffic began to move again.

> It was so moving as to be unbelievable, and the counter marching of the Honourable Artillery Company was something I shall never forget. Off to the Law Courts in the coach, where we were received first by the Lord Chief Justice, who was not terribly gushing, and then Tom Denning [Lord Denning, Master of the Rolls] who was terrific and remembered occasions when we dealt with matters in his courts. Full of praise and very comforting. Wonderful show, the best I have ever seen. Terrific performance. Back to the Mansion House for lunch. We waved to the crowd and I was so impressed and so emotional.

I had to make my way round all the tables in the dining-room and welcome people, but by the time I had done so the meal was practically at an end. I managed to grab a few mouthfuls and then made my way up to the Old Ball Room to greet and thank the teams which had been running the Show, and into the kitchens to thank the staff and waitresses, which seemed to be greatly appreciated.

At the British Legion reception in the evening I felt my GBE made me look somewhat overdressed when everyone else was only wearing medals. This was followed by a reception at the Dorchester Hotel in Park Lane outside the City of London, where we take second place to the Lord Mayor of Westminster.

The church service in St Paul's Cathedral on Sunday was spoilt by having the congregation stand up while the choir chanted the psalms instead of allowing them to sing them, too. It was a great mistake; if we must *listen* to them and not sing, we ought to do it sitting down. But one soon learns to reconcile oneself to things like that, and to learn not to take your hat off to everybody who salutes you.

The difficulty of saluting with your hat is that when you have taken it off and stretched it right out you have got to put it back again. With your ordinary hat – a bowler, for instance – you put the hat on, and your hand practically touches your forehead. With the Lord Mayor's large hat, you have to become accustomed to putting it down with your hand about three inches in front of your head.

The final ceremonial in the long process of being inducted was the Lord Mayor's Banquet in Guildhall preceded by a reception in the Library. This provided an early opportunity to practice what for so long I had been preaching about the need to bring City and Corporation together. The financial City regarded the Lord Mayor as an important person but totally irrelevant to their business activities – and the feeling was mutual. When they told me it was the duty of the Governor of the Bank of England to visit the Lord Mayor as soon as possible after his election, I thought it ridiculous. I could not stop him coming but I made sure it was no mere formality, done as a matter of traditional courtesy. I got the Bank of England to tell me when the Governor was leaving and made a point of being at the front door to greet him personally. Presumably no other Lord Mayor, generally not so closely associated with the City as I was, had done this, because to them the Governor of the Bank of England was a remote personage of little consequence to the Corporation. For me, however, he was a friend. Whenever I was going to speak at a bankers' dinner and say something controversial – which was always – I sent an advance copy of the script to the Governor and someone at the Treasury asking them whether it was nonsense. I usually got an answer to the effect that it was far from nonsense but they would prefer me not to say it!

I was in a good position therefore, rare for a Lord Mayor, to proclaim the need for a closer association between the City and the mayoralty. The City, and not just the top people, should feel that the Mansion House belonged to them. That was to be the theme of my mayoralty. And, to start as I meant to continue, when they brought me the official guest-list for the Lord Mayor's Banquet, I deleted the names of a large number of the people traditionally invited year after year (the Great and the Good and the Useless), and replaced them with those of bankers and the heads of the big City institutions. In addition I filled my personal guest-list with similar people – people with whom I had been associated in my professional life and who had become my friends. Through my attendance at the sessions of the Harold Wilson Committee – and I never missed one throughout my twelve months at the Mansion House – I had got to know more City people than probably any other Lord Mayor.

As a sheriff I had always thought the Lord Mayor's Banquet rather long, but as Lord Mayor it seemed to go at a much smarter pace. I found both the Prime Minister James Callaghan and Mrs Callaghan very easy to talk to.

In spite of the slight contretemps with my speech, while I was Sheriff and Harold Wilson was Prime Minister, I got to know Ken

Stowe very well. He is an extraordinarily nice person. He is now of course Sir Kenneth Stowe, and he had, I think, been Private Secretary to Heath, Wilson and was to Callaghan and maybe even for a short time to Mrs Thatcher, and he said he had to see that the Prime Minister's speech was in order, and it would be very helpful if he knew what I was going to say. Would I send him personally a copy of my speech. He was a friend, and I thought this was very fair, so I sent him a copy of my speech, and in it I had put my remarks about British management, which I will refer to later, saying that there was nothing wrong with them. The Prime Minister apparently looked at this, and remarked that his speech was going to say something critical about British management, and would I consider altering it. I received the message via Ken Stowe, and sent the message back: 'This was sent for information, not for discussion!' And that was that!

However, the actual speech on the night went quite well; but, then, the Lord Mayor's speech always goes down well, because there are seven hundred or so people wishing him well on his first night, which is always a help. In the speech I told the gathering in Guildhall that the City always made a profit and was still the greatest financial centre in the world. I told them there was nothing wrong with British management. What other nation other than the British, I said, could maintain this great trade and financial centre in the face of fluctuating currency rates, rationing of the money supply and high inflation? Others might well have given up, but we went on and still made a success of it. But we had to find a way of rewarding people for risks taken in new ventures. I grumbled at the Archbishop of Canterbury for remaining silent on the subject of inflation, which was another word for greed and against Christ's teaching. It was trying to make out of the community more than you put into it. Greed and inflation, I said, were nearly as great a danger to the community as war.

The Prime Minister got a little back at me, very nicely, in his speech. He said he always liked to start with a light-hearted remark, and therefore had asked his staff for something funny about Chartered Accountants. He said they spent some time with no result, and then came back to him and said the funny thing about Chartered Accountants is that there isn't anything funny about them! I thought that was rather a witty reply to my note to him.

He dealt a little with the problem of inflation, but spent more time on the Common Market and the monetary system. The Archbishop of Canterbury was good and so was the Lord Chancellor. Though I was not expecting to, I thoroughly enjoyed the dancing. On the whole a very good day. More fun than I expected. With the launching ceremonial done with, it was now a matter of plunging into the mayoral routine which began the very next day with joining the royal party welcoming the President of Portugal and his wife at the start of his state visit.

We met the President at Victoria Station, which had to my mind rather an amusing touch. Victoria Station is in the bailiwick or province of the Lord Mayor of Westminster; but apparently Queen Victoria decided that, as her Lord Mayor entertained her visitors, when they were met at Victoria Station he would have precedence over everybody except the Cabinet, and of course royalty, so the situation at Victoria Station is that on one side are the royalty, with the Queen to greet her guests, and facing them starting nearest to the railway line is the Cabinet, then the Lord Mayor and the two Sheriffs, then the heads of the Army, Navy and Air Force, and then, I think, the Lord Mayor of Westminster and other important people. However, when you get outside the station to say goodbye, the precedence changes as far as the Lord Mayor of London is concerned, and he gets into the back row, behind everybody else.

I must say it was rather nice to stand on the right-hand side, and more senior to the Admirals of the Fleet, and the Air Chief Marshals and Field Marshals – something my sergeant-major at the HAC never could have dreamt would happen to the rather indifferent recruit into whom he had tried to knock military sense.

The second night of the visit of the head of state there is always a banquet in Guildhall, given by the City of London, at which the Lord Mayor presides. On this occasion, as in many, the evening started off a little stiffly, because the Portuguese president and his wife spoke no English, and so the conversation had to be carried out through an interpreter. A great mistake, when talking through an interpreter, is to try to make a light-hearted remark. I said as a joke that the statue of Wellington was specially put there to greet him, as he was a great friend of Portugal and had done so much for Portugal. This was treated with a very straight face. 'I am very surprised', he said, 'because it looks much older than that!' However, things went very much better with his wife. I discovered she spoke French, and I speak French very ungrammatically but reasonably well, so we were able to speak in French. She was a very attractive lady, and I told her that we knew we were expecting an attractive lady but we did not expect to see such an example of Portuguese spring on a grey November day. Her eyes shone, and she felt very much more at home after that.

The Queen told me the next day at the dinner given by the President that I seemed to have made a bit of a hit with the President's wife. In any event, they asked Nina and I to go and stay with them at the presidential palace in Portugal, but of course you cannot do it during your mayoral year, and it would be inappropriate to do it afterwards.

At the banquet at Buckingham Palace I sat between the Leader of Her Majesty's Opposition, Mrs Margaret Thatcher, and Lady Cameron, wife of the Chief of the Defence Staff. It was quite splendid. Everybody made you feel entirely at home; you were never left alone for a moment. I had a talk with Angus Ogilvy and Princess Alexandra, who were both very charming. Angus told me he was anxious to hold a dinner at the Mansion House in connection with some charity he was interested in, but he did not really explain what it was.

Apart from the President of Portugal, the Vice-President of the People's Republic of China, Mr Wang Chen, was also on a visit to Britain, and he came and saw me at the Mansion House the following day. I gave him a book on the City, and in return he gave me a little China plate.

The life of a Lord Mayor of London is one of continual contrast. Early the next morning I was presiding over proceedings in the Justice Room at the Mansion House, for the first time as the City's Chief Magistrate, to hear charges against a drunk and a bomb hoaxer. The police asked me to refuse the latter bail, but he seemed to me a perfectly respectable man with a chip on his shoulder, so I remanded him on bail, much to the fury of the Customs and Excise man who was involved in the case in a way that escapes me.

Before I could give City University students degrees the Vice-Chancellor had to give me an honorary degree, which he did somewhat reluctantly, I thought, pointing out that unlike my predecessors I was not an academic. Surely *all* the previous Lord Mayors since the City University was founded have not been graduates? Once endowed with my honorary academic status and all set to present the keen young men and women with their fully earned degrees, I ran into the snag of the Hat.

I did not realise, as I was now being made a doctor, that the hat which I had to put on was in fact a velvet squashy hat. I expected a mortar-board. The hat as it was lying on the table looked like a rather up-market piece of blotting paper, so I said to the Vice-Chancellor: 'Where the hell is the hat?' He then pointed to it, so I put it on. I had heard the story about the Lord Mayor wearing one back to front, so I hopefully tried to put it on the right way round, which in fact I did, but I tried to get a moment to ask the Vice-Chancellor whether I had it on the right way round, but as the graduands – or graduates, whichever they are – came pouring by one after the other without interruption I could not get a word in, so I sat there with this doubt in my mind.

It is quite an exhausting morning. There was a very good lunch in the middle of it, but there are so many people receiving their degrees, and it all goes in such a hurry, that you hardly have a moment to breathe, but it is very impressive and a great honour.

Miss South Africa managed her presentation to me of a model elephant and calendar with much more aplomb; but there was further confusion over dress at the service in Westminster Abbey to mark the 150th anniversary of King's College in the Strand, outside the City boundary. Peter Milo, the Lord Mayor's Secretary, advised that we should go in morning suits; but we had a request from the Chancellor and from the Lord Mayor of Westminster that we go in full gear, together with sheriffs. I agreed. I was told this looked good. But the service was a disaster – appalling sermon, lousy service and again just the clergy talking, playing and singing to themselves. And at the end of it all a snub from the Dean of Westminster, who bid goodbye to the Lord Mayor of Westminster, turned and disappeared accompanied by his red crows without a word of farewell to us. We walked out in what I hope was a dignified way. I was hopping mad. But all was soon forgotten – though I did drop the Dean a note of protest at his discourtesy – on finding myself the next day presenting the prize to the best producer of beef cattle at the Smithfield Exhibition at Earls Court. Going round the meat section was uncomfortably cold. I felt distinctly uneasy at the thought of those wretched animals being judged by one judge alive, and soon after their dead carcasses being judged by another. No wonder they all had a rather sad look in their eyes. I was grateful that roast beef was not on the menu for lunch at the Savoy with the Malaysia–Singapore Commercial Association. In my speech I told the Malays that if they wanted us to invest in their country they would have to be more helpful to our expatriates; and that it did not create a good impression when unwise takeover bids were carried out from Malaysia and Singapore. I also pointed out that Advance Corporation Tax enabled them to buy the assets cheap in London. I thought perhaps the Malaysian ambassador would walk out at these remarks, but he not only sat through them but also asked for a copy of my speech. He said he thought what I had had to say was very helpful.

Surprisingly my letter to the Dean of Westminster also found its mark, for the next morning I had a note to say that the incident at the Abbey had upset him very much and he wished to come and see me about it. I agreed to receive him, and he came on his bicycle. He apologised; he agreed it was a terrible service. He had not organised it. We talked about health and exercise, and I told him that I used a Champneys exercise bar every night and morning. I asked him if he would like to try it. It was difficult for him to say anything else but

Yes. So I had it brought down. When Peter Milo came in he found me laughing and the canon lying on his back doing push-ups with the bar, and thought I had made him do penance. Anyhow, we became good friends.

I do not think I am unreasonably sensitive on matters of etiquette, but it is essential in public to preserve the dignity of the Lord Mayor. I am probably more intolerant of people who appear to have no sense of the boring and inappropriate at official dinners. If ladies are asked to official dinners, as opposed to luncheons, they should expect to find themselves at social functions at which no speaker sees fit to launch out on a long dissertation of the kind the chairman had no qualms in giving at the so-called Port Health Dinner at the beginning of December. To my horror, his boring speech was followed by an equally lengthy one from the chairman of the Medway Ports, who made very derogatory and condescending remarks. I had my usual swipe and was probably equally boring. It was a Friday evening, and everyone ought to have gone home hours before. I told the chairman as much.

A controversial matter which pursued me throughout my mayoralty was determination of the salary to be paid to the Recorder of London and Common Serjeant, both servants of the Corporation for the dispensation of justice at the City of London Quarter Sessions held in the City's court at Old Bailey. I had received both a formal and an informal letter from the Lord Chancellor, expressing his views, which I showed Norman Hall, the chairman of the appropriate committee, and Bernard ('Bunny') Morgan, a past Chief Commoner, who were pressing for higher emoluments for these two. I told them we really could not expect our friends in government to support us if some of our committees thought they could assess the judges' salaries better than the Lord Chancellor. The Policy and General Purposes Committee, which had pronounced on the matter, had not had the full facts. We would be in great political trouble if we handed the Old Bailey back to the Government, as was being suggested. The trouble is that some people are too certain that they have the answer to everything. The silly compromise suggested of giving the judges a clothing allowance would never work, I told them.

Putting the Old Bailey under the jurisdiction of the Lord Chancellor's Department would follow from the suggestion made in the Labour Party manifesto that the Corporation of London should be disbanded altogether. I took the opportunity provided by the annual Royal Society of St George Dinner in the Mansion House in December to fire a salvo or two at those who would undermine the office and the ancient governing body of which for a year I was the head. I gave them the full treatment and finished by misquoting King Harry's St Crispin's Day speech by calling on the company to 'Cry God for Bunny! England and St George!' 'Bunny' Morgan was President of the London Branch of the Royal Society of St George.

I told them the Square Mile was one of Britain's greatest assets, creating wealth throughout the country and affecting the lives of every man, woman and child in it.

Yet some people want, so I hear – and it has started again – to abolish it. God only knows why. Lord Tennyson said 'The old order changeth, yielding place to new, And God fulfils himself in many ways, Lest one good custom should corrupt the world'. Well, God might do it, but I doubt if he wants to. But I can tell you, no misguided twit is going to do it while I am Lord Mayor.

We were running our industries against a background of legislation which frowned upon success and penalised it, I said. Not just by the present government or the last one, but by a succession of legislators who meant well. It was the failures which made the headlines. In a difficult economic climate there were bound to be failures – and nobody knew that better than I. But for every failure there were so many unsung successes. For every company which got into financial difficulties, hundreds were prosperous.

Apart from anything else, abolition of the Corporation would mean disappointing the 700 or so little people who so looked forward to the Children's Party held every year just after Christmas in the Egyptian Hall. I spent most of the time being photographed with each child either on my knee or beside me sitting in the Lord Mayor's chair. I finished the party by leading the conga, which the officers tried to dissuade me from doing because they thought I was too old but which I thought rather fun. I declined to make the customary speech at the final Grand Parade – they are tired of being talked to. So I got them to give three cheers for the entertainers and the Master of Ceremonies and the band, and three cheers for God who had provided the goodies for tea.

With a general election in the offing, educating the politicians and the civil servants who advised them on the rôle of the City in the nation's financial affairs became high priority. Eric Faulkner, chairman of Lloyds Bank, with whom I discussed the matter, agreed that aldermen should know much more than they did about the financial City. Because of the Harold Wilson Committee, however, and, to a certain extent, because of my connection with it, the mayoralty was much more connected with the financial City.

The lay magistrates on the other hand had always resented being kept at arm's length by the Corporation and not being allowed to become members of the Guildhall Club. It seemed a pity that when everybody was wanting to join the City and be nice to it we were giving them the cold shoulder. That the lay magistrates would want to join had been the excuse for trying to exclude the Harold Wilson Committeemen from the Club. I saw no harm in allowing them to bring a guest to the Club and drink at the bar on the day they sat. After all, only six were on duty on any one day. I also saw no objection to their holding a reception to mark their ten years as lay magistrates; they were willing to pay for it themselves.

Essential but unpompous part of the ceremony connected with the mayoralty was the team of horses which pulled the drays and the coach in the Lord Mayor's Show; and one day in February I went to see them at Whitbread's old brewery in the Barbican and fed them with carrots. I saw the police horses, too, and banged a traditional horseshoe in the forge. I had a word with the Lord Mayor's coachman, and I suggested to the Whitbread directors that the Corporation might present him with a silver salver as he was retiring. I agreed to send the mayoral Rolls-Royce to the brewery to fetch him to the Mansion House for the presentation, so that he came in style.

Going to the Mansion House for a presentation is always an occasion, and it was something which the very pretty Celia Freshwater was unlikely to forget when she came with her mother and father and boyfriend to receive a medal of the Royal Humane Society. She had jumped in to rescue a boy who had fallen into the Thames while her friend, who could not swim, had gone off to get ropes and a lifebuoy. The police came with her, and we gave the whole party champagne.

I liked having young people to the Mansion House – particularly when they were as pretty as Miss Freshwater. One Monday at the end of February I received a party of Belgian participants in 'Young Enterprise' in the Long Parlour. They spoke no English, so I had to chat them up in my very poor French and told them my old and well-rehearsed story of the *vache espagnole*. In return they gave me a very nice pewter plate made in Liège.

That was the start of a hectic and, with its great variety of activity, fairly typical 'Day in the Life of a Lord Mayor of London'. When it was all over I dictated to my diary:

After that [receiving the young people from Liège] the Irish Ambassador came in, who turned out to be very much nicer than I thought. He told me they were very worried about this new car factory in Northern Ireland because they think the chap is a con man, and it will fall flat on its face. This I agreed with. I said I would mention it when I went out there. He wants me to go to Dublin, but I do not think it is possible. Certainly a very pleasant chap and very friendly.

And then to the Savoy for the lunch given by the London Chamber of Commerce and the Japan Trade Advisory Group of the British Overseas Trade Board in honour of the Import Mission from Japan, in the Abraham Lincoln Room. A lousy lunch. The smoked salmon was stuffed with cotton wool, the chicken was cotton wool and not chicken, and the Japs went on endlessly and incoherently, so nobody knew what the hell was happening. It really was rather a bore. Got back late not in the best of tempers.

Then at four o'clock we had the Chairman of the Bar Council, David Hurst, and an admiral who is his secretary, to talk about Inner and Middle Temples; and we had them in the Venetian Parlour. In the end it is quite clear that they cannot get their own way and with present fees have buildings at a price that counsel can afford. I suggested that all they wanted was subsidised tenancies, and they had better think again about their general policy. They said it would be difficult to put up their fees most of which were paid for by Legal Aid. However the Corporation has clearly not been very helpful about converting some of the living accommodation to offices, and I think we will be more helpful in future.

Then we had the Scripture Union Bible Reading meeting in the Mansion House where I talked about the Bible being the best missionary. After that I had a dinner for my neighbours at Great Missenden. Couldn't get them to go home until after 12 o'clock. Was absolutely dead tired, but they all enjoyed it, I'm sure.

In contrast to such activity was regular attendance at sessions of the Harold Wilson Committee in Guildhall. At a recent dinner I said it seemed nonsense to me to have a Wilson Committee appointed by the Government to decide how it came about that banks declined to lend money to industry, while everyone knew that the Government's financial adviser, the Treasury, had forbidden them to do so. Were we just going through the motions of trying to find a solution to our embarrassments, or were we saying that 'circumstances' were things which none of us could ever influence? If you ask someone at the Treasury why they deter banks making loans to industrial enterprises, they blind you with economic gobbledegook which is supposed to be indisputable – which indeed it is, because it is incomprehensible. They say 'M3 Sterling' is out of line; there is too much money running round the coffers. Such 'clever' talk means that, because they believe everyone thinks the Government is borrowing too much money, they have decided that the interest rates will go up. The Government borrows too much, so other people have to borrow less to stop inflation.

At one session of the Committee at this time we discussed control of industry. We had a heck of an argument about whether industry was well run or not well run, and David Orr, chairman of Unilever and an able and very nice man, put up some compromise statement saying we had no evidence either way, which was true. I think a bit of sense was knocked into them, but the trade unions are still batting hard on Prince Charles's wicket that business is badly run. There was a lot of talk, too, about institutions controlling industry. The trade unions want representatives on boards of directors, and those directors to represent them; whereas everyone else of course wants a director on a board to represent the company.

It was surprising how much mayoral business was concerned with matters not only outside the City but also outside the United Kingdom. On the agenda of Common Council at the beginning of March was the so-called 'Resolution to Malta', the official message I would carry from the Corporation to the government of Malta, which I was shortly to visit.

John Yates opposed it at the private meeting on the grounds that we were always turning our cheek to the enemy; that Mintoff's government had been throwing the British out and we ought not to be nice to him. It was appeasing him, said Yates. Not a bad argument I suppose, except that it is very difficult to have a goodwill visit and start it by kicking the Prime Minister in the teeth. At my request Bernard Waley-Cohen defended the Resolution by saying we had a number of residents in Malta and we wanted to give them support and a lot of British investment. The point was taken up by others, and the Resolution was passed. I was also scheduled to pay official visits to Romania and Yugoslavia, and members of Common Council pointed out that we were not too enamoured of their governments, either. However, though it was difficult to go around saying everyone was nice when they were not, the visit was designed to help convert the *people* of these countries not their governments.

After all that I received a Delegation of Mayors from America who presented me with a very effeminate belt with an agate in the middle which God knows when I will wear. I had hardly thanked them and ushered them out when Peter Wood, the Mansion House PR man, came in without being asked with a woman from the BBC who wanted my reaction to the view that no one would be doing any work in twenty years' time since it would all be done by silicon chips. 'How would it affect the theatre?' she asked. We tossed the idea around for a bit, but I think people who hold such views are round the bend. I cracked my usual joke about the economist who spent twenty years learning what went wrong last time so he could get it wrong next time, and left it at that. Personally I cannot believe anyone will ever be out of work in the theatre because 'the work' has been replaced by machines. Electronic devices will create more wealth, and that will mean more entertainment and more people being entertained.

I suppose the Isle of Man can hardly be called 'overseas', but my first official visit across the water was as part of that offshore island's millennium celebration. The first morning we signed the Governor's visitor's book at Government House, and then drove in an open coach with footman and outrider to meet the mayor at the town hall. The extraordinary thing about that drive was that we passed no one on the way. The town seemed to be entirely empty. Although the weather was perfect and the sun shone, there was no one on the promenade, and scarcely a soul in any of the streets. It was the emptiest place I have ever seen at that time of year.

But there were a great variety of people to meet at the reception. What seemed to interest them more than anything else was the absence of politics in the governance of the City of London. The socialists had just brought politics to the Isle of Man apparently.

'How do you get a project through', asked one good lady, 'if you have not got a party to back you?'

'If a project is worth having', replied the Lord Mayor of London, 'what do you need a party to back you for?'

She was, I think, shaken but unconvinced. I did not pursue the argument, which was getting dangerously political, and went on my way to sample other Manx opinion. In my more formal speech to members of their parliament, the Tynwald, in reply to a very charming one from the Lieutenant-Governor, I quoted my usual bit from *Richard II* about this country which was wont to conquer others making a shameful conquest of herself and going on to create the greatest empire and wealthiest country in the world. We could do it again, I said, in spite of the detractors and rumour mongers.

For this grand occasion we paraded in all our finery with the Chief Commoner and the Sheriff, the Sword and the Mace. On arrival we were a little confused, since I expected a seat to walk into. Normally, when the Sword Bearer lowers his sword, I take off my hat and bow. But because there was no chair I was not sure I had arrived at my final destination, so I only did half a hat-off. They brought the chair later. After my speech I presented them with the scroll containing the Resolution, which we had difficulty in getting out of the casket.

In the address I gave to the Chamber of Commerce in the afternoon I kept to the script which had been written for me in London, but could not resist adding to it my favourite warning about the difficulty of creating wealth. If they were to do so, I said, they would have to be careful to see that the people who came over to the Isle of Man did not come merely for themselves but for the Manx community. Otherwise they would get some 'wrong people'. The low tax system on the island in no way harmed Britain, I said, because it brought people to it along with their wealth who might otherwise have gone abroad. What I did not say, but thought, was that the Isle of Man could well become a spiv's paradise unless they were very careful about the standard of people they allowed in.

There was nothing I could do to mitigate the 'organised chaos' of the celebration in Stratford-upon-Avon on 23 April of William Shakespeare's birthday. As we were approaching the town in the mayoral Rolls a ramshackle old car pulled up in front of us, bringing us to a halt. Out stepped a little girl, who came to the door and presented my wife Nina with a bouquet of flowers in the mistaken belief, I imagine, that she was the Queen. However, the Lady Mayoress took it in good heart, thanked the girl, and we drove on. After a somewhat muddled reception attended by a host of ambassadors, we rambled through the town with the sheriffs and the people from the Memorial Theatre, with the Light Infantry in front of us doing a jog-trot. I found it very difficult to keep awake during the lunch in a very stuffy tent. The ambassador of one of the African countries droned on and on in a muddled way but he obviously meant well. It was very tiring. I could have done with one of the Motability vehicles, the first of which I gave to a party of disabled people the following Monday. One of the cars you could drive even when severely handicapped – but I must say I would not have liked to be in it if anything went wrong. It was marvellous giving these people their shiny new motor cars. They were so full of joy. Their eyes glistened as brightly as the Queen Mother's diamonds at the City of London Sheriffs Society Dinner a few days later, at which I thought I was to make the only speech, with Edward Howard merely proposing the Silent Toast. But in the event Edward got carried away and said everything I was going to say. So I scrapped what I had written and made up another speech. In it I told the Queen Mother that from a distance I had watched her diamonds and I had watched her eyes and wondered which were the brighter. I could see now, I said, it was her eyes. I had seen her wearing the most beautiful furs and I wondered which were the warmer, the furs or her heart, and now I knew it was her heart. It was all a bit corny, but she was obviously pleased, and so was everyone else, although one is not supposed to comment on the dress or appearance of the royal family; but the Queen Mother is everybody's mother or grandmother, and she does not seem to mind a compliment, particularly if it is sincere.

While upsetting the rulers of the Isle of Man would have been discourteous – and I was at pains to keep my thoughts to myself – offending the man who governed the island of Malta would, discourtesy apart, have had repercussions of a much more serious nature. I was determined therefore to play this second overseas visit well within the bounds of discretion.

The visit had a slightly difficult start, because my son was a member of the Bowyers' Company, and at that time, they had never had a Lord Mayor to dinner – at least, not for many years. He wanted to produce his father as Lord Mayor at the Bowyers' dinner. They were very pleased to have a Lord Mayor, and so it was agreed that we should go. When the date was fixed for Malta, unfortunately it was the night we were going to the Bowyers' dinner.

The household officer said: 'In that case, we will send a Lord Mayor *locum tenens* to the Bowyers'.' I said: 'No! I have agreed to go, and I will go.' As I knew the planes to Malta quite well, when they complained I said: 'No. There is an 11.30 p.m. flight to Malta. We'll catch that.' They said: 'But it does not arrive until about half-past one in the morning.' I said: 'So be it!' They said: 'Also it is a tourist-class flight.' And I said: 'Well, so be it.' So we caught the 11.30 plane.

There was rather an amusing sequel to the Bowyers' dinner. The Pope had just been to Ireland, and had spoken out against terrorists, I thought very courageously, so in my speech I congratulated the Pope on his visit to Ireland – not that he was likely to ever hear about it – and said how much we agreed with him and admired him speaking so clearly. I got a very ferocious letter from a professor at either Oxford or Cambridge, I forget which, complaining that a Lord Mayor should not talk politics, and that it was totally wrong for me to praise the Pope at a livery company dinner.

What I had not noticed was that the Pope had also spoken against birth control, and that was the part which upset the professor, who was also a priest, and he did not seem to have noticed that the Pope spoke against terrorism. So I suppose it proves you always notice the things you want to notice! There is a moral in it somewhere!

With regard to the flight, it was not uncomfortable. We had the whole of the front part of the plane to ourselves – first class at tourist prices. Mintoff had arranged that we had a state reception in Malta. I of course had known Dom Mintoff for many years. He was the architect of the hotel my brother and I and Ladbrokes built at the Dragonara Palace, so the morning after we arrived (very late at night) we got up early in the morning and drove in state to the entrance of Republic Street, where we were met by the Chief Justice with whom we walked in procession between cheering crowds to the President's Palace to be greeted by the Speaker. In the speech I made to their Parliament I said we could get sun elsewhere but nowhere else could you find the happiness you got in Malta. I had dinner that night in the old Byzantine palace with the President and his Scottish wife. I dressed for the occasion in knee breeches and a lace frill at the neck which we call 'Old Bailey'. I knew the palace – and Malta for that matter – well. The last time I had dined there had been with Sir Maurice Dorman, who had been Governor-General after independence from 1964 to 1971.

In his speech the President said how much he and the Maltese wanted to be friendly with England. In mine I said I had always regarded Malta as part of England, and did not care who they were friendly with so long as they were friendly with us. The next morning we had a friendly talk with the Prime Minister – after he had kept us waiting for half an hour. Dom Mintoff made it clear that he did not want money but British expertise and British participation in industry.

Mintoff had been criticised, unfairly in my view, for not allowing imports. Many of the British residents complained that they could not buy British cars and other things, but Malta adopted what was called the 'basket currency' – each month they decided how much they had exported, and importers were allowed to import up to that amount. This is the way they stopped inflation and kept the monetary situation under control. This resulted later on, to the intense irritation of the British, including myself, in the British pound being discounted to the Maltese pound, and British tourists were obviously very upset. If they had called their currency by some other name, the tourists would not have minded, but to see a tiny economy with their own pound at a discount was not something which made them pleased with Malta.

We went officially to the main hotel of the town and had lunch and dinner with the Chamber of Commerce, etc.; and on this occasion I changed the rules, because Admiral Ellis, who was Secretary, had been stationed in Malta with his wife, so I took in our party not only both Sheriffs (one for part of the time as he had duties here at the Old Bailey) but also the household officers and Admiral Ellis. It was a very pleasant time indeed. Admiral Ellis and his wife were charming company, and they thoroughly enjoyed the one opportunity they had to go on a foreign visit, for which they did so much planning.

Within a few days of our return to England we heard that the Conservatives under Mrs Margaret Thatcher had won the general election. I wrote to James Callaghan, the outgoing Labour Prime Minister, thanking him for his co-operation, and to the new lady Prime Minister, congratulating her on her victory. The next day we left true blue Britain for red Eastern Europe by British Airways who, unbelievably, served cold salmon and salad for breakfast on the first leg of the flight to Frankfurt. 'Really! We are out of our minds!' I told my diary. 'Breakfast is the best meal we serve on a British aeroplane, and who the hell wants to eat fresh salmon at *that* time of the morning?' Our destination was Bucharest for the start of our good-will mission to Romania. We were received on arrival by the Mayor-General, the British ambassador, the Vice-Mayor and a crowd of photographers. 'The hotel is very comfortable but far too hot.'

During my journey in the car with one of the ministers, we were having a happy discussion which was unfortunately interrupted. I have a watch which I can make *ping* every hour, which keeps me in time, so that I do not have to keep looking at it. As soon as we had been driving for about ten minutes, it *pinged*. The minister clearly thought that he was being bugged and that was the end of one tape. It took me a lot of explanation, through an interpreter, to persuade him it was just an ordinary watch, with nothing sinister inside it! We were warned that we would be bugged in Romania. Maybe it was equally imaginary – I just do not know!

According to Peter Wright's book I later learnt that everybody bugs everybody else. How one's illusions can go!

> There aren't any lights, the loo falls on you when you sit on it; it's very difficult to see and there's nowhere you can find the electric light switches. Extraordinary when they want to sell goods to us that their home affairs are so badly organised, although the hotel is beautiful and the rooms are beautiful, and we have a very nice balcony.

However, the balcony had a sort of iron curtain which came down, with shutters – presumably so when anybody wanted to dine there with his mistress nobody could see them. The only snag was the thing had rusted down, and could not be moved, so you had a balcony from which you could not see. The other problem in this splendid bedroom was that the one light was a 25-watt lamp hanging beside the chandelier on a piece of wire. It was so dim that you could

not see to write your speeches or do your work, and you had to go into
the bathroom where there was a fluorescent light, and sit on the loo,
and this was the only place where you could clearly see at night.

There were about forty at the dinner we gave in the hotel dining-
room that night, which began with the Mayor-General proposing the
health of the Queen, to which I replied and then presented the Mayor
with a scroll and a piece of plate. They were extremely nice people
and did everything to make us happy. We did not start the meal until
the speechmaking was over, and we ate to the music of an orchestra
which entered the room with a great flourish accompanied by singers
dressed in costume who sang regional folk-tunes. New singers and
orchestras kept turning up during the evening.

The ambassador later told me that they had taken nearly every
group from the restaurants in Bucharest, so everybody else had no
entertainment for the night.

> I am very impressed with the kindness and good will. They
> want to do business with us and they want to be friends, as we
> do with them. I think it is going to be a very successful visit,
> though we must talk to them about the kind of goods we buy,
> because we don't obviously want to buy those in competition
> with our own.

M. Pana, the Mayor, told me that up to twenty years ago the
average annual income in Romania was $98 a head but now was
$1,200. They were keeping the population of Bucharest down to 2
million for the time being and would never let it be more than $2\frac{1}{2}$
million. They were bringing a certain amount of light industry into
the town and building flats so that people could live near their work:
47,000 that year and another 50,000 next year. In my talks with them
I made a point of emphasising 'working partnership', and telling them
about the balance of payments. My view on these matters is the simple
one that you cannot sell goods to people unless they buy from you. It
is no use having an unfair balance of payments. I got the impression
they got the message and agreed to it. I also told them about the tax
system in Britain, and how advanced corporation tax would make it
difficult in future for people to take a participation overseas.

At the lunch given by the British ambassador, I sat next to the
Chief Professor of English at Bucharest University, who told me that
the British came from Romania, which, he said, was proved by
Falstaff's horns. In *The Merry Wives of Windsor*, Falstaff certainly
enters 'disguised, with a buck's head on' and invites Mistress Ford to
divide him like a bribe buck, each a haunch, 'and my horns I
bequeath your husbands'. Just how this makes the British originate

in Romania I am not entirely clear, except that the Romanians apparently had the same country entertainments as the Merry Wives in remote parts of the kingdom.

The President of Romania, Nicolae Ceausescu, whom I saw on the Tuesday morning, was not entirely sold on the desirability of keeping the rubber market in England. He gave me a lecture on the need to look after the developing countries and their right to sell their own rubber. He did not think it right that he should have to buy copper through London instead of in the producing country in Africa. He was of course peddling the orthodox communist party line. I said if he wanted to be able to quote a firm price for his manufactured goods he must be able to buy forward; also if they bought copper, say, at a different place each time they could never be certain they got it at the right price – the 'market price'. I do not think he understood what I was talking about. The industrialist present did and kept nodding. The President, however, was unconvinced, but the ambassador seemed to think the talk went very well, especially when we discussed helping to get together with Third World countries and those to which Romania could gain entrée and Britain could not, such as Iraq and Syria, by using their labour and our skills. We left on very good terms, and the ambassador was delighted.

The Archbishop of Canterbury, who had recently been to lunch with me at the Mansion House, heard I was going to Romania, and asked me to give some support to the Church. I asked: 'The Church of England?' He said, 'No, the Orthodox Church,' which was only barely tolerated, so he believed, in Romania. When I had a spare afternoon, and was asked what I wanted to do, I said I would love to go and see their cathedral and meet the Bishop. They said yes, this could be arranged, as though they were about to achieve a miracle! Off we all went to the cathedral, and the Metropolitan was produced, looking slightly worried, presumably only having been told at the last minute. However, the effect on the people sent to look after us was quite extraordinary. They did not really very much want to go inside the building. When we got inside, they said: 'You would not want to go behind the altar, would you?' I actually had no particular desire to go behind the altar, but immediately they said that I said: 'That's just where I want to go.' So we all went behind the altar. The Metropolitan bucked up considerably. Then there was somewhere else they said I wouldn't like to go, would I? I said, 'Yes,' so we went there, too! The last one, they said, 'You don't want to go and visit the Saint, do you?' and I said, 'Yes, that's just what I have been waiting for.' They had a saint, as far as I can remember, preserved in a glass case, so we went and looked at that. Then I thought I would put the final boot in, so to speak, and said to the Metropolitan: 'As we were not able to go to church on Sunday, because we were travelling, would you be kind enough to bless us?' He was absolutely delighted, and to my surprise we were not only blessed but also got a very whiskery kiss, because Orthodox priests, as you probably know, seem to be totally unshaven. They look very good, too!

However, the effect on those coming with us was very surprising. They said, 'Well, we do not usually go to church except on Sundays,' and they were very uncomfortable. I got the impression that, although they were meant to be atheists, they still had a healthy respect, and were frightened of being inside a church unless they were extremely respectful.

Our party which was blessed consisted of a Jewish Chief Commoner, one Roman Catholic, two Presbyterians, and the good old Church of England! Outside, we had our photographs taken with the Metropolitan, and I gathered also with the minders in as well, so what kind of trouble they got into when they went back and these pictures were received I do not know. Nor was I too much bothered. I told the Archbishop on my return to England what I had done, and to my surprise and amusement he said: 'Kenneth, I do not know whether you did this out of Christian responsibility or sheer devilment.' Anyhow, he was very pleased.

It was a fitting finale to our Romanian visit before setting off on the second prong of our Eastern Europe goodwill mission, which was to Yugoslavia. This began as before with a presentation dinner, with me dressed in 'Old Bailey', at the hotel in Belgrade. My speech in reply to the Mayor's was translated sentence by sentence. It is difficult to make it flow!

At the 'neighbourhood unit' for 10,000 which we visited the next morning we watched some thirty children going through their routines in a gym class. We were welcomed by the little girl who was head of the class. I astonished them all by putting my feet under the rail and joining them in the exercise they were doing. This amused them intensely. At the neighbourhood centre its leader told us how they ran their affairs and elected their ruling council in a way that it represented every type of work which those who lived there undertook – tailors, shoemakers, doctors, lawyers and the rest.

He gave us a long lecture about how his team of councillors altered the course of politics, as for instance when they found it was costing more to dispose of waste and sewage. His councillors had thrashed the matter out, he said, and got the cost reduced. I said, if it was costing that amount of money to dispose of the waste, who paid for the shortfall? And at that there was a deathly silence, and he went red. Well, he said after a bit of thought, they had had to divert money they had saved up to buy equipment to paying the extra cost of waste disposal – and they had had to forget the hoped-for garden seats or whatever it was. Even the Town Mayor smiled while this was going on, because he saw how my intervention had thrown the council leader in the middle of his set spiel approved by the party. He really did not know what he was saying.

The whole of our Barbican Centre could have been put inside the enormous Conference Centre at Bucharest with a main hall for 3,000 and several others to hold a thousand each. It was not attractive to look at but it had everything. It took ten months to design, eleven months to build, and cost £50 millon. The smaller Barbican Centre took eight years to build and cost £120 million. As I told my diary when I got back to the hotel, 'it makes you wonder which kind of system you want'.

Regrettably our ambassador had not managed to persuade any government ministers to attend the reception he had organised for us at the British embassy. It seemed they were all buzzing round President Tito, who was off to Moscow in the morning. Much of my time was wasted with having to calm a fretful chap from ICI who had heard we were paying a visit to a Yugoslav firm which was doing work for ICI but looked like breaking the contract. He had not been told we were going and he blew his top. When he had cooled down I agreed that the ambassador should have known and warned us away. But I said that in the circumstances we could not call it off, so would he like to come along with us? When we got to the place next day we found he had been there twenty minutes ahead of us and had had to leave for a more important engagement elsewhere. So it was obviously not a matter of life and death for him to be there. But from what I saw and was told I think he had good cause for concern. I got a very evasive answer when I questioned someone about the particular drugs ICI were worried about. They told me in answer to a question I put that no payment was made possible for product liability on any drugs they sold in third markets or in France, say. It was a criminal offence.

'That would never do, surely, if as a result of taking your drugs people developed deformed limbs like thalidomide babies?' I said.

'Well,' they said, 'that has never happened.'

'What happens when you get sued overseas?'

They did not know the answer to that one, and said they would have to make enquiries. I made a note to ask ICI about it when I returned home, which was the next day, Thursday, 10 May. But there was very little time at the Mansion House for anything of that sort, or indeed anything at all, for I was up at six o'clock on Friday morning in time to drive to Luton airport to catch the plane for Aldergrove for the start of a visit to Northern Ireland.

I of course knew Northern Ireland well, as I had run the Northern Ireland Development Agency, and the NIFC before it, as chairman. We landed at the aerodrome and drove in police cars, which I called 'Q cars'. They had no markings on them. When I got in, as the Lord Mayor always sits on the right-hand side of the car – it becomes a habit – I sat on the right. I was politely moved to the left-hand side of the car. I thought they wanted to balance the car for some reason.

The next time I got in, I sat down on the right-hand side of the car as usual, and I was politely moved to the left. The third time the same thing happened, so I said to the inspector in charge: 'Why the hell cannot I sit on the right-hand side of the car?'

He said: 'Well, sir, it's like this. I am responsible for your safety. We know that the devils know you are here. Although we have good security, we cannot be one hundred per cent certain, and if they open up on us, and you are sitting by the driver, you and the driver are killed, and I have to go back and explain why I lost you. But if you sit behind me you and I get killed, and I am not there to do any explaining!'

I thought it was a lovely Irish touch, but it also shows that we just go there for one day, or two days, and come back, but those security people have their lives in danger every day. They are very brave men.

We drove the seventy miles to Derry in a police car. It prepared us for what was to come. There were soldiers on every corner, and we were guarded wherever we went. The Mayor of Derry was a Protestant and his deputy a Catholic. So, as I told my diary, 'they have the art of living together'. The trouble was the oddballs who were trying to prevent such a state of affairs ever becoming permanent. The police reported that the car parked further up the road which we took that evening from our hotel to Hillsborough Castle to dine with the Secretary of State for Northern Ireland probably carried a bomb. So we stopped, turned round and took the longer route.

The police sirens started screaming and we shot down the other side of the road. On the way we learned that a bomb had exploded outside the town hall, supposed to be 500 lb, but they told us later it was 150 lb. It had made a hell of a mess and was close to the town hall from which we were going to watch the Lord Mayor's Show tomorrow. Some people were injured but no one badly.

At the castle we were greeted by the new Secretary of State appointed by Mrs Thatcher's administration. He was very nice but knew nothing about Northern Ireland. The dinner was in my honour, and it was a very good meal. I talked at length with the Secretary of State about the problems facing the Conservative government in the province and what might be done to solve them. I found it very gratifying that he made a point of attending the dinner in person.

In the question time after the talk I gave to students at Belfast University I had an argument with a professor who told me I had got my figures wrong.

'Surely, sir, the National Wealth includes the work of schoolteachers, police, judges?' he said.

'Of course they don't,' I said. 'They are paid from the wealth created by other people.'

'You've got it all wrong.'

'If that is what the universities here are teaching, then they are teaching codswallop. No wonder Ulster is in the mess it is! The people who create wealth are the people who create saleable goods and saleable services which earn income in Britain or earn overseas income.'

I ended by giving my definition of an economist, which I introduce into all the talks I give of this type: the man who spent twenty years learning what went wrong last time so he could get it wrong next time. An enormous roar of laughter went up at that, and my questioner retired somewhat discomfited.

The Lord Mayor of Dublin was with us to watch the new Lord Mayor of Belfast's Show from the balcony of the town hall which had been badly holed by the bomb of the night before. We had just taken our seats when a posse of the Royal Ulster Constabulary roared by. Someone had shot at a policeman directing the parade 250 yards up the road, but he had not been killed. They were cheered to the echo.

I was in 'Old Bailey' for the Lord Mayor's Show and again for the Junior Chamber of Commerce Dinner that evening. In court dress I expect to be at the high table and in the line-up that enters. When I arrived for this I learnt that I was not in the line-up, and I refused to go into dinner unless I was. It was an insult to the City of London. I insisted, and they could do little other than give way. However, the dinner was indifferent, the speeches appalling and tediously long. Everybody seemed to think it was necessary to speak, and by the time it came to my turn the diners were pretty word-drunk. Anyhow, I told them how greatly we in Britain admired them for standing up to their troubles, but it was no more dangerous in Ulster than crossing Piccadilly Circus in London. They were part of the United Kingdom and nobody was going to bully Britain into giving the province away until they wanted to be given away. The Minister of State for Northern Ireland who was present joined in the standing ovation they gave me which, to my surprise and that of everyone else, went on for five minutes.

Our days in Romania, Yugoslavia and Ulster may have seemed exhaustingly crowded, but on returning home the appointments began piling up in a way that made life very hectic. And of course that meant plenty of opportunity for things to go wrong.

May 14. After the Queenhithe Ward Club Luncheon, we came back to the Mansion House and rushed straight into the annual general meeting of the Lifeboat Institution. We then had tea, and rushed straight off to the Tower of London for their At Home. It was incredibly hot – so hot you could hardly breathe in the place. Fortunately we could not stay long as we had to be back for the Spectacle Makers' Dinner. Had about 720 people in the room, so it was a great occasion. It was their 350th anniversary.

May 15. Town Clerk came in; practically everything he had to report was Bad News. We have got the problem of the judges' salaries and how to deal with them at Thursday's Court of Common Council. Then off to the House of Lords to see the Opening of Parliament. Everything went wrong. Hans didn't turn up with the bag – he had gone to sleep as usual in the staff room. Traffic down the Mall was terrible. Sat next to the Lord Mayor of Westminster in very cramped quarters. But it was a fascinating ceremony and a very good Queen's Speech. At the Speaker's Reception afterwards I had a chat with the Prime Minister, Willie Whitelaw her deputy, and Geoffrey Howe Chancellor of the Exchequer. When we came to leave we couldn't find the car, so we arrived back at the Mansion House in a hell of a rush to get to the Court of Aldermen and made it by one minute – 17 minutes to drive from the House of Lords to the City, change dress and enter. I was however half an hour late for the meeting of the Royal Shakespeare Company and we had to get through the business in five minutes. Photographers were waiting for me back at the Mansion House for a 'Day in the Life of the Lord Mayor' photograph to illustrate an article in the British Tourist Authority's magazine *In Britain*. I left them to attend the Festival for the Sons of the Clergy at St Paul's where the Archbishop of York preached a better sermon than usual, but they had an endless *Te Deum* with all of us standing in our gowns until I was absolutely exhausted. The day ended with dinner at a company, which again meant a long time standing. The speeches were quite good but the food indifferent. And so exhausted to bed.

May 16. We had a hell of a rushed day – it is getting worse every day. The Vice-Chancellor of the City University came in and we rushed through the ceremonial. Then we dived off to the Insolvency Law Review Committee [see page 184] where I stayed for an hour and a half, already dressed. From there to Airey Neave's memorial service where Mrs Thatcher gave the oration, and I must say she was very good indeed. The service was packed, people standing everywhere. Over lunch at the Stock Exchange they were very concerned about the Harold Wilson Committee starting to ask about self-regulation and reference of the Stock Exchange to the Unfair Business Activities Committee. I agreed to write to the Government supporting their case, and they are preparing a letter for me. I had an appointment with my tailor at the Mansion House before visiting the Spectacle Makers' Exhibition which was extremely interesting but beyond me entirely. I am now going to the Annual Parade of the Special Constabulary, and after that we have got a private dinner party for the professionals.

At the end of this last entry I added: 'If the pressure goes on at this rate I think I'll resign. We have not time to do our post, no time to listen to anything, no time to write speeches and hardly time to sleep. Let's hope it quietens down.'

But of course it did nothing of the sort. The following week saw me swinging in a hammock with Lady Soames in the adventure playground at the Hyde Park Children's Party. We looked pretty undignified, they swung it so high. But it was harder for Lady Soames in her frock than it was for me, especially getting out of it.

Chapter Eight

Lord Mayor as an Amateur Diplomat in the Far East

After so much being received by foreign dignitaries abroad, it was a nice change to find myself on a fine morning in June on the welcoming side of the fence as one of the party at Victoria Station meeting His Excellency President Daniel arap Moi of Kenya whom I already knew. Mrs Thatcher was already there when we arrived, along with Mr Whitelaw and Lord Carrington, the Foreign Secretary, whom I quizzed on how friendly he was prepared to be with Dom Mintoff. I got the impression he thought the Maltese prime minister a tricky customer. I asked the Prime Minister when she would like to pay us a visit at the Mansion House, and she said in September. Princess Anne and Prince Charles joined the party on the platform, and we all lined up in order of seniority. On these occasions the Lord Mayor of London takes precedence immediately after Cabinet ministers and before field marshals. If President Moi was overawed by the high-powered group who had come to greet him, he did not show it.

At the dinner-party at Buckingham Palace that evening I sat between Mrs Duncan Sandys, who is French (née Marie-Claire Schmidt of Paris), and the ambassador of one of the African countries, who was a lady. It was a very splendid affair – an extremely good meal and served on gold plate. So there were some ways in which the Palace could beat the City! At the end of it we had the Scots Pipers, and we mingled with fellow-guests – perhaps the most interesting part of the whole evening. Lord Carrington came and said how grateful he was to be able to have the Mansion House for the dinner he was giving London's ambassadors and high commissioners. I told him he could have a free hand to make whatever arrangements he liked and stay at the Mansion House if he wished.

The next day it was my turn to entertain President Moi. While I was standing in front of the table receiving the guests, the Remembrancer rushed up to say the Duke and Duchess of Gloucester had arrived – which was earlier than expected. The crowd were being held back from mobbing their car, but I must come at once. So I went out with all my train, but I forgot my hat, so I had nothing to sweep off, and it had to be sent for. The Duke and Duchess were already on the pavement when we got down – and it was pouring with rain. No sooner had we welcomed them and gone upstairs than news came that President Moi was just about to drive up, too. Anxious not to miss the bus, the Honourable Artillery Company band at once struck up the National Anthem of Kenya, while the men presented arms. But they were too quick off the mark. By the time the President stepped from his car they had finished. However, I had recovered my hat by then and I was able to doff it to him in the most respectful way I knew.

He was a splendid chap with an ivory knob on a stick which he waved like a field marshal's baton. He went out into the rain carrying a large umbrella and inspected the guard of honour. At the end of the inspection the guard commander ought to have asked permission to dismiss but he didn't. He just buzzed off. I suppose the wet got into his heart. We then formed up to go through the front door. The Corporation officials had decided that as he had no wife, he, I and my wife Nina would walk in three abreast. Well, the door was not wide enough for that, so there was a bit of shoving and pushing in which sometimes I got left behind and sometimes Nina.

In the library upstairs I presented the president with a casket containing a scroll. He gave me my present after the speeches at dinner. It was stoutly wrapped in plastic. I made a great show of not being able to open it, at last pulling it out and showing it to everyone. In thanking him I said we in the City greeted him as a friend and told him how impressed I had been by the way he went out and inspected the guard of honour in the pouring rain. I would like everyone to know, I said, that he was that sort of man.

Speeches on these occasions can be a little boring, and I thought I would add to the official speech, which had been agreed by the Foreign Office. At the end I said that when I had finished my year of office I was going to go on a holiday in Kenya, which was true, shooting big game, which is of course unlawful! And rightly so. There was a horrible gasp at a clanger being dropped by the Lord Mayor, and I waited a decent interval for people to become very cross, and then said, 'With a camera of course!' at which everybody laughed, particularly the Kenyans; and later, when I went to Kenya, they still remembered the joke and how I pulled their legs. They have a great sense of humour, and were most amused.

At the end, President Moi made another speech – not a prepared one – extremely charming, and really got people behind him. It was such a sincere friendly speech. The second one was much better than the first. The first had no doubt been prepared by civil servants.

At midsummer I staged a get-together in the Mansion House at which, unlike a dinner where you only talk to the people on either side of you, everyone could meet everyone. In other words a ball of the kind which was commonplace not all that long ago, with people in full evening dress – white tie and tails and long evening dresses – dancing in each other's arms to tuneful and not over-loud music played by the band of the Honourable Artillery Company, my old regiment. It was not only an exercise in nostalgia. I did it to show that the Mansion House was the centre of the City. We had Cabinet ministers, top civil servants, financiers and bankers, City aldermen, the Town Clerk and his colleagues at Guildhall, mayoral staff and officers, all mixed up together letting their hair down and enjoying themselves. I have never seen Sir Geoffrey Howe, the Chancellor of the Exchequer, looking more relaxed; his wife Elspeth was having a great time.

I had breakfast served in the Mansion House kitchen at midnight. Everyone went down and collected their eggs and bacon and sat on the stairs and in the hall with their plates on their knees as we used to do in 'the old days'. People could mingle and talk as on no other occasion. There was no protocol; all met merely as guests of the Lord Mayor of London. Lord Armstrong, chairman of the Midland Bank, had a copy of the *Financial Times* delivered carrying the announcement of a knighthood for Anthony Tuke, chairman of Barclays Bank. I read the news to the assembled company and then kept Anthony's wife dancing so he could not slip away. He had kept it secret from her, and I do not know which was greater, her astonishment or his embarrassment.

I was glad not to be too late to bed, for I had to be fresh and wide-eyed for the Trooping of the Colour on Horse Guards Parade next morning. I would have looked – and felt – more in keeping with this colourful occasion if I had been allowed to wear a grey waistcoat and grey top-hat instead of sombre black. Apart from that, it is difficult to get rid of a silk hat; every time you touch it you spoil it. I had no need of a hat of any hue, however, for the less strident but equally colourful Ceremony of the Knollys Rose. At the end of the fourteenth century one Lady Knollys had a bridge built so she could walk from her garden to her house in the middle of medieval London without getting her shoes dirty. She had, however, omitted to get the permission of the City Corporation and was summoned to appear before the Mayor. Her husband, Sir Roger Knollys, spoke in her defence with all the authority and menace of the great national hero that he was, having raised armies and fought in France and Flanders. The Mayor got the message and, in dread of being hauled before the other court in Westminster and facing the wrath of King Richard in person, he allowed Sir Roger and Lady Knollys to keep their bridge in perpetuity – provided they paid the Corporation an annual rent of one red rose from their garden. The land has never been built on and is now a Corporation Garden from which every year for 600 years a Knollys Rose has been ceremoniously presented to the current Lord Mayor of London. My turn came on 21 June 1979.

I like flowers, and I insisted on having them, and not the horrid plastic name-labels suggested by the staff, for the buttonholes of the thirty senior civil servants and thirty top brass from the City whom I invited to the reception in the Mansion House. The idea was to have a social occasion, like the Midsummer Ball, on which people from two different worlds could meet each other, almost certainly for the first time, on neutral ground. I was not having lapel labels in the Mansion House as if it was some grotty sales conference. I had the civil servants wear red carnations and the City people white ones. They were handed out at the door. Everyone then knew which camp people came from, and it was up to them to introduce themselves and start talking. It had never been done before, and worked like a treat. Afterwards I realised that of course we should have given the men from Whitehall the white flowers!

Not that all arrangements at the Mansion House went as smoothly. It was one big muddle the morning at the beginning of July when the attractive coloured singer Patti Boulaye and a troop of others swarmed into the Salon and started demonstrating the exercises being recommended in their 'Fitness for All' campaign.

Mary Donaldson was meant to be there but she wasn't. We had our photographs taken, first on one foot and then on the other, and nobody knew what to do. Peter Wood, who presumably had arranged it, was hovering around very vaguely. They said they would like photographs outside because it was a fresh air thing. So we all stood outside the front door, but once more we had nothing to do. Someone suggested I might like to do a press-up dressed in a morning suit, wearing my big mayoral badge and in the street! Thankfully no one thought it a good idea, and Peter Milo was adamant. In the end I stood still while Patti Boulaye gave a high kick in front of me. After that we came back in.

That was the only photograph to appear in the press, complete with my astonished expression.

It was a pity I was not going to the West Indies for my next overseas tour, as that would have given me an excuse to entertain the delightful Miss Boulaye and get her advice. It was to Spain, however, that I was scheduled to go, and the next day I was due to confer with the somewhat less glamorous delegation from the Corporation of Madrid on the subject of their proposed sewage system and how the building of it was going to be financed. They had been to Germany on the same mission where, it was said, they had been offered money at 8 per cent. In London banks had offered some at $9\frac{3}{4}$ per cent. The civil servants from the Foreign Office and Department of Trade who came to brief me on Spain had very little to say on the matter. They had no idea what rate of interest the British government would offer, but people were investing in Spain, they told me, in order to get a foot into the Common Market which she was shortly expected to join. British Leyland, Ford and Fiat were already there. I got the impression that Britain was only interested in selling capital goods to Spain, and we would have to take a stake in whatever operation we set up.

Professor Don Enrique Tierno Galvan who was Alcalde-Presidente (Mayor) of Madrid spoke little English. Did I have problems with London's sewers? sewer-conscious reporters asked me on my arrival in Spain's capital. Once again I had to explain the difference between Greater London and the City of London. London's sewers, I told them, were not my responsibility but the GLC's. I was not the mayor of Greater London with its 9 million population but of the Square Mile inside it which was the capital's financial centre. The Minister of Finance whom we saw a couple of days later was also an academic. He told me if a company in Spain borrowed abroad it had to deposit a quarter of the amount with the Central Bank. He would receive interest on it. It seemed that they had too much money in Spain in 1979, particularly in the holiday season. I told him they would do better to have discount houses and a money market. He agreed. Sometimes, he said, the rate of interest rose to 40 per cent overnight. He wanted us to help them reorganise their stock exchange and have British banks open branches in Spain.

'They are academics playing with financial toys,' I told my diary.

The Minister of Trade was more down to earth. He talked of their energy problems, their inflation and their lack of investment. Industry, he said, was not investing because of the uncertain political situation. On the contrary, I thought but did not say, it was lack of incentive.

Our ambassador to Spain was Sir Antony Acland, and absolutely brilliant. He was trying to get firms interested in investing in Spain before it came into the Common Market, because they would have to open their markets to British goods, as well as all other European goods, and he wanted the British to be first. He had written to many firms in England, and got no reply. He really was on the ball, and I agreed a list with him of people I would write to and point out the advantages of getting into Spain before the others and before Spain actually entered the Market. I am glad to say, as I could write to many of the chairmen by their Christian name, most of them contacted the ambassador and many of them made investments and took part in the opening up of Spain to foreign industry.

I also wrote to the Foreign Secretary, and said what a brilliant ambassador they had in Spain, and how impressed I was with the work he was doing, which was true.

Many of the ambassadors are under-rated. They do an enormous amount of work for industry, and their praises often go unsung. Sir Antony later on became the senior civil servant at the Foreign Office.

What would these Spaniards, whom I had patronisingly dubbed impractical, have thought of the ritual I performed the day after my return to England in the crypt of Guildhall: the Early Evening Reception for Corporation Benefices? This was one of the Corporation's principal lunacies. The idea was that, having the gift of the benefice of all the City churches – the ecclesiastical living, that is – the Corporation had the right to nominate each vicar. So, naturally enough, the Lord Mayor had, by reason of his office, to take an interest in the affairs of the Church of England. There were some ninety people in the crypt that evening. The only thing we gave them was the idea that we had got money for them, which we had not. No one else ever took any interest in the Corporation's Benefices, except when we had to appoint a new priest, who was always the one the parishioners wanted anyhow.

At the annual service in St Paul's Cathedral of the Order of St Michael and St George I paid tribute both to religion and to chivalry. This was a traditional engagement for every Lord Mayor, but I wonder what would have happened if, for whatever reason, I had declined to go. A fair rumpus, I imagine. Not that I would have wanted to miss it. It was a fascinating service. I met the Duke of

Kent, who is Grand Master of the Order, at the gate and took him to
his seat. He had a splendid collar, but I thought his gown was rather
poor compared with the others'. Sort of short back and sides, and slit
up like a girl's frock.

This was right in the middle of the Season, and at the Buckingham
Palace Garden Party I was with royalty again. In fact Nina and I
were among the guests in the Queen's Tent. We were escorted there
together with the Archbishop of Canterbury whom we met coming
in. We were among the first few to arrive, which I suppose was not
very good. Walking round afterwards I met all kinds of interesting
people. The Lord Mayor of Westminster for some reason took me for
the Lord Mayor of York. But I soon sorted that one out. We left early
for a less exalted engagement at the Mansion House, the 'Gilding of
the Lily' Fashion Show. The model girls who took part changed in
the Drawing Room. They asked for drinks, and when one of the
caterers' waiters brought them he found one girl absolutely starkers
and nearly dropped his tray. He rushed out declaring he would never
go there again, 'it was dangerous'. Not everyone, I thought, would
have taken the same attitude.

More dignified was the Kennedy Trust Fund Reception. This was
for the young people who had won scholarships to Harvard and
would shortly be leaving to take them up. With them were those who
had just come back after finishing their time at the American
university. And what a difference there was between the two! The
students on their way out seemed terribly gauche and unsophisti-
cated, whereas those who had completed their stint on the campus
were full of self-confidence and thoroughly adult. One rather nice
little girl brought her small child because her babysitter had let her
down. So we had this little thing, who was an absolute sweetie,
running round the Mansion House. One of the nicest things that
happened that day.

The City Arts Trust Carnival Procession which rounded off this
hot and clammy week should have been the entertaining event its
name implied but was a dismal mess-up. As soon as Basil Watson our
chaplain began reading the prayers which were to open the proceedings, the Chinese Dragon appeared with its train of noisy followers.
Bernard Miles launched into another series of long prayers, all
exceedingly complicated and about as cheerful as a funeral. A cadet
unit of the Rifle Brigade is hardly the stuff that carnivals are made of,
and they were hard put to it to compete with the drum majorettes,
one of whom added to the jollity by fainting from the heat. What
could I do to liven things up? Not much. I walked over and shook
hands with one little girl and kissed another. I congratulated the
band and tried to put a bit of pep into the hymn-singing by beating

time for them. I called for three cheers for the carnival. But it was a
forlorn effort.

That such occasions should fail to come up to expectations was of
little consequence. What was worrying me was the small progress I
seemed to be making in preparing for the tour I was about to make to
Malaysia and the Far East. I had kept Monday, 23 July clear for
drafting some of the speeches. But it was hard going. As I told my
diary:

> the ambassadors and high commissioners and the Foreign
> Office have given us damn all in the way of information. Their
> plea that they are busy with the Boat People is a load of
> nonsense because most people have to find time to do things in
> life, but the Foreign Office seems to go into a complete trance
> and does anything to avoid work. I wonder what the country
> would be like if everybody took the same attitude over business?

The Anglo-Malaysian Trade people who came to brief me were
very anxious that we kept a low profile in Malaysia. The Malays, they
said, were very sensitive. Several British firms, notably BP, had
satisfactory arrangements there. Though Malaya was a capitalist
country, as soon as an enterprise became successful parts of it were
transferred to Malay ownership. Moreover the FIC in Malaya did so
at the wrong prices. It was a pity we did not stand up and be counted.

To brief me on the Far East the Foreign Office sent me a young
man who was obviously very important – the McIntyre of McIntyre
or some such name. He was just a boy who, poor chap, knew nothing
about anything. He had had to take the place of the official who had a
meeting at the Foreign Office about these wretched 'Boat People'
from Vietnam.

> It is absolute nonsense that the Foreign Office can really
> persuade people, because they have got a particular problem,
> that nobody of any understanding on the Far East desk can find
> time to talk to the Lord Mayor of London on a visit which is
> costing a considerable amount of money, and which both the
> Foreign Secretary and his Permanent Secretary Michael Pal-
> liser tell us is of great importance. Parts of the Foreign Office
> are absolutely dead beat. Michael Palliser told me this was true
> about the South American section when I went out with
> Lindsay Ring, and they were all changed. I should think it is
> about time they changed the Far Eastern section.

The man who came from the Department of Trade and Industry
on the other hand was very helpful. If Malaysia wanted investment

from Britain, should we not spell out that they had to behave themselves? Or would it be more politic to lie low so as not to upset the people who were already there? I was probably going to have to aim at a compromise between the two. There was no such problem in Thailand, Korea or Japan, which I was also to visit, except that I had no information on which to base any intelligent formal speeches. Nothing was volunteered. None of the ambassadors on leave in London at the time bothered to come and talk to me. Moreover Our Man in Malaya was not going to be in the country at any period of my tour.

> I cannot understand people who have got careers do not think it worthwhile just flying back for a few days when the Lord Mayor of London is out there, particularly when I am able to get them into places to which they would not otherwise have access. If this country's Foreign Office is run like some sections of it are, God help Britain! Fortunately, as my experience with my previous tours showed, other sections like those dealing with Spain and Romania, are run extremely well.

An unnerving experience just before we set off for Malaya was preaching a sermon in St Paul's Cathedral. When you climb the ladder to the pulpit to speak there are detailed instructions on how to use the microphone. Put it round your neck. Wait for the red light, count to ten, then start. What they do not tell you to do is take it off afterwards, so you can be nearly decapitated as you escape from the pulpit. I never want to do it again. It was a terrifying experience. Getting airborne at Heathrow, on the other hand, was not so much intimidating as infuriating. Our party consisted of myself, my wife Nina, the two sheriffs and their wives and the Chief Commoner and his wife – eight in all plus one of the Mansion House staff. Normally Lord Mayors took a small party on overseas visits whose expenses would be covered by the official allowance. If the Lord Mayor wished to take a large one, he could do so, but he would have to pay the extra cost himself. If I was to go at all, I wanted to make as big an impression as I could on the heads of state and ministers to whom, after all, I was on a diplomatic mission. So I bore the cost of taking an impressive train of supporters.

For the nine of us at Heathrow that morning, as I told my diary, it was 'sheer absolute inefficiency and chaos, and really Ross Stainton, the chairman of British Airways, a very able man, must be ashamed of his bloody airline'. We should have left at 5.30 in the afternoon, and in fact we took off five minutes before midnight.

There was supposed to be some trouble in Turkey – I have

forgotten what it was – and, although we were in the VIP lounge, no one was there who knew anything at all about what was happening. We could get no intelligent person to say why there was a delay, or when we were likely to take off. After about four hours of waiting, we were told we were about to take off and they had found an aeroplane. When we got on board, the crew were out of time, so while all the passengers sat on the plane the crew very reluctantly had to march off. We then had to wait for another crew to be found. When that was done, we finally took off. We should have flown direct to Karachi – certainly India. However, we were informed that the new crew were not properly in time, and therefore could only fly as far as the Gulf States! We put down at one of the Gulf States, where we were assured there was a crew waiting for us, to take us on. While we were sitting on the ground with no crew, we were then told that the crew would not be in time for another hour or two, and so we had to wait for them.

Finally, we took off, and the Captain said he apologised for the delay, which was through no fault of British Airways. I sent a message to him asking if he would see me. I said: 'I think you would be very much better advised just to say you are sorry you are late, because it was quite clear to the people on the plane that it was the responsibility and the muddle of British Airways, and it would be much better not to make silly excuses.' He was very nice, and then apologised to the passengers again for the delay. When we took off finally for Kuala Lumpur the new skipper got the message and just apologised for the delay, and realised how inconvenient it had been for everybody. We finally touched down at midnight – twelve hours, as far as I recollect, late.

The welcoming party of course had been waiting since twelve o'clock midday. This cannot have been very convenient for the Mayor and the entire town council and their wives, who – good for them – gave us a rapturous welcome. And it did not end at the airport. For across the dual carriageway for us all to see as we entered the town from the airport was a colourfully festooned arch on which was written in English and Malay: WELCOME TO SIR KENNETH CORK, GBE, DLITT, LORD MAYOR OF LONDON.

I was so astounded and impressed that I had the driver stop the car and I got out to have a closer look at it to show my appreciation. Looking back on this, Lord King and his staff have done a wonderful job on British Airways, which is now the best airline in the world.

It was Ramadan, the month of fasting in which Muslims refrain from eating and drinking in daylight hours. I knew Malaysia fairly well and had been there many times. So I was prepared for not being offered anything to drink at the lunches and dinners and the meetings with officials and ministers. Datuk Bandar, the Mayor, told me they wanted help from Britain over town planning, anti-pollution measures and traffic control. And what about a loan for Kuala Lumpur? A training course for their law officers? At the dinner he gave in our honour in the Regent Hotel I read him a message from the Common Council and gave him a silver plate. He gave the Corporation a huge aluminium plaque. Though there was no drink, we managed to down a Planters Punch or two in the lounge bar before it all began.

The pro-British Minister of Home Affairs spoke of the communists on their Thai border and hoped the City of London would help develop Malaya. To the Governor of the Central Bank, with a reputation for being short-tempered and having once been very rude to Sir Hartley Shawcross, I hinted that if he wanted investment it was no good vaguely shouting for it and holding seminars. He had to identify the objects for which he wanted finance and make specific approaches. I suggested pharmaceutical manufacture. Though the country was too small to provide a home market, the product was small and easy to transport across the sea for export. He seemed to take all this in good part, and was extremely polite and helpful.

I reminded guests at the British Malaysian Industry lunch that Britain had a hard currency. There were people there who would be happy to invest in Malaya so long as the conditions were right. Those with industries in Malaya should stop taking everything and stand up and be counted. My listeners did not seem unduly put out by this. And to my astonishment they cheered my answer to someone who queried the high fees being charged Malaysians who came to Britain to study. 'Well,' I said, 'Malaysia is a wealthy country with a surplus of payments and twenty thousand students, and I don't see why they should not pay the right price for their education.'

We went to Penang where at the civic reception I told them that only the British could have founded it – it received its charter direct from Queen Victoria. It was a great venture at the time, and Britain, I said, was still great. Moreover we did want to invest in Malaysia and, by jingo, if we did, we had the skills, we had the men and had the money, too – a piece of British arrogance which went down well. Rex Hunt, the Deputy High Commissioner whom everyone was to know later when the Argentinians invaded the Falkland Islands where he was Governor, believed the whole world was going to be taken over by the Chinese and Britain could do nothing about it. Overseas ministers like Hunt should spend more time in Britain. Living all the time with an expatriate community gives them the idea that there is no future for Britain – a misleading impression.

The most famous resident in Penang could not come to my lunch because of Ramadan, so I took the presentation gold cufflinks to him at his house. He cut my wife a beautiful spray of orchids from his garden before we left. In his small museum-like room where the walls were hanging with photographs, the eighty-six-year-old former Prime Minister Tunku Abdul Rahman, who was an honorary Freeman of the City of London, talked brightly about everything under the sun. They wanted us to finance the building of a big new hotel, and we went to see the site. It was said that the Bank of Paris were interested and the Peninsular Hotel Group of Hong Kong would like to run it. But surely it must be more British than that!

So back to Kuala Lumpur airport under my triumphal arch, which this time I stopped to photograph, and away to Bangkok where we were met by the Governor, who had only been appointed five days before. For the Thai Foreign Minister whom we saw the next day the insoluble problem was infiltration of Cambodians trained since childhood to do nothing but kill. They could not be resettled, for no one else wanted them. All the Thais could do was to push them back across the border.

Conditions for investment were better in Thailand than in Malaysia, yet there was only about £9 million worth of British capital in the country. It was a point we made to the Prime Minister, who seemed somewhat hazy. British investment and Cambodian refugees were the main topics of conversation, too, with the charming King of Siam, to use a more familiar but incorrect title. We were met by an elderly chamberlain straight out of operetta. The palace grounds were indescribably beautiful. All the hedges were cut in the shape of animals. The chamberlain respectfully instructed us on the correct way of approaching and withdrawing from His Royal Highness.

The King was obviously more nervous than we were, but slowly the conversation got going. He told us, as others had done, about the Khmer Rouge refugees who had been taught nothing but how to kill people, but added gruesome details. He described how they beat people to death with a hammer and threw babies up and caught them on bayonets. In those places where they had them in camps and treated them kindly, he said, they improved. But the locals who lived in the vicinity of the camps and were very poor could not understand why their former enemies were being shown such kindness.

At the lunch I gave at the end of my stay in Thailand I found myself advising the chairman of their Securities Bank on – of all subjects – insolvency. One of their deposit banks had become insolvent, and he had withdrawn its licence. It was now closed. I told him what he should have done was to freeze the deposits and then run the bank down slowly to get the best realisation. If I had not been off to Seoul in the morning, and if I had not been Lord Mayor of London, I said, I would have stopped and given him a hand.

South Korea was a country with an only just balanced economy. In fact it was in slight deficiency. It was not pumping out goods like Japan, Singapore and Hong Kong. It imported a considerable amount of goods from Britain with whom, with invisibles, it was roughly in balance. I agreed with their Minister of Economic Planning, with whom I had a very interesting chat shortly after my arrival in his country, that we in Britain had got it all wrong. I promised to help to make this clear when I returned. This was the least I could do after receiving from his Prime Minister, Mr Choi Kyu Hah, only an hour before, the Korean Gwanghwa Decoration Class 1, a beautiful sash with a star, for Meritorious Service in Promoting Trade between Our Two Countries. Afterwards I had a Korean-style lunch with the chairman of the Korean British Business Promotion Committee sitting on cushions on the floor. I am glad to say, however, they had backs to them. We were served by attractive Korean girls in national costume. The one who served me was greatly amused at the way my legs stuck out on the other side of the table where they knelt and handed us the dishes. Each time she prodded them with her knees, which she thought extremely funny. I must say she really was quite beautiful. Nina said that was why I always put my legs where I did.

At Panmunjon 'Armistice Centre' on the frontier of the Defence Zone we peered out over 'enemy country' where North Koreans dressed in Russian-style uniforms peered back at us. It was very, very hot, and my shirt was wringing wet. Tallboys, the chargé d'affaires, had arranged a very full programme for us. He got us to see the Prime Minister and a number of other ministers. But he really worked us far too hard. Apart from anything else, because of fuel shortages, the air-conditioning was only turned on half-cock. We did not have a single gap, and we were grateful for a few days' rest in Kyongju.

When we left the hotel in Seoul we came down in the lift a little early. From the lift door to the front door was laid a very expensive carpet which all the guests were avoiding, so Nina said: 'Don't walk on it. It is for some important visitor.' So we carefully walked beside it. The Koreans were most upset and came rushing up to point out that the carpet was for us. So we hastily went back to the lift and came down again, walking out on the special carpet. Perhaps modesty is not a virtue after all.

But that was after we had seen the famous Korean Pedal

Motorcycle. If the British government could agree to allow people to ride without wearing a crash helmet, it might be something the Viking works in Northern Ireland could manufacture. We also saw another of the magnificent cultural centres with a fine theatre, restaurant, art gallery and the rest, which was far better than ours at the Barbican, took only four years to design and build, and cost a mere £25 million.

It was stiflingly hot, too, in Pusan in the south-east of the Korean peninsula for the promised recovery session. Here we relaxed before the final leg of the Far East tour, which was to be Japan.

The air-conditioning was working full blast in the magnificent Hotel Okura where we stayed in Tokyo. 'We had in fact come to a place where efficiency reigned and we enjoyed it very much,' I told my diary. Our number 2 in Tokyo, Mr Gifford, was for some reason convinced that I would drop the most appalling clangers when I talked to Japanese government ministers and to the chairman of their Confederation of Industry. I did nothing to disillusion him. If he thought I was a twit, it was best he continued to think so. So I bid him farewell after our talk, leaving him in a state of great anxiety. He had offered us a drink, but I was too tired and just wanted to relax. When I did feel like a glass of something and ordered some wine for dinner I saw that drinking in Japan was going to be somewhat expensive. A half-bottle of wine cost around £15. Indeed, everything in Tokyo was excessively dear.

I had met Shigeru Okada, the manager of Mitsukoshi, the Tokyo equivalent of Harrods, in London when he came with a trade delegation. So I telephoned him and said we would all like to come and see his store. He sent a car to collect us. I imagined his inner sanctum being decorated in supreme oriental good taste, full of silk screens, jade and lacquer, and superb Japanese prints on the walls. But, surprise, surprise, it was all Louis XIV and a genuine portrait by our own Joshua Reynolds over the mantelpiece. Mitsukoshi sells *everything*, including Rolls-Royces. The company's agent in Japan allows them one car a month. Mr Okada put it in his window priced at £75,000, which was £25,000 more than what one would have to pay in London. Officials at the British embassy told me this was due to tax and duties and handling charges. The Rolls agent's story was that because he could not take delivery for three years he had to give a fixed price, because the Japanese accepted it. He had to load it high so he could afford to sell it at that price when it was delivered. This was clearly nonsense, since he had thirty-six cars in stock and anyone could buy one off the shelf from the window of Mitsukoshi's. However, it explained why everything was so costly.

At the reception given to us by the British ambassador in the garden of the fine British embassy opposite the royal palace I was interested to see the range of British business represented in Japan. I spoke to agents for Marks & Spencer, Barclays Bank, Thorn-EMI, you name it; they were all there. I began to get an entirely different view of the situation in Japan. At that time the balance of payments was 3 to 1 in their favour, but I could not see that lasting. However, with the difference between our imports from and our exports to Japan in 1979 being something in the region of £600 million a year, so huge an embassy staff was surely non-productive and difficult to justify. If we could not get our trade to turn round fairly soon, it seemed to me that we should close the embassy and reduce our representation to a chargé d'affaires. But that was not the kind of heresy a guest of honour aired at an embassy garden party. Besides, the British government owned the ground and the building. What else could they use it for? If they gave it back, it went to the Emperor.

I explained the difference between the Greater London Council and the City Corporation to the Mayor (or Governor) of Tokyo with whom we had a very formal meeting sitting opposite each other in two lines of chairs. It was the last of many times I had to spell this out. The tour was over.

I had a steam bath locked in a kind of sweatbox, had my back scrubbed and massaged. After that I felt much more relaxed. It was 16 August, and I wondered whether it was equally hot and muggy in London. I hoped British Airways would not let the side down as they had done on the outward journey. Their representative had called on me in Bangkok. He had had a telex from Ross Stainton saying how sorry they were for the delay. But it was not the delay they should have been apologising about, which was not their fault, but the muddle, which was. However, the seven-hour flight to Anchorage in Alaska went without a hitch. We left right on time. Anchorage consisted of nothing but moss and water and a big mountain in the distance cloaked in mist. Everything in the airport shop was exorbitantly priced – even more expensive than in Tokyo. They asked two American dollars for a postcard – more than a pound. A belt would have cost me £40. We arrived at London Airport on the second leg of a very comfortable flight two minutes early. It was six o'clock on a Friday morning. We had only been away three weeks, but it seemed like three years. I felt absolutely drained. It was not a long drive home, but we were out of phase. But there was the whole weekend to recover, and gradually I eased back into the world I had left on 28 July.

I was determined not to rush things, not to be too precipitate in allowing myself to become immersed once more in the affairs of the

Mansion House, Cork Gully, the Harold Wilson Committee, Insolvency Law Reform, *et al.* In any event 21 August was my birthday, and the staff of Cork Gully had commissioned David Poole to paint Nina's portrait, and they all assembled in the boardroom to present it to me. I do not think I have ever been as touched as I was then. It was extremely kind of the staff, and I shall never forget it and the number of people who contributed. In mid-week I went down to Hamble to see my new little boat, *Rum Run*. It took me half the morning to get it sorted out, but I was then able to launch out and sail it on my own. It sailed beautifully. The engines were a bit noisy, but with *Gander* I was used to well padded engines. The self-furling head sails on *Rum Run* worked marvellously, and it cut through the water at a remarkable pace for a little boat. It was amazingly stable, too. I told myself I would have to get used to *Rum Run* having very much smaller quarters. But I came back to the landing-stage feeling very refreshed after a day out at sea on my own, and well able physically and mentally to engage gear once more in the programme of engagements which Peter Milo and Brian Wright had planned for my final months as Lord Mayor of London.

Muddle characterised the first one, the memorial service at Westminster Abbey for Lord Mountbatten who had been the victim of an IRA bomb outrage while fishing in a boat off Holyhead. Nina and myself were the only ones asked from the City, and the police escorted us in our official car along the Embankment and past the House of Commons to go into Parliament Square. At that point our car and its police escort were stopped by a policeman on the street who said no one was allowed through, 'even field marshals'. So we had to get out and walk. We fought our way through the seething mass on the pavement, and I was very conscious of the fact that round my neck was the golden badge said to be worth £50,000, and the priceless chain. Finally we found a policeman who solemnly walked in front of us and took us to the entrance of the Abbey – just in time. There we were told that if our police escort had brought us in the proper way our car could have drawn right up to the door. When we were in our seats someone came and apologised to us for not having been given the right priority and for having to walk.

It was a very moving service. Prince Charles read the lesson extremely well. Clergy of every denomination spoke. When it was over an official came up and said: 'You know, Lord Mayor, you will come out after the Lord Mayor of Westminster, who takes priority in his parish.' Having said that, we were escorted out in front of all the Cabinet ministers and everyone else. We got the right priority then – or was it? We had a long wait, however, before we could leave while the royal family said their farewells. It enabled my car to be in the right place, though, and we were whipped back to the Mansion House in no time.

In the mean time the Governor – the Mayor, that is – of Cairo had come to stay at the Mansion House, and he had been to see the new town at Bletchley called Milton Keynes. By the time we gave him his banquet I had got to know him very well. In my speech I told everyone what friends we had become. The Minister of State at the Foreign Office was surprised how we could be so formal at one moment, as we were when we processed in, and manage to behave so informally at dinner.

The actual election of Peter Gadsden as the 652nd Lord Mayor of London took place in the Aldermen's Court Room on 2 October. I knew him well, and he was a good friend. Peter Delaney, who was to become my chaplain, preached a first-class sermon but appeared to be suffering from St Vitus' Dance. I was to witness another but very different sort of dance that evening by the girl who constituted the cabaret at the London Retail Traders Association reception at the Fan Makers' Hall. No one could stop Rita the Belly Dancer from waggling herself and all her accoutrements upside down in front of me for almost her entire act. What a contrast to the morning's staid election ritual in Guildhall! The new sheriffs were flabbergasted. It had all been organised by the man who ran the Arab restaurant in the old Turkish Baths frequented by Gully, my father's partner. I was told that shortly after I left the fan dancer went topless, so I think the sheriffs were able to congratulate themselves on having got me away just in time – or perhaps not!

Whether it was overdoing it at the Fan Makers' Hall or the accumulation of nine months' non-stop junketing, I do not know, but at the end of the week I woke up with terrible pains in my chest which having to go through the cold room at Billingsgate fish-market early next morning can hardly have alleviated. I went to Barts Hospital for an X-ray, and they told me I had a spot on my lung and to take it easy. Some hope! My officers tried to persuade me to pull out of parts of my programme, but I felt unable to let people down when so many were involved. So I finished my day by seeing a Hindustani newspaper correspondent; giving a lunch for an Armenian, a Greek and two Roman Catholic bishops and the Vicar of Great Missenden; receiving a deputation from Sabena apologising for mucking up the return flight from Brussels; giving a lecture to the Royal Naval College at Greenwich on economics; and attending the annual dinner in the Mansion House of the Horners Company, my own, principal guest Sir Harold Wilson. By that time I was feeling pretty ill. My next day's diary ended with the words: 'My chest by now was absolute bloody agony, and I couldn't sleep.' My local doctor saw me in the morning, said I had pneumonia and told me to stay away from the Mansion House for two weeks. I settled for two days – the weekend.

My main reason for not wanting to absent myself from the Mansion House was the visit of the President of Penang Town Council. I should have vetted the top guest-list for his reception, for they seemed to have invited a whole lot of quite irrelevant people – except for Field Marshal Templer whom the President was delighted to see. But for the most part the days were filled with telling the Magistrates Association not to knock Willie Whitelaw's Short Sharp Shocks scheme for young offenders before it started, and telling the Establishment Committee meeting, at which Michael Heseltine proposed the civic toast, that the Government should make sure the tax system did not drive investment away from industry and into the secondary market on the Stock Exchange.

And then it was the last weekend but one. Other Lord Mayors, I was told, regretted the end. I had enjoyed my year but I certainly did not want it to continue a day longer. I had an end-of-term feeling and a prospect of 'freedom'. On Sunday, 28 October I was telling my diary I would hand over to Peter Gadsden with a sense of relief. But the events came crowding in up to the very last moment: half an hour at the Banqueting House in Whitehall for Mrs Thatcher's reception to Chairman Hua of China; the last Livery Dinner in the Egyptian Hall for the Shipwrights; the White Ensign Association's Dinner in Guildhall welcoming Prince Charles (who had no relief from *his* round of duties after a mere twelve months); receiving the Mayor of Las Vegas and the Mayor of Stuttgart, Field Marshal Rommel's son; our reception for Chairman Hua, whom I got interested in the National Enterprise Board's Monotype Printing Process then being demonstrated in China. That was my last big function at the Mansion House. Nina and I were at the top table at Chairman Hua's dinner at the Chinese embassy. When Margaret Thatcher asked me how long a speech should be, I told her fifteen minutes. If I had known she was not going to use chopsticks I would have offered to show her how, but I imagine whatever tongs one used the nine-course meal would have tasted like solid glue. I do not know if my bad lung was affecting my palate, but at the Wine Tasting for Spastics at the Grocers Hall next day the wine tasted quite awful – except for the English wine, which was absolutely excellent.

We had the car up from home to move our junk out of the Mansion House. I had bought crates of champagne in November the year before. I was glad to see there was still some left, since the price had now doubled. At the dinner given that night by Thames Television, newspaperman Bill Barnetson threw out suggestions on what I might do when it was all over. Chairman of the Crown Estates? Join him at Hill Samuel? And, as if you could just ring up and ask to be a member, 'Why don't you go to the House of Lords?'

At eleven o'clock the next morning (8 November) I received all the Mansion House staff in the Drawing Room, had a drink with them and made a farewell speech. At that stage I still felt little sadness. But then the parting did not seem real. We had had a wonderful year. Staff like Teddy Ellis and the household officers had become my friends, as had the girls, the footmen and Peter Ricketts. But I had come to the end of the road. It was continuous giving out, and you have to take in some time. I believed I had done all the things I had set out to do. I had made the commercial and financial City and the Corporation very close. Many of the letters I received referred to this, so it looked as if I had got the message across.

I had a farewell drink and lunch at the Old Bailey. We were met by the two new sheriffs who take office six weeks before a new Lord Mayor takes over, the Recorder Sir James Miskin and Ralph Snagge, the Secondary and Under-Sheriff at Old Bailey. I had attended lunch four times during my term; most Lord Mayors never went at all. At lunch I sat between the Recorder and Judge Alan King-Hamilton whose father had been one of the founders of the Automobile Association. Back at the Mansion House I went up to 'our' Dressing Room, Bedroom and Boudoir, and then, I confess, I *did* feel sad. They were no longer ours. The beds were turned down – by mistake, I think – and Peter Gadsden's clothes were in the wardrobe. For the first time I became all sentimental.

When on the really Last Day, Friday, 9 November, the BBC Television interviewer asked me whether being Lord Mayor of London was all just pomp and show, I ran through a typical day and he had to agree it was not. My advice to the new Lord Mayor? Don't get fat on things you don't like. I had my thirtieth and last session as Chief Magistrate in the Justice Room and gave the staff a farewell chat. At the Last Lunch I sat beside Belinda Gadsden and Nina sat beside Peter, whose toast I proposed. I wished him good luck and off we went to the Silent Ceremony when I handed over the badge. We returned to the Mansion House, no longer Lord Mayor and Lady Mayoress. After tea in the Venetian Parlour with the two who were, we went downstairs to find to our surprise the whole of the staff and the girls, led by Teddy Ellis, waiting to say goodbye. It was an emotional moment for both of us. Indeed, I could hardly speak. Since we had to take part in the Lord Mayor's Show on the morrow, we stayed the night in our own flat in the Barbican. So we should not feel too depressed, I had booked seats at the theatre and we laughed our heads off at *No Sex, Please – We're British*. We were made to feel that all glory had not yet departed from us by the manager of the Strand Theatre, smartly dressed in black tie and dinner jacket, welcoming us in the foyer and inviting us to take drinks with him in the interval.

The next morning I rode to the Mansion House from Guildhall in the Green Coach which looks as if it had been made for a king's mistress. On the balcony I stood on the left of the Lord Mayor and watched the march past. On arrival at the Law Courts ahead of the Lord Mayor several shouted 'Good old Sir Kenneth!' and 'There's the old 'un', which I hopefully took as referring more to the fact that I was the retiring Mayor than to my age. It was the same excellent steak and kidney pudding at the Mansion House which followed. We said goodbye to Peter and Belinda Gadsden; Stanley the doorman was so overcome that, to Nina's astonishment, he kissed my hand.

So that really was the End, apart from the Lord Mayor's Banquet in Guildhall, given incidentally in honour of the *departing* mayor not of the incoming one. The Prime Minister spoke for almost double the fifteen minutes I had told her was the ideal, but her speech was outstanding and she was given a standing ovation. In my reply to the Archbishop of Canterbury, who had proposed my health (but spoke mostly about himself), I referred to Margaret Thatcher's use of the word 'wireless' and said I did not believe, from the way she looked, that she was that old. We had one or two dances after dinner, and then Andrews drove us to our flat in one of the Mansion House cars. Unlike Dick Whittington, who served four times, I shall never be Lord Mayor of London again. But for Nina and me the memories of those extraordinary twelve months will live with us for ever.

Chapter Nine

Tracing the DeLorean Millions

Removing myself for eighteen months from Guildhall House in Gresham Street, which was then the headquarters of W. H. Cork Gully & Co., for the six-month run-in followed by the year at the Mansion House gave me a legitimate opportunity to find out how they would all get on without me. And how the work would continue to come in. Michael Jordan was left to run the firm, with Walter Tickler in charge of administration. The partners, who were mostly of the same age, reacted to my absence in different ways. Like the lady who shed her corsets, some were pleased with the freedom, others were worried about the lack of familiar control. We were receiving an increasing amount of business requiring investigation work. For this we needed extra staff, for whom there was no work once the investigation was completed. Michael Jordan was keen to merge with a bigger firm, while we wanted it to keep the name which attracted the insolvency business. I agreed, and so did the rest of the partners. Not unnaturally, they were worried about what would happen after I retired in 1983.

In 1980 we were the largest insolvency practice in the United Kingdom and a household name in that field. We had developed the handling of insolvency to a fine art. This was one of the reasons, I imagine, why I was the recipient of the first Centenary Award given by the Institute of Chartered Accountants to a practising Chartered Accountant. Cork Gully had made insolvency work not only respectable but up-to-date.

I did not want to link up with a firm which had too much insolvency work, set in ways which were not our ways. I believed we had a way of handling insolvency that was better than anybody else's, and anyone who joined us would have to agree! Maybe that narrowed the field somewhat and, indeed, preliminary discussions with several firms soon foundered. For many years I had had a very friendly relationship with Lord Benson, the retired senior partner of Coopers

& Lybrand, with whom we had carried out a number of joint receiverships. It seemed to me that they were likely to suit us best. So I had a word with Donald Chilvers, the partner who ran their financial investigation and insolvency departments, and who was a very good friend of mine. He suggested having a preliminary canter over lunch at the Savoy. I was taking my usual week at Champneys at the time and said on no account could I abandon my orange juice diet, but if they would provide me with rabbit food I thought this would be an excellent way to start negotiations which I knew would be amicable but probably difficult.

Their offices were near us but in Gutter Lane. When they had joined with the American firm some years before, the Americans had been horrified to hear that their address was 'Gutter Lane', and I am told that they applied to the City Corporation to change the name. The City was equally horrified to hear that anyone should be other than proud of being in such an ancient street and told them so. So there was no change!

What was proposed was a merger of their insolvency activities (based at 1 Noble Street) with W. H. Cork Gully & Co. in a new partnership to be known simply as 'Cork Gully'. I would be its senior partner, and it would act as a 'division' of Coopers & Lybrand. There was to be an equal number of partners on the insolvency committee, and in the event of a disagreement the senior partner of Coopers & Lybrand would have the right to arbitrate. Coopers & Lybrand, with their twenty-nine British branches and worldwide representation, less their insolvency operation, would of course continue as before.

We worked on an agreed cash basis and had considerable cash reserves in the form of work in progress, much of which had not yet been paid for. We had an extremely close relationship with the banks and good connections throughout the City, but unlike most large firms we also acted for the major body of creditors throughout Britain. Provincial liquidations mainly came from the creditors' end, and it was a trend that was likely to grow. For us a great asset of Coopers & Lybrand was the number of branches they had in the provinces. It was suggested that we establish Cork Gully offices only in any branch of theirs which had a partner who understood insolvency and would operate the Cork Gully way. A disadvantage of being so closely associated in the public mind with insolvency was that any company we went into tended to be scared. Though understandable, it was not justified. Our record showed that far more of the companies we investigated did not end up with a receiver. We gave a clearance to many more companies than we 'took in'. Be that as it may, we felt it would be greatly to the advantage not only of ourselves but of the banks, too, if it was not Cork Gully but

Coopers & Lybrand who did the investigation. Only when the investigators showed that liquidation or a receivership was inescapable would it become a Cork Gully operation.

Norman and I would retire at seventy, and our share – after giving us a pension – would in reality go to Coopers & Lybrand. David Hobson, the senior partner of Coopers, and Donald Chilvers saw the wisdom of this and, with agreement on the main issues among Michael Jordan, Walter Tickler, Gerry Weiss, my brother Norman, Roger and myself, an announcement was made on 16 April 1980 that the new Cork Gully would come into being on 1 July. Its partners were to be the thirteen partners of W. H. Cork Gully & Co., with myself as senior partner, less Anthony Jolliffe, who ran our audit firm (see page 000), together with Coopers & Lybrand partners David Hobson, Donald Chilvers and Paul Shewell and the four who handled their insolvency business in London, Manchester and Birmingham. Michael Jordan, Gerry Weiss and my son Roger Cork became partners in Coopers & Lybrand. I was the only Cork Gully partner not to become a partner of Coopers & Lybrand, apart from Walter Tickler who was sixty-four in 1980. I did not feel the need and, anyway, at sixty-seven I was above their partnership age-limit.

'We believe', I said at the press conference launching the new partnership, 'that insolvency must be carried out in the interests of the community which is indeed in the interest of creditors. We share with Coopers & Lybrand the philosophy that every step should be taken to save the actual business so that it can be sold as a going concern. For this not only realises the best price for the assets but at the same time keeps the business, which is a national asset, in being.'

In the press notice issued at the same time we emphasised the unique rôle of receivership in the difficult 1980s.

There have been forecasts, official and otherwise, that the outlook for the commercial sector of the community is not encouraging in the medium term. Inflation continues to erode the capital base of industry and commerce. Receivership can play its part in rescuing businesses from difficulty; there is already a current need to provide advice to the business community in cases where it is believed that financial problems are pending. Although it is hard to foresee future developments already offered by way of prompt action to preserve assets and to effect reconstitution of viable elements of business will continued to be recognised, at least as much as in the past. Both Cork Gully and Coopers & Lybrand have demonstrated that a receiver's responsibilities towards creditors can often best be fulfilled by maintaining a business for sale as a going concern;

and banks who have so often appointed receivers have supported them.

Even more we saw the rôle of the new Cork Gully as embracing the *prevention* of financial difficulty. We looked to providing alternatives to receivership and liquidation. The service we offered for identifying the symptoms and causes of a company's financial plight so that we could hopefully take corrective action before it was too late we called 'intensive care'. It was designed to help clearing banks respond to the problems of the business customers whose directors, unaware of their true financial position, had failed to diagnose their illness, let alone take remedial action. We could quickly marshal the facts and pinpoint what needed to be done to avoid receivership or liquidation. We could put an immediate bung on the flow of further funds, and then draw up a longer-term programme to nurse the patient back to health and former prosperity. Once the decision was taken to apply this kind of treatment, the company's condition was carefully monitored week by week to detect and arrest any signs of further deterioration. There was no formal arrangement. We operated with the bank in a purely advisory capacity. By their leave we offered the ailing enterprise a helping hand to trade out of trouble.

'Intensive care' worked extremely well. The analysis of problems was undertaken by Coopers & Lybrand's management consultancy side, and many companies were saved from the brink. I had been able to apply the technique personally a few years earlier when I came to the aid of Hugh Bidwell, the son of an old army friend, whose company, the old-established food manufacturer Pearce Duff (founded 1847) had let its overdraft become very much higher than the limit set by its bank the National Westminster who, not unreasonably, had become worried. I persuaded NatWest to allow Pearce Duff time and money to pull out of their temporary embarrassment and hold off the appointment of a receiver. We cut away the unprofitable part of the operation and concentrated on their traditional food-processing activity, particularly custard, in Dunstable. In due time it recovered. It was a good example of how a bank, properly consulted, will give aid and support. Barings Bank had been a shareholder in Pearce Duff, and after the rescue they sold me their holding, which, when I came to sell it later, turned out a good investment.

I had of course been in and out of my room at our Gresham Street offices on many occasions during my time at the Mansion House, but from 1980 I took up the reins in earnest. The amount of work coming in had dropped, and I felt we were losing our place in the market. I was not particularly keen to become personally involved in insolvency work during the three years leading to my retirement, but willy nilly I did. I was of course anxious to show our new partner that we had it in us to get new business, and the first of the big cases which landed on my desk as senior partner of the new Cork Gully was that of Foden.

This company, located in Sandbach near Crewe, was renowned for making steam traction engines and steamrollers, and of course for its brass band. At about this time they ran into difficulty. Some 150 years after they had been founded, they were now making tank transporters for British and NATO armies and for Commonwealth countries. Though they had a large business, they were making a loss. Every effort was made to find someone to take them over but, because the liabilities were too heavy, without success. The National Westminster Bank felt obliged to appoint a receiver. They chose us. It was the first appointment of the new Cork Gully. I took over the running of Foden as receiver jointly with Philip Livesey, senior partner of Coopers & Lybrand's Manchester branch. Martin Iredale was to be in charge on the ground. That the truck industry was in depression I could see from the rows of Vauxhall trucks which had remained unsold through the winter of 1979–80 and were lined up on what had once been the airfield of Handley Page at Hatfield – scene of an earlier Cork Gully rescue (see page 00).

I did not need long in Sandbach to discover why the company was running at such an enormous cost, out of proportion to what was coming in. They had always taken pride in the quality of their vehicles. They still designed and produced in their own workshops the axles, suspensions and all the heavy equipment which other manufacturers had long ceased manufacturing themselves but bought in from GKN and the rest and then assembled. But that was not in the Foden tradition, and it was not something which as receivers we could order them to change. It was obviously a valuable business and one which should stay British. If the place had to be closed down, Britain's Ministry of Defence and NATO would have to buy from Mercedes and Volvo, etc. So we worked very hard to keep it going. A team from Coopers & Lybrand management consultancy went up to advise them on cutting costs. But eventually we had no alternative but to sell. If the works shut down, the company would only be worth around £5 million. We aimed at getting £14 million for it as a going concern. The Foden management had a list of potential purchasers like British Leyland, Volvo and SAAB, and insisted that I wrote to all of them. They all seemed unlikely customers to me, and I was right. I did not receive a single favourable reply. In my book the only people likely to look twice at Foden were the Americans, who would like to get into NATO. It would have to be a group with interests other than truck-making as the American truck industry was also doing badly. So we scoured around for an enterprise in America who made heavy trucks but had another part of their business which was being profitable and would carry them through the depression. Moreover owning a plant in Britain would give an American firm entry into European, NATO and Commonwealth markets. I had a computer programmed to come up with an American company which met these requirements. It produced one only: Paccar of Seattle. It had been built up by one Chuck Pigott, son of the founder, to manufacture vehicles and equipment for the timber industry. I sent Chuck a telex to say that Foden was in the market and it was something he could not miss. Would he be interested? He sent one back saying he had already considered buying it but decided against. It was my one chance of achieving a reasonable sale, so on the Friday night I sent him another telex: 'Thank you for your telex in view of which I am arriving Seattle Monday morning.'

I caught a plane, and to their intense astonishment arrived in Seattle as threatened and stayed there three days. In that time I not only persuaded their Pat Young and Chuck Pigott, who turned out to be an extremely nice man, to buy Foden – we signed a heads of agreement before I left – but returned with the present of two home-canned tins of smoked salmon. He had a boat in which he sailed up the west coast of Canada and the United States salmon-fishing in inland waters.

After a great deal of negotiation Paccar bought Foden and transformed the business. Pigott sent his engineers over to Sandbach, including their design engineer for these heavy vehicles who, to the amazement of the British lot, turned out to be a woman. Paccar paid the asking price of £14 million, which not only left nothing owing the National Westminster Bank but also meant there was a good sum of money over for other creditors. If Paccar had not bought it, the bank would never have got out, and Britain would have lost a very valuable business. They cut the workforce down to two-thirds of its former strength and with it substantially increased the turnover above that of 1980, keeping the Foden employment at Sandbach which otherwise would have disappeared altogether.

Chuck Pigott asked me to go on the board, but it was not ethical for anyone to become a director of a company of which he had been the receiver and had then sold. I did, however, produce two directors for him: Tony Jolliffe, a partner of W. H. Cork Gully before the merger and later a Lord Mayor of London; and the man who had just retired as the Commandant of the Royal Corps of Transport. The Foden family directors resigned, but certain of their technical directors remained. It was a sad example of people dedicated to running a business but unable or unwilling to move with the times. Having worked so hard and so desperately, being unable to continue must have been soul-destroying. Even the Foden name disappeared. The company was renamed Sandbach Engineering. And the band? Long disbanded. But it was a good start for our new partnership.

I decided to handle the Foden case with a former Coopers partner, not a Cork Gully partner, in order to consolidate the new-look Cork Gully – and, as I said, show Coopers & Lybrand that we were able to get the work when we wanted it. Our position was further cemented by a second receivership from the National Westminster Bank which again I took on personally with Paul Shewell of Coopers & Lybrand as joint receiver. This was a canning enterprise in East Anglia which we were also successful in disposing of as a going concern but only with the greatest difficulty. It was the third job, however, which demonstrated to any doubters that we were still top of the top league.

Just before I began my stint as Lord Mayor of London a proposal was put to the Northern Ireland Development Agency of which I was unpaid chairman – I had declined the Government's offer of £10,000 a year to leave myself free to tell them whatever I felt – that we should deal with a Mr John Z. DeLorean, an American who was trying to find a site for a factory in which to manufacture a two-seater sports-car he had designed. One of the places he had been looking at was Northern Ireland. NIDA looked at it and said No. We came to the conclusion that it was not a project we should support. He would have to form a company in Ulster and it would be a subsidiary of his holding company in the United States which held the sole distribution rights for the car and was wholly owned by John DeLorean. So the Ulster unit would be purely for manufacture, and every car it produced would have to be 'sold' to John DeLorean's American company. So we in Britain would have no control of what was happening in America, nor any financial hold on the DeLorean Motor Company Inc, the Michigan corporation – though it was shown later that we could have done.

So, taking my informal advice, NIDA decided to take no action. In fact my advice was the wrong one. The factory built at Dunmurry, West Belfast, and the company which owned it, DeLorean Motor Company Ltd, could both have been successful. The British government had faith in the project and decided to finance it. As part of the package, John DeLorean agreed to have two British directors on the board of his Michigan corporation to represent British interests, but the British government would no more have insisted on having a financial stake in it than they would have in Monsanto or any of the other big international groups whose subsidiary companies they were glad to have operating in Northern Ireland. This was the way the officials in the Northern Ireland Office were geared. For them the DeLorean Motor Company was just another operation of a type which had already proved profitable for all concerned. At this time, however, it was inadequately financed, a circumstance which unfortunately escaped their notice. Moreover the Michigan corporation was completely under-capitalised and had no business other than to be the head office of this manufacturing subsidiary in Northern Ireland.

The first winter after the Dunmurry car factory went into commission, sales of the vehicle in America went splendidly. There were the inevitable few engineering problems to start with, and the workforce, which had been carefully trained by former Chrysler experts, were on a 'learning curve'. But soon the whole unit began functioning exactly as prescribed, and John DeLorean saw all his dreams coming true. He had already taken as much money as he could out of his Michigan holding company to set up the unit in West Belfast, so his plan now was to 'go public'. In optimistic mood promoted by the high American sales, he engaged another thousand men for the factory and threw them into the assembly-lines. But, unlike the original expertly instructed team, none of them was properly trained. So, though production doubled, many more cars left the factory with faults which had to be sorted out in Michigan before they could be sold. At the same time a freeze-up seized America, and sales fell right off. A sports-car became low priority, a fast toy for bright young men but hardly a necessity at a time of a winter freeze. The $30 million credit with the American bank ran out. The Belfast factory produced another $10 million worth of DeLorean cars to be paid for by DeLorean Motor Company, to find, however, that their sole customer had run out of money. Asked to grant extra facilities, the bank took over the documents in anticipation of doing so, but in view of the declining sales thought better of it. The bank held on to the documents as additional security for the money they had already lent John DeLorean, but offered him no more. Where was the cash coming from to pay the Northern Ireland staff, the electricity bills, the component suppliers? It was this very serious crisis which led James Prior, who had taken over as Secretary of State for Northern Ireland, to enlist our help.

Jim Prior was a good friend of mine and he knew of my connection with the province through my chairmanship of the Northern Ireland Development Agency which had brought me a good understanding

of the manufacturing scene there. Since there had been criticism of
the British government's behaviour in Ulster, he wanted someone
known for his reasonable independence of view to advise them on
what to do next.

Cork Gully's brief was to do an investigation into the DeLorean
set-up in West Belfast and declare whether in their view it was
capable of surviving. Was it something the British government
would be justified in putting more money into?

Coopers & Lybrand did the major part of the investigation with a
management consultancy team. Through their American connections they reported on the marketability of the car in the United
States. They went through the manufacturing process at West
Belfast with the proverbial fine-tooth comb. They sent staff to
DeLorean's depots on the west coast of America and the east coast. It
was an extremely valuable and thorough report, and it was completed in three weeks.

I was made the special adviser to the Government. The Northern
Ireland Office told me that DeLorean was over here and wanted to
see me. I was also told the only time he could fit me in was for
breakfast at 8 a.m. the next day at the Connaught Hotel off
Grosvenor Square where he was staying (at British government
expense) before leaving that evening for the States on Concorde. I
told his office that I lived at Great Missenden, some way outside
London, and that it would be difficult to get in by eight in the
morning; I was more used to people coming to see me than my going
to see them. However, they hinted that Mr DeLorean was a Very
Important Person, and could I stretch a point and be there? Which I
did.

I managed to arrive dead on eight, and he swept into the room with
three of his henchmen dead on half-past. He made no apology for
keeping me waiting, but I suppose it never occurred to him. He was
immaculately dressed with an extremely commanding presence, and
had the air of an exalted Person of Importance irked at having had to
put up with a lot of incompetent civil servants and their minions
whom someone of his eminence should never have been asked to deal
with in person. The day before he had had a session with Jim Prior
and his advisers who, in spite of having backed the project in
Northern Ireland initially, had told him they were unlikely to
continue their support. The Secretary of State's instincts led him to
believe that things had now gone too far.

DeLorean will have dined on that unwelcome piece of news the
night before with his colleagues who were now attacking the Connaught's English breakfast. The two main ones were Roy Nesseth, to
whom I took an instant dislike, and Don Lander, the nice Canadian

who was managing director of the Irish company.

'Well, Sir Kenneth,' began the Great Man when we were all settled round the table, 'I want your advice.'

'Yes, Mr DeLorean?' I said guardedly, not knowing quite what to expect.

'I'm going to sue your government for fifty million dollars. Should I do it before or after you write your report?'

I was rather flattered by this, as presumably he assumed I was a man who would be frightened by $50 million, and smaller men by a smaller amount. But it was too early in the morning to think of an appropriately bright but snubbing riposte.

'Well, Mr DeLorean,' I said, 'it depends on how much money you've got.'

'What's that got to do with it?'

'Well. You're going to lose your money eventually. But you will keep it a little longer if you sue after my report.'

There were no more would-be clever remarks after that.

When he read our report a few weeks later he learnt that it was our belief that, in spite of increasing faults having to be corrected in America at great expense, the car was saleable. A turnover of 8,000 cars a year for sale in America was justified, but no more. In addition he might sell another 1,500 in Canada and ultimately some 2,000 in Europe. A major drawback was – and is – that the cars were made to run on lead-free petrol, which was only found in America at that time. There would have to be an expensive 'homologisation' exercise on cars for Europe and to fit each country's different specification.

In the circumstances, we said, it would not be right for the British government to refinance the DeLorean subsidiary company in Belfast. It had now accumulated debts of £60 million. The only thing we had a charge on in Britain was the factory plant and machinery and the stock of work in progress; the dealers with their stocks of high-priced cars were in America. We recommended that the British assets be sold to a newly created organisation, 'DeLorean Motor Cars Ltd 1982', which would take over existing management together with ownership of the distribution rights in America. DeLorean did not agree to this. In no way, we said, should the Government continue to finance a unit which was a subsidiary of a foreign holding company which itself was now in financial trouble. The bank had cut the line of credit, and an insolvent corporation in Michigan would not have the wherewithal to undertake distribution.

Acting on the advice in the report, the British government decided that the DeLorean Motor Company Ltd had no chance of survival and intended to appoint a receiver. Jim Prior summoned John

DeLorean to London to tell him what that implied. Though probably not fully aware of what a receivership meant in Britain, John
DeLorean knew it would be humiliating, and set his mind to prevent
it with all the energy he had poured into creating his car. He
commissioned accountants Peat Marwick to produce *his* report on
the situation. This showed that all talk of receivership would
disappear if he could lay hands on a mere £20 million. So he set to
work. Tiny Rowland of Lonrho? No, *sir*. The 'head of an Arab
state'? Who knows? An American on the West Coast? Maybe. He
was clearly a drowning man clutching at straws when in all the
confident affluence of a onnaught suite he desperately tried to
impress me with the 'certainty' of at least one of these hoped-for last
resorts coming to the boil.

The climax came when James Prior and I confronted him at the
Northern Ireland Office in Whitehall in the middle of February
1982. It was a fraught meeting. We insisted that he *ask* for a receiver
to be appointed for his Irish subsidiary. I explained to him the
difference between our receivership system and the so-called Chapter 11 of the Federal Insolvency Code of the United States which in
due course he had to apply to his holding company in Michigan.
Under the American system the proprietor stayed in possession and
lawyers acted as trustees. In Britain, I told him, the receiver had
absolute control in the management of the company without
reference to any court. The directors could only do what the receiver
wanted them to do. Though he could not dismiss them, the receiver
could stop them managing. In the light of this, I think John
DeLorean realised that, if a new investor could be found, a constructive receivership gave his company its only chance of resuscitation.

Though it was a blow to his pride, he could only accept the
situation and submit to the remedy prescribed. But at this eleventh
hour he pleaded with us to allow him *just one more chance* to stave off
this receivership thing which for his friends and colleagues back
home could only have one meaning: failure. Once again he took off
into the realms of fantasy, assuring us that it only needed time before
one of the three sources he was negotiating with came up trumps. We
knew about Alan Blair's Californian consortium, a non-starter if
there ever was one. The unnamed 'Arab head of state' had yet to turn
him down; but surely there was more than a glimmer of hope in
General Electric. Jim Prior, who knew its chairman, Lord Wein-
stock, could not help laughing. The Secretary of State then became
serious and insisted that DeLorean, as chairman of the Irish company, formally request the British government to appoint a receiver
by signing the letter he then placed in front of him. There was
nothing he could do now but sign it. We also got him to authorise a

press statement announcing the appointment of a receiver, and to assent to the text of what the Secretary of state would tell the Commons in the morning.

But – and it was a big But – he wanted to delay the appointment, so he was given a last chance to the extent of agreeing to delay the actual appointment of the receiver until seven o'clock the next morning. If before then he was able to produce the Arab money, we would tear the letter up and there would be no receivership. But at midnight I had a call at Great Missenden from his solicitor in Belfast to say that all his telephoning had drawn a blank and his client was reconciled to the fact that the receivership must take its course. But the minister agreed that it was to be a 'constructive' receivership and we were to try to save the business if possible. No one wanted to close the factory if it was possible to keep it going, because of the distress it would cause in Ulster.

John DeLorean flew back to America; Paul Shewell and I as joint receivers took over the DeLorean Motor Company Ltd with its factory in Dunmurry. It was to be a constructive receivership which gave an opportunity for new investment or for the company to be sold as a going concern – in other words, our Way. It was agreed that we should continue running it at least for a limited time, not making any new vehicles but merely converting the 500 or so half-completed cars into finished ones. This, we reckoned, would take about three months. It would at least raise the value of the assets – unfinished cars are worthless – but without it there would be little opportunity for refinancing. If we could not get the operation refinanced or sold in that time, then that was the end. The company would be wound up and the factory closed.

The first thing was to tell everyone at Dunmurry exactly what the position was. Fortunately, one of the members of the Northern Ireland Development Agency while I was chairman was John Freeman, head of the Transport and General Workers Union in Northern Ireland. When he heard that I had been appointed joint receiver he sent me a message saying he would meet me when I came to Belfast and promised his assistance and that of the workforce in anything that I wanted to do. He had told them that he knew and trusted me, and I was his friend, and that they were to give me all the support they could. If they did not, they would be answerable to him. So my first appearance at the factory was with the head of the TGWU at my side. He had got the twenty or so trade union representatives into one room and introduced me to them. He asked them to trust me; he knew, he said, that I was going to do my damnedest to save the business. I told them that I was now running the factory and the object was to get it refinanced or sold. To do that

we would be making no new vehicles from scratch, and could only
employ people who could be usefully employed in the job of
completing the stock of two-seater models in various stages on the
assembly-line. We then went and met the entire workforce and
explained exactly what was going to happen. If I had not been able to
meet and talk to the men with John Freeman at my side, there would
almost certainly have been trouble. John DeLorean left the very
good British management, mostly former Chrysler people, to carry
on the business and we established a good relationship with them,
too. Our efforts to make ends meet were still thwarted, however, by
our having to sell the cars we were going to complete through the
DeLorean network in America. Possessing the sole selling rights, he
had a stranglehold over us.

   In his grand Park Avenue office in New York, DeLorean worked
away at trying to find an investor and devising one scheme after
another, each of which he optimistically hoped I would agree was
just what we had been waiting for to save the day. I made several
visits to New York in this period and, from one to the other, I never
knew how I would be greeted or treated. One week I would be God's
Gift to the company; next week I was the Devil Incarnate. Each time
I had a go at trying to persuade him to let us have some control of his
distribution company, he always refused. Whenever I raised the
matter of the millions of dollars he owed his British subsidiary for the
vehicles sent to him from Dunmurry, he jumped in with a counter-
claim which showed we were not creditors at all. On my second visit,
when he again had Roy Nesseth with him, I told him point-blank I
was not prepared to sit in the same room with the man, and he asked
him to leave. So from then on my sessions were always with John Z.
alone. On most occasions he paraded before me at least two prospective purchasers who always expressed great interest to start with but
never came to the boil. There was the day when he gleefully
presented a 'report' on the profitability of the car which had no
relevance to reality whatsoever. Between confident declarations that
'I've got a wonderful business' (as if saying so would make it so) he
would abuse the British government for letting him down and failing
to carry out their promises. Every time I started to talk about time-
limits for producing the $10 million which we had agreed was the sort
of initial investment which might postpone the closure of the Belfast
factory, he changed the subject. So I made him find the money for
the continuation of the factory *week by week*. If he wanted to
continue for another week, then he had to pay for it. For the final
week he borrowed the money from his own lawyers in Belfast, who
were never repaid. And then there was no more. The British
government ran out of both patience and money.

There was a last-minute drama, the would-be *deus ex machina* which came out of the blue with a promise of a loan to the American DeLorean company not of $10 million but $100 million. This was 'Minet Finance Management', a connection of Minet Holdings of London, a Lloyd's insurance broker which, as Ivan Fallon and James Srodes explain in their book *DeLorean* (Hamish Hamilton, 1983), specialised in high-risk, high-yield investment outside the reach of the Inland Revenue. That amount would have settled the Belfast company's $30 million of creditors' debts, bought the assets of the Northern Ireland plant and paid for the now finished cars. I said I would be happy to consider this on the condition that DeLorean himself at once invested $20 million of his own capital in the Belfast company, which would stay there even if the proposed Minet loan failed to materialise. When John Z. said he could only raise half that amount, Minet contacted an American woman, Jeanne Farnan of an organisation called Financial Services Inc. of Virginia, and asked her if she would be interested in making him a short-term loan of $10 million. She said she might, and on her way back to Virginia dropped in for a quick look at the Dunmurry operation. The next day her firm offered John DeLorean a standby loan of $10 million for ninety days at 12 per cent and he accepted it. Whether or not she knew that he would not be able to retrieve the sum he was investing in the Belfast Company, of which the $10 million was part, if the Minet loan fell through, I do not know. I put the deadline for wrapping up the whole transaction as 20 October.

All this time a subplot to the DeLorean Drama was unfolding on the other side of the Atlantic of which I was unaware, and by sheer coincidence had its climax the day before my deadline.

Apparently for some time the FBI had been suspicious that DeLorean was about to become involved in a plot to distribute drugs, and they had been observing and watching his movements. They were also watching people known to be in the drug trade and they considered it possible that John DeLorean was about to deal with those people. On 18 October in Los Angeles, one of them was apparently arrested by the FBI and a quantity of cocaine was found in his possession.

The next morning over on the East Coast, John DeLorean arrived for work in his New York office where Jeanne Farnan's document requiring DeLorean's signature was delivered in the course of the morning. He opened the package and presumably recognised its contents as the papers which would bring him the ninety-day loan of $10 million, but for some reason he postponed signing them. He was due to fly to Los Angeles later in the morning. However, on arrival there, he went to the Sheraton Plaza Hotel and was apparently arrested by the FBI and charged with dealing in drugs. I felt rather sorry for him when I saw his picture in the paper, but the sympathy did not last long!

I had a surprise too that morning! I was hoping our transaction would go through later in the day, and the business continue, but I was woken by a telephone call at 5 a.m. from a newspaper reporter. Everything seemed to happen with DeLorean at the wrong time of the day, because of the difference in time between America and the UK. As I answered the telephone the reporter said, 'Did you know that DeLorean has been arrested for dealing in drugs?' I said, 'No.' I was then asked, 'What is your reaction?', to which I replied, 'I am bloody astounded', which indeed I was! However, later that morning when I opened the letter from FSI saying the money was in place I sent a telex to DeLorean's office in New York enquiring whether the financing was still on. The reply I received was in the negative. I was soon to learn officially what had happened, and it all came as a bit of a shock. When, as receivers, Paul Shewell and I had to realise the British company's assets and wind it down, that involved us in enquiring into what had happened.

We discovered that the American DeLorean company had undertaken to put up the cost of completing the engineering of the car. When it came off the end of the assembly-line it was to be a complete working vehicle. Unfortunately it was not. It had to go to the British firm of Lotus in East Anglia who, it was arranged, were to 'develop' the car. It could not go under its own power but had to be taken to the Lotus works on a car-transporter. This was of less financial consequence than it might have been, since part of the deal was that the British government through the Northern Ireland company would finance the tooling and the glass-fibre process for the body to the tune of about $5 million, but the Americans would finance the *engineering* of the car. For this the American DeLorean company formed The Research Partnership in which John Z. persuaded friends to invest some $18½ million. Though Lotus were to do the actual work, the contract to 'develop' the car was between this Research Partnership in America, with the British subsidiary in Belfast, and an organisation in Switzerland called 'GPD Services Inc.' incorporated in Panama in 1977 as ILC Inc. The initials are supposed to stand for General Products Development. GPD has been described as a 'shelf corporation' and a 'cash laundry'. It appeared to have no assets and no office premises, and was run by a woman called Marie-Denise Juhan Perrin ('Juhan'), an associate, so I am told, of Colin Chapman of Lotus for twenty years, and whose husband worked for Lotus.

GPD signed the contract to develop the DeLorean two-seater sports-car and subcontracted the development work to Lotus. I never learnt why it had not been possible to have the work done by Lotus direct. But in the course of our inquiry we found the minutes of a board meeting of the Belfast company at which John DeLorean had informed directors that, though his American friends had put up $12½ million, a little more money would be needed to develop the car. It would not be fair therefore for his American colleagues to continue to pay out money for this, as they had made their contribution. The rest of the cost of development should fall on the Irish company, he claimed. Since the British directors had agreed to this and had paid out another $17 million I was anxious to see how far the car had in fact been 'developed' by Lotus at that stage. I wrote to Lotus asking for this information but got no reply. So I telephoned Colin Chapman, the head of the firm, told him I had to have an answer and was coming to see him. Chris Hughes of Cork Gully, who later took over from Paul Shewell as joint receiver, came with me, and we took with us all the receipted invoices making up the $17½ million. What had the Belfast company got for the original money? Moreover what had been done by way of Lotus 'developing' the car at the time the arrangement had been made that the Americans should stop paying for it? It was uphill work. We tried painstakingly to go through invoice by invoice with Chapman and his finance director Fred Bushell to discover precisely what work had been done for each sum of money paid. At one point Chapman became exasperated.

'What are you trying to do?' he exclaimed.

'We are trying to find out what the DeLorean factory in Belfast got for its $17½ million.'

'People keep on talking about $17½ million. I know nothing about any such sum. Lotus has never received $17½ million. All we had was $5 million from GPD to show good faith, which was later returned to them. All the costs for the development of the car have been invoiced to the Irish company. We here know nothing about $17½ million.'

'I can't understand it. Seventeen million dollars was the money put up by the American "Research Partnership" and the Irish company to develop the car.'

'If that is so, then we at Lotus know nothing about it.'

'So far as I remember, you signed a contract to carry out all the work under contract with GPD. You must have seen the contract, surely?'

'I did not see it,' claimed Chapman.

On my return to Belfast I dug out all the contracts, and there was the one from Lotus declaring: 'We undertake to carry out the work which GPD has contracted to do "according to the contract attached".' I telephoned Chapman at once and read this out to him.

'I really am rather puzzled,' I said.

'Oh,' said Chapman breezily, 'we only saw that bit of the contract, the bit about what was to be done to the car. We did not see the rest of it.'

In view of what he had said, I told him, I would have to come and talk to him again. He agreed to see me, but before I could go he had a heart-attack and died. The true version of this tangled sequence of events died with him. Though during my visit Bushell had certainly seemed concerned, Chapman was perfectly happy and relaxed. So I do not think his heart-attack was in any way related to the problem we had been discussing. The British government, through the Irish company, had paid for the whole cost of developing the car, in spite of the fact that in the contract it was very carefully spelt out that invoices for the glass-fibre tooling *only* should go to the British government; and that any surplus money required over £17 million should be paid for by The Research Partnership in America, the general partner of which was John DeLorean or rather his DeLorean Motor Company in America.

It appeared that in spite of everything which had been said in the past the whole of the money put up for the development of the DeLorean Car had disappeared – or 'gone walkabout', as I told the parliamentary committee. Where had it gone? To find out, Chris Hughes and I journeyed to Geneva to see Mme Juhan, the woman reputed to be running GPD.

'Can you tell us, madame, what has happened to the seventeen million dollars paid out by the DeLorean Motor Company Limited of Belfast, for which we have receipted invoices?' I asked her.

'It is none of your business,' she said without flinching.

'So you won't tell me?'

'It's not that I won't tell you. I'm just telling you that it is nothing to do with you.'

'On the contrary, I am afraid it is.'

I hammered away for a few minutes in the same vein, but got no change out of her whatsoever. She resolutely refused to divulge what she obviously knew.

'Will you at least tell me whether anyone who signed the contract got any money out of it?' I said in an attempt to leave Geneva not entirely empty-handed.

'Yes,' she said, 'I can tell you that they did not.'

I did not believe her. We subsequently were able to find out, however, that of the money which went into GPD some $8\frac{1}{2}$ million found its way via various other banks including Rothschild's in Zurich, the Chase Bank in New York, the Pierson Heldring Pierson Bank of Amsterdam, to John DeLorean's personal account. This transfer was made in the form of a long-term loan with no payments due for ten years, and the interest accruing to the lender. We only discovered this after DeLorean's arrest at the Los Angeles airport hotel on 20 October, because when that happened Pearson Holding called in their guarantee. Up to then we only knew that the $8\frac{1}{2}$ million was deposited in a bank in Holland who declined to tell us anything about it. But as soon as the money had to meet the guarantee we were able to see that it had gone to John DeLorean, and the connection was complete.

Armed with this information, we returned to Mme Juhan in Geneva. We thought we had got her.

'You knew you were not telling the exact truth when we last met,' I said, 'because the money we were talking about had already been released to you on a bearer warrant to DeLorean, which you then signed and sent to Mr DeLorean – or, rather, to his lawyer in Geneva.'

'I did nothing of the sort.'

'Oh, but you did.'

'My signature was forged,' she declared without batting an eyelid. 'What is more, I am going to take action against my lawyers for releasing my money on a forged signature.'

'But your signature was certified by Rothschild's.'

'Well,' she said, 'it is not the first time that a bank has certified a forged signature.'

We knew we could not expect much co-operation from the Swiss authorities in tracing money belonging to a Panamanian company trading in Switzerland which therefore did not have to file any accounts. But when Mme Juhan denied her signature on the cheque we went to see the Swiss lawyer to whom she had given it, Jacques Wittmer, with whom John DeLorean and his partner Tom Kimmerly had negotiated the deal with Colin Chapman and Fred Bushell of Lotus. He was horrified.

This seemed to us grounds for bringing the matter to the attention of the Swiss authorities. Forgery was certainly fraud in every country, and here was one of their nationals alleging someone had forged her signature on a cheque. We were right in thinking the Swiss police would be interested. Their whole banking system was based on signatures of people that no one ever saw. They produced a handwriting expert who certified that the signature on the cheque *was* in Mme Juhan's writing.

Her delaying action backfired. Whereas the Swiss authorities were not, it appeared, too interested in foreign companies trading in Switzerland swindling each other, the banking system in Switzerland depended on signatures of people which were certified by their banks. They immediately started proceedings. It was as a result of these proceedings that Mme Juhan had to produce the records, and we were able to trace where the remainder of the $17½ million had gone.

At one time she asserted that the money represented GPD's commission. A very high commission, I said, $17½ million on $17½ million. All right if you can get it, she replied with a glimmer of a smile. Lotus would not deal with DeLorean, she claimed, unless GPD were intermediaries, which was odd because I knew that John DeLorean and Chapman had been in very close communication. Indeed, at one time DeLorean had plans to acquire Lotus. It was evident to me that GPD's only rôle was to launder the money – something which should have come out at the trial of John DeLorean for fraud down for hearing in the American courts in September 1986 and expected to last at least two months. It did, but he claimed that the money was a loan from Chapman. I find it unbelievable, but the court accepted that it might have been.

We were able to establish to our satisfaction that the other $8½ million had gone to two directors of Lotus. The $5 million which had been paid to Lotus and returned by the company to GPD was handed over to the Lotus directors who however deny this and claim that they have no interest in the money. Writs have recently been issued against the Lotus company, the estate of the late Colin Chapman and Fred Bushell for the return of the $8½ million which we the receivers are claiming belongs to the DeLorean Motor Company Ltd of Belfast. The *Sunday Times* 'Insight' team discovered a second GPD company, 'Grand Prix Drivers Services', also registered in Panama in 1978, but I know nothing of that and it has no bearing on the DeLorean case.

Whatever the outcome of the fraud trial, there is incontrovertible evidence that the whole of the $17½ million put up to develop the DeLorean two-seater sports-car was misappropriated. The Irish company, having paid royalties to The Research Partnership and having paid for the development of plant and machinery in Belfast, actually paid twice. It is the only time in the whole of my professional career that I have met a case where the entire capital subscribed to develop a project was misappropriated.

And nobody noticed. Because nobody looked.

Was it a plot from the word Go? The development contract was carefully drawn up by both the Irish and American lawyers. Yet no one in the Irish company apart from the chairman, John DeLorean, appeared to know where the money went. No one asked what they got for their $17½ million. We as receivers thought some of it was likely to go astray, but it never crossed our mind that the company had got *nothing* for it. Accounts were all certified, yet the whole misappropriation was successfully concealed. The concealment was helped by the fact that at that time, owing to exchange controls, the Bank of England had to approve the transfer. So when any questions were raised outside the company the answer was given that it had received Bank of England approval – which was of course to transfer the money to Switzerland, not as to the manner it was spent. That everything was above board was taken for granted. Whatever was due to be paid should first of all have been paid by the up-front money. The Irish company paid for all the work chargeable to The Research Partnership as well as the money they paid for the development of the tooling. They should not have paid anything for the engineering of the car – certainly not, that is to say, until they had passed a resolution saying that the Americans had paid enough. Whereas what happened was that the Americans paid nothing towards the development of the car. The company applied the lot dishonestly to other people's use – which is what misappropriation means.

Chris Hughes and I, as receivers of the Belfast company, and the British government were the main creditors of the American DeLorean Motor Company Inc. We have no alternative but to leave the investigation to the American attorney Malcolm M. Schade of New York whom we and the British government instructed, and to the 'trustees' of the American DeLorean Company who, as I have explained, have the rôle of what we call liquidators. Our own lawyers, however, have given them very great assistance. We are reasonably hopeful of recovering some of the money owed to us – particularly for the cars supplied to the American distribution company by the Belfast manufacturing subsidiary and never paid for – since John DeLorean himself is far from bankrupt. Indeed, he has considerable assets, one of which is a company which he bought with the money he took from the British company.

When we all heard that Mrs DeLorean was filing for divorce, we all smiled wryly to ourselves. Silently, we congratulated him on a clever ploy for dividing his assets. Later, of course, it was clear that she really *was* divorcing him. Well, we all got it wrong that time.

The whole episode is a real tragedy. To me one thing is dead clear: he was genuinely dedicated to producing his own motor car and being the head of a motor corporation. Yet at the same time he could not wait for the project to mature before milking it. He could not resist draining out money while the project was still going through – on the side, as it were.

In this he showed his amateurishness. If he had run it economically and in a thoroughly professional and businesslike way, the enterprise had little chance of being a roaring success, but he could have gone on manufacturing, say, 9,000 cars a year in an unspectacular way for the American market and a few more for Canada and Europe. The proposed limousine which would have been a more useful car than the two-seater sports model would also probably have sold reasonably well. If he had been content to settle for this kind of reward and avoided the wild extravagance of the Big Tycoon, if he had dismissed the idea of doubling production to achieve the dream of going public and building up a really big corporation, the enterprise would never have been in jeopardy and no one would ever have found out about the missing $17½ million, and he would never have been called upon to explain what happened to it. It would have been repaid and there would have been no trace of the whole complicated transaction.

DeLorean was desperately trying to raise money to keep DMCL going. He was dedicated to having his name on a car. He knew that if the operation was finally shut down any investigation was bound to uncover the missing $17½ million and he would have to produce a wholly credible explanation, otherwise it would lead to the story becoming public. If it had not been for his greed and an inflated *folie de grandeur* which made the whole thing a tragi-comedy both the American and British DeLorean Motor Companies would still be ticking over today.

Subsequently John DeLorean was found not guilty on the drugs charge, but by this time action had had to be taken to realise the business, and there was nothing anyone could do to stop it.

The British government's decision to let an American manufacturer have a car factory in Northern Ireland and become its major shareholder was not as silly as some would like to think. If they had succeeded in controlling him, and someone who was not dazzled by his grandiose manner and his so-called 'charisma' had said to him firmly, 'You don't go and double production with untrained labour until you are absolutely certain you can sell what you make – and not in the middle of winter anyhow,' the likelihood is that the operation would have been kept on the rails, and employees, suppliers, dealers, customers and shareholders would have continued to benefit for many a year. His lieutenants like Mr Kesseth, and the rest of his 'advisers', presumably had no wish to risk imperilling their well-paid jobs by questioning their paymaster's judgement, even if they had known what advice to give. 'Colourful characters' who lack self-discipline, with little more than a 'flair' to guide them, need strong-minded colleagues to keep them on balance, particularly when they have made themselves dependent on other people's money. The kindest word to apply to the DeLorean fiasco is *mismanagement*. As

George Bickerstaffe wrote in *International Management* in May 1983, 'the undisciplined DeLorean failed to manage hs own talent'. That is what made the whole affair so tragic – and unpredictable. No one can be blamed for failing to anticipate how John Z. would behave under stress. Such projects are always a bit of a gamble. It was just unfortunate that in that case the British government backed the wrong horse.

Chapter Ten

Reforming the Insolvency Laws

When all the half-finished cars were completed the Dunmurry factory was closed, commendably with very little trouble from the workforce, and we sold the building back to the British government. We also disposed of the machinery, and of the 500 two-seater sports-cars which had now acquired an artificially enhanced value as collector's pieces. The trial of John DeLorean on fraud charges was due to start in New York at the earliest in September 1986 and was expected to take several months. Whether he was sent down for a term of humiliating imprisonment or allowed to return to the jet-set lifestyle which, seeing the risks he took to maintain it, must be of paramount importance to him, was of considerable concern to Chris Hughes and myself as receivers of his company's Belfast manufacturing subsidiary. A conviction would have enabled us at last to get our hands on the insolvent American company's liquid assets, the money so long owed us. With it we would have repaid creditors in Britain such as suppliers and banks. And then for us the DeLorean case would have been closed. However, at his trial DeLorean claimed that the money transferred to his account was a loan from Chapman, and he was acquitted. If this was true, he owes the money to Chapman and he owes it to DMC. I cannot claim that it is the best illustration of the effectiveness of our way of handling insolvency, but at least there was no immediate seizure and sale of assets, which had hitherto been regarded as normal procedure. By the 1980s it was no longer the norm – a state of affairs due, I hope, to some extent to the reasoned argument submitted in the report of the twelve-man Insolvency Law Reform Committee which I was invited to chair by Edmund Dell in 1976 and which he set up the following year. The unanimous Cork Report published in 1981 was for me endorsement by the Establishment of our approach; which, after so many years crying in the wilderness, was extremely gratifying.

The brief was to investigate and co-ordinate and bring up to date the whole of the insolvency law of this country – a formidable task. I was told that the civil servants in the Official Receiver's Department had been asked to consider doing it themselves, but they had said they would not have the time to undertake so major a review. Moreover, they said, they did not have the experience outside the Compulsory Liquidation and Bankruptcy sectors. I was the first person I think who was neither a High Court judge nor a Queen's Counsel ever to chair so important a committee.

Two years previously of course I had been chairman of the Government's Advisory Committee on the Co-ordination of the EEC Draft Provisional Insolvency Law of 1970 whose report had been 'Cork 1'. In preparing Cork 2 we had no formal brief on the matter, but were asked to keep an eye on aspects of the reform of the British code which might affect harmonisation with the EEC. The trouble was there was no European *system* as such. Each member nation has its own way of ordering these matters. Under the French system, for instance, directors of failed companies were then virtually guilty until they were proved innocent. They took a very different view of limited liability. Moreover we were the only country to countenance voluntary liquidation by which a company's affairs could be wound up without the jurisdiction of a court.

The EEC's suggestions for a single insolvency law for all members was drafted by a French professor, and completed though not signed before Britain joined the Community. In Cork 1 we thought the only co-ordination worth attempting was determining, where a multi-national went insolvent, in which country should be the so-called 'Centre of Bankruptcy'. We gave up trying to work out a principle on which to base a commonly accepted system of preferential claims. For one thing, whereas in Britain we accepted foreign creditors on the same basis as our own, which we considered only fair, we got the impression that in other countries in the Community foreign creditors were a long way down the queue. One might have thought it would have been comparatively easy to reach agreement within the EEC on a simple procedure to prove a debt without swearing affidavits and the rest. But in practice it was well-nigh impossible to find common ground on the several different systems with several different backgrounds. For one thing there was the language difficulty. Words had different meanings. Try to translate 'liquidation' into French! There was no exact counterpart in France or indeed any other country to our system of 'distress' where a landlord can 'distrain'. If you are not paid in Britain, you can obtain a 'judgement and levy execution' which means you can put the bailiffs in and collect the property. What phrase is there in German or Italian for all that? The foreign words you managed to find for such terms could at best be an approximation and probably misleading at that. When we submitted the Cork 1 report some 250 or so amendments were made to the English translation, and within weeks another fifty arrived. We were getting nowhere.

American insolvency law was more akin to ours, but it was based on the fact that 'trustees' were lawyers. The 'Chapter 11' of their Federal Bankruptcy Code, as I have shown, was entirely different from anything we had in Britain. It was a method by which an insolvent company bought time. Nine months after the American DeLorean Motor Company Inc. went into 'Chapter 11', John Z. was still in possession. So when there was any argument over there between trustees and lawyers the creditors brought their lawyers, the British government theirs and DeLorean theirs. Result: utter confusion.

In the Cork 1 report published in August 1976 we proposed that preferential creditors should be allowed whatever preference the law of their own state provided. We criticised Europe's failure to acknowledge the concept of either the floating charge or voluntary liquidation; and exposed their confusing the punishment of culpable debtors with the business of distributing assets which were insufficient to make 100 per cent repayment.

Our operations over the years brought home to us at Cork Gully the need to act and think internationally, not only in EEC terms but also, with the growth of the truly multi-national trading corporation, in a way that truly embraced the world. The big British firms of Chartered Accountants such as Peat Marwick, Price Waterhouse, Coopers and Deloittes had been operating in other countries since the 1950s. In December 1975 therefore accountant Anthony Jolliffe linked with our auditing arm Cork Porritt Sunderland which became Jolliffe Cork & Co. Two years later at a meeting in Barcelona of the senior partners of accountancy firms from thirty-one countries, it was agreed to form a new partnership to be called Jolliffe Cork International to cement even more firmly links which we had established with overseas accounting firms. In Britain, Jolliffe Cork extended its activities into the field of management consultancy by forming an association with the Economist Intelligence Unit which already operated internationally. Anthony Jolliffe also established an agreement with lawyers Nabarro Nathanson & Co., who were represented in fifteen countries.

So in 1977, on the eve of embarking on Cork 2, I had close links with Jolliffe Cork, the nucleus of an international service offering accountancy (mostly audit), management consultancy and legal advice. Through this connection therefore and my chairmanship of Cork 1, I was not wholly unfamiliar with insolvency outside Britain, and was well briefed on the aspect of the subject to which the Government were anxious that Cork 2 should also give some attention. I realised, however, that any chance of reconciling the two systems still seemed slim. In Europe they still could not visualise any form of insolvency that was not carried out in a court and under the supervision of lawyers. They still only recognised a fixed charge on assets such as a mortgage but had no equivalent of a floating charge which crystallised on the stock and debtors. All we could do was to make it clear that a meeting of creditors in Britain which appointed a liquidator should be regarded in the EEC as a court order.

I accepted the appointment as chairman of Cork 2 on certain conditions. I realised that the Government would wish to include certain 'statutory members' such as representatives of the trade union and the Co-operative movements – though not, to my regret, a Statutory Lady! The others, I told them, I should wish to choose myself, and they agreed. However, when I suggested including a well-known member of a different firm of accountants specialising in insolvency the Department of Trade said that a number of people had raised an objection. They did not wish me to have that particular nominee, they said. This was somewhat unfortunate since some of my friends in other firms of accountants thought I was deliberately keeping them out.

The three I chose personally and was allowed to keep were Edward Walker-Arnott, a partner in solicitors Herbert Smith & Co. which had a lot of receivership work; Alfred Goldman, another solicitor, whose firm had dealt with bankruptcy for more than seventy years, as well as acting for trustees in bankruptcy and the Official Receiver; and Muir Hunter, QC, a leading expert on insolvency, the author of many books on the subject and a Department of Trade counsel. I also suggested that as we were dealing with small bankruptcies we ought to have a registrar at a county court.

At first I was not at all sure that such a committee could cope with the enormous volume of work which would be required. We had after all to revise the *whole* of the insolvency law of the land. And it was a job which I felt could only be done by writing a new Act. So, without the permission of the Department of Trade but later with their consent, I set up a legal subcommittee composed of my committee's lawyers. I asked them to study the legal implications of the changes we proposed and recommend any changes they themselves would like to see. I had an accountancy subcommittee of insolvency practitioners, most of whom were Chartered

Accountants. I had an insurance consultant. I was given an observer from Scotland. And then – again, without particular authority – I co-opted two outsiders. One was Gerry Weiss, who had worked with me and Cork Gully for a long time as already seen, and we called our legal partner. The other was a leading silk, David Graham, QC, whom I also co-opted on to my committee reviewing EEC insolvency law.

We had an extremely efficient civil service secretary in Commander T. Traylor, and I was also able to enlist the help of barrister members of the committee to write the report. The members who were lawyers and accountants, and their firms, provided back-up work, investigation and other facilities, which, if paid for, would have cost the Government a fortune.

We are a strange country. All the members worked for nothing. All the back-up work provided by the major firms was provided free; yet when I organised the HAC (my old regiment), which was close by, to provide lunch for members at one-third of the price of any City restaurant our secretary got into serious trouble in getting it agreed – whereas the Germans, who set up a committee to see if the German insolvency law should be revised, were given remuneration and a budget of many hundreds of thousands of marks.

It was a large and varied team, and I must confess when I was first confronted with them I thought: I've got an odd lot here! But it soon became evident that each one of them had a valuable contribution to make. It took about two or three sessions for them really to start to understand what insolvency was all about. It was quite extraordinary, however, to see how people who probably had never opened a book on insolvency law in their lives soon became experts. All of us were heavily involved in the subject, and in doing so became great friends – so much so that every now and again we have a reunion dinner! We went on sitting of course right through my year as Lord Mayor of London, and I must admit that that put an extra strain on me. Having to come back to the Mansion House after a livery banquet with its table-chat, speeches and rich food and turn my mind to reading the detailed discussion paper on which we had to quiz the chairman of the Confederation of British Industry next morning at that late hour needed all the willpower and concentration I could muster.

Once the composition of the committee had been settled, I devised our plan of working. We were not going to take the existing law and jigger about with it. We were going to set our objectives and write *a new law* to carry them out. They were short and simple. We sought to simplify present procedures; to provide the means by which an insolvent business could be continued and disposed of as a going concern so as best to preserve jobs for employees and preserve the nation's assets; to reduce the emphasis on 'selling up' the individual debtor and make it more possible for creditors' claims to be met out of the debtor's future income; to increase the amount available in an insolvency for ordinary creditors and make for a fairer distribution of assets; to relax the severity of the law towards the individual debtor, who might be incompetent rather than dishonest, and increase the severity towards those who traded under limited liability but had acted irresponsibly.

Previous insolvency law review committees had taken the existing Acts and merely tried to amend them – and their reports had all been ignored. That was not to be our Way. Obviously the major part of existing law would need no alteration, and where that was the case we would incorporate it into our proposed new Act. But in so many places it was unclear and confusing and had references to conflicting case decisions. So we asked the barristers on the committee to write into our report a detailed summary of what the law was in 1977, so that people could understand what was being altered. Anyone wanting an up-to-date specialist review of English insolvency law at 1977 would find it in our report.

At our first meeting it was made clear that, if nothing else, it must be *readable*. It was no good our issuing a boring and dry-as-dust report which was of interest only to lawyers and accountants. We should be able to express ourselves adequately without resort to would-be 'impressive' long words and legal jargon which would be incomprehensible to the layman. In this I think we succeeded, for even a senior official of the Inland Revenue, whom we hammered by trying to cut down their rights, agreed it was a very readable document. We knew that if we were to get the Government to accept it and legislate in accordance with our recommendations a large number of people would have to read it and *understand* it. And that included Members of Parliament, who are not renowned for the detailed knowledge they have of the varied matters on which they legislate.

The Stern case had greatly reinforced the views I had formed over thirty years as receiver and liquidator about the inadequacy of Britain's insolvency law. I had had a long time to pre-judge the case for reform. I had a whole cupboardful of prejudices, and as impartial chairman I knew we were going to have difficulty in putting across views which we felt we were obliged to put. But we were determined at the outset to set members' minds thinking on the right lines; to make them see, for instance, the distinction between the company which administered the business and the business itself – the bricks and mortar, the workforce, the plant and machinery. I laboured to make them appreciate that, if a company had failed and was beyond saving, the business it had been running was something that others might transform. I endeavoured gently to bring them round to seeing the benefit of thinking twice before destroying the business of a company which had already destroyed itself. This I saw as the essence of our way and hoped that the good sense of it would appeal to them and colour the approach they brought to the difficult deliberations on which we were to embark.

I had never made a secret of the fact that I regarded the law as it stood in 1977 as too penal with regard to bankruptcy, but too often lacking teeth in penalising directors who had acted without scruples though perhaps within the law. The stigma attached to bankruptcy inhibited a businessman from admitting to his true state of affairs, so that he often continued to incur credit, adding to his losses and trading recklessly, so that when the crash came it was much greater than it need have been. It was thoroughly wrong that the awesome procedure of bankruptcy should engulf the small man whose failure was due to nothing more than bad luck. My view was that the insolvency laws would be more equitable and effective if they softened the penalties on the little people and made it harder for people who committed real abuses. I believed more businesses could be saved, or partially rescued at any rate, if the existing rules on receivership were extended.

In 1977 the law provided that a receiver could only be appointed if there was a floating charge on the company's assets. If there was no floating charge, the company almost invariably went straight into liquidation, which meant a break-up was unavoidable. I had always held that it should be possible to appoint a receiver without a floating charge, either by application to the court or under some other official procedure. For long I had been thinking in terms of a new kind of insolvency court with the power to make an administration order on any individual who chose to appear before it. In that case the vast majority of bankruptcies in which comparatively small sums were involved would be disposed of instantly and without fuss. I was convinced, too, that the duties of liquidators should be enlarged to give them responsibilities to shareholders and other groups, particularly where there was a suspicion of fraud.

Little could be done as the law stood then to prosecute people who, probably acting under pressure, found themselves involved in fraud. Only a minute percentage of the bankruptcies, liquidations and receiverships Cork Gully were handling in the Fringe Bank Crisis in the 1970s had an element of fraud in them, but that was not to say that many smart operators did not take advantage of ignorance to act just within the law. A familiar scenario was the elderly honest businessman with a sagging trade and mounting debts who decided to advertise his business for sale. He was delighted to receive a visit from two charming young men who looked at his books, his premises and his stock, and with an ingratiating smile said: 'Yes, we like it. We'd like to buy. Creditors? Yes, we noted that. Don't worry. We'll take them over. We'll pay for the debts with the money advanced and transfer assets to another company.' The relief on the face of their victim told the wide boys they had effected another killing. The ageing seller probably only cleared £50 or so, but he was rid of his liability and able to sleep at nights. The new owners moved in, took away the assets and shipped them off. But they did not shift the old man's debt. That stayed where it was – with creditors unpaid and clamouring for their money. They went and saw him at his home. He told them the story. He no longer had any assets which he could realise for repaying them. He had been conned and so, without their knowing it, had his creditors. There was nothing either could do about it.

Equally fraudulent I considered to be the directors of a diminishing business who went on trading and drawing their directors' fees until they had doubled and trebled their credit and there were practically no assets left at all. At the meeting of creditors tempers got frayed. There was talk of fraudulent trading. The accountants promised a detailed investigation, but time passed, the case lost its urgency and people forgot. There was in any case in practice no legal redress for anyone.

But there were worse cases than these which the law of the 1970s could not reach. One January a firm of wholesale grocers had a look at their accounts and found there was a deficiency of assets against liabilities of £1,000. So their accountant advised them to stop trading and close down before matters became worse. The directors said the deficiency was the result of neither mismanagement nor the state of the market; goods were being stolen from their warehouse. They had since found the culprits and taken measures to prevent a recurrence. It was unlikely they would ever have another deficiency. They decided to continue trading until April and review the situation then. But their accountant and their lawyer saw a deeper cause for their failure to make a profit and advised them to close without further ado. The directors took no notice, even when the April accounts, which were not ready till June, showed a deficit of £5,000. Their large bank overdraft became larger, and enabled them to trade until August. They again took stock and again, against the advice of accountant, lawyer and banker, decided to soldier on. They incurred further credit and reduced the bank overdraft guaranteed by the directors. Creditors multiplied. The August accounts which came in October showed a gross trading loss of −3 per cent when it should have been in the region of +8 per cent. Their debt was up to £20,000, and by November to £35,000, when some of the leading creditors asked us to see what we could do. In the three weeks before the creditors' meeting we took what we thought was a crafty move. We had heard that the stealing had continued and we engaged a private detective agency to keep a watch on the warehouse. When they caught the thieves red-handed, the creditors congratulated us on our cleverness – but it was the worst thing we could have done!

At the meeting of creditors a gross trading loss of £35,000 was revealed, though purchase sales invoices showed a profit of 4 per cent. Some £20,000 had disappeared into the blue. We went back over the balance-sheets which showed continuous trading from February to November, and all the while insolvent. It was an open and shut case, we were told. We took counsel's opinion, which was that we had a good case. He advised having the directors up for private examination, and holding a private investigation also of the officers of the company. There must be no question of a voluntary liquidation.

When we interviewed the director and his wife, all they would say was that they had had trouble. They had had this outbreak of stealing and they had given people the sack. After that they thought they could make a profit. Though their lawyers implored them to stop, they believed that continuing to trade would enable them to pay off their creditors. As for the unexplained deficiency of £20,000, had not Cork Gully's detectives revealed the reason for that by catching the thieves? That proved it was no fault of theirs.

We reported back to counsel. 'It is quite clear from their answers', he told us, 'that they are saying that the intention for which they went on trading was to make a profit. The fact that they did not is nothing to do with their *intention*. It would therefore be very perilous to pursue them for fraudulent trading.'

We went back to the Committee of Inspection, and they confirmed counsel's opinion; so did a second counsel. Some creditors also took counsel's opinion, and they got the same answer.

We, too, were convinced by now. In order to prosecute, the Act said, the *intent* for which a man carried on his business must be to defraud the creditors. It did not indicate how anyone could look into the working of a man's mind who either said only what he chose to say or said nothing.

What I hoped to see was the word 'intent' taken out of the Act, and prosecution made possible 'where the business is carried on resulting in the fact that the creditors are defrauded'. Until they received the protection of the law it was up to those who supplied on credit to protect themselves. But so many were in the habit of calling up the man who owed them £10,000 and telling him he could take another £2,000 worth of goods, adding: 'You have got to reduce that to put us right.' Nearly every firm did this, but it meant that the debtor obtained £500 worth of credit somewhere else. The misguided creditor was merely giving him another six months of trading during which he made his losses even bigger. Although the creditor was assured of part of his debt – £500 or £1,000, say – he would find there were no assets left to cover the rest of it. Whenever we had the opportunity, we insisted that if a man wanted to go on trading when he could not meet his commitments we must call an informal meeting of creditors and deal with *figures*.

Ordinary people could no longer respect the insolvency law of the 1970s. More and more irresponsible people and criminals were getting away with it. The bankruptcy law worked reasonably well for big cases, but the little debtor had to go through the whole stigma and difficulty of official bankruptcy, public examination and the rest, which was quite ridiculous. Apart from that, it was an enormous waste of money and time for the Official Receiver. It was a silly way of dealing with small people who were incompetent and not dishonest, and were unlikely ever to become bankrupt again. And it took an inordinate time for them to obtain a discharge. So we on the Cork Committee recommended a very much simpler procedure where the bankrupt would go through the local County Court, and his contribution to creditors should be part of his future earnings, if adequate. He would then be discharged unless he had been bankrupt before. But the Government would have none of this. They thought it would take work off the insolvency service and transfer it to the courts, which were already overloaded. Both we and the then Government (Labour) agreed that bankruptcy procedure should be as close to the procedure for liquidation of companies as possible and as simple as possible, so that everyone could understand (particularly foreigners) how to make their claims in any insolvency.

That the Cork Committee set out to do, and that is why it took us so long. It would only have taken us four and a half years instead of five and a half, had not the Tory government which took over in 1979 published a Green Paper halfway through our review which set out their reasons for wanting to abolish the Official Receiver in Bankruptcy. They asked us to stop the work we were doing and give them a report commenting on their proposal. So we did as we were told and took eight months to spell out to them what a lunatic act it would be to abolish the Official Receiver. To get any discipline into

directors you have to make them personally liable, and unless
someone could then make them bankrupt afterwards and collect the
assets it would have no power. The abolition of the Official Receiver
would in effect have abolished bankruptcy. For when someone
wanted to go broke he could only do so if a creditor provided a trustee
and paid for the trustee to act. But what happened to the man who
filed his own petition? He would have to find the money to provide
his own trustee.

We rejected the Government's proposal out of hand. None of us
wanted to see the removal of the Official Receiver. We convinced
them, and they threw the idea out. It was what we wanted them to
do, but it seriously delayed our main task, to which we now re-
addressed ourselves.

Of course the proper disciplining of directors – and, if needed,
prosecuting them – was very germane to insolvency law in general.
The provisions for dealing with fraud and prosecuting directors as
they stood in 1977 just did not work. For after the debenture had
been paid out and the company had gone into liquidation there was
no money for the liquidator either to investigate or to prosecute. Moreover a British jury and a judge would not send someone to prison
unless, as seen, it could be proved that they had an intent to defraud.

We thought a new discipline should be brought in, and we
suggested calling it 'wrongful trading' where the penalty would not
be a custodial sentence but unlimited liability. We invented the
slogan 'limited liability is a privilege not a right, and if you abuse it
you lose it'. 'Wrongful trading' was where assets fell short of the
liabilities and further credit was incurred. It was where someone
incurred credit when no reasonable person would think he had a
certainty, or near-certainty, of repaying it. We suggested that if a
person was a director of two companies which became insolvent and
then became a director of a third company which then became
insolvent he had unlimited liability.

Most directors distrusted the idea of wrongful trading. They
thought it would make holding a directorship too dangerous. But, as
I told so many, they would only be liable if they traded insolvently.
Discipline, I reminded them, was useless unless it hurt. They also
disliked the idea for 'business doctors'. You would never get anyone
to take the risk, they said; it would therefore never work. It was an
objection we had anticipated, however, by providing safeguards.
Anyone who was in doubt about the solvency of a company could
apply to the court for dispensation in advance.

The main innovation we suggested was the concept of an 'administrator'. During the Fringe Bank Crisis there was no way of holding a
moratorium or reconstruction of a company in financial difficulty

unless it had a floating charge or went through a complicated legal process. Various schemes were allowed for in the Companies Act, and at Cork Gully we tried to get one of them going for the Stern Group. But by the time it came through it had cost us something around £¼ million in legal fees. We had the greatest difficulty in getting everybody to sign up; so, while waiting for it to surface, we ran an informal voluntary scheme of our own with the backing of the Bank of England until the job was nearly finished. If we had done nothing until the official scheme was ready, the company would have been dead and buried. This made us realise that, if there had been a floating charge on all the companies involved instead of on just a few, it would have been easy to get a grip on the situation and keep the business going until it could surmount its troubles.

We also saw that if a company was to be saved action should be initiated a long time *before* the time when a bank normally appointed a receiver. In the Fringe Bank Crisis many companies were not necessarily broke but were seen to be tottering and in need of immediate financial help. Above all, they needed a period when the dogs were called off and they were able to recover a degree of equilibrium. They needed, in other words, a moratorium for which existing law made no provision.

Our idea of an administrator was designed to remedy this situation. If there was a floating charge, he would only go in instead of a receiver if the debenture holder did not want to appoint a receiver. If there was no floating charge, he could act pretty well in the same way as a receiver and take immediate control of the business. The appointment of an administrator, we suggested, would not constitute an 'act of insolvency'. None of the things would happen which happened when a company became officially insolvent. For an administrator should be brought in *before* a company was declared insolvent, where for instance the directors were obviously incompetent or dishonest and the ordinary processes could not remove them; or where in the national interest the Government should take a hand, as happened in the case of Rolls-Royce, without going through the trauma of bankruptcy. He would have all the powers and more of a receiver, but he would have to realise the assets *for the general good*, if indeed it was deemed necessary to realise them at all. He would be responsible to *all* parties who were interested in the particular debtor company, whereas under the law as it stood a receiver was only responsible to his debenture holder. A request to the High Court for the appointment of an administrator could come from shareholders who thought their investment was at risk, from creditors or from the Secretary of State at the Department of Trade if he thought it was in the public interest. But we anticipated that in the majority of cases it would be the directors of the company themselves who would make the application. The appointment would be immediate.

Who would choose the man for the job, and what should his qualifications be? We suggested that whoever requested the appointment should be the person to go to the court and nominate the person he had in mind. We stipulated that the appointee should be recognised by the Department of Trade as eligible to take *any* insolvency appointment. That, we hoped, would keep the cowboys out of it. Once appointed, the administrator would have to produce a plan of action. He might decide that the only thing to do was to put the company into liquidation; it might be to continue trading under a moratorium and 'trade out' of the difficulty. For that the procedure would need to have been started early enough. The more likely decision would be to continue trading and then sell the business as a going concern, distributing the proceeds to the creditors and shareholders.

After six weeks he would have to give a report to all creditors and shareholders and call separate meetings of them both, at which he would put his plans. Both would have the right to accept or reject his proposed plan of action. If more than half the total number of creditors and shareholders accepted his plan, he would stay in place as administrator and put his plan into action together with the Committee of Creditors appointed at their meeting. If they totally rejected his plan, the company would at once go into liquidation. They could, however, accept it in part and offer amendments.

Subsequently, when the Insolvency Act came into being, the Department of Trade misunderstood our plans for an administrator, which was *not* to be necessarily an *insolvent situation*. They therefore, in spite of our protest, enacted that an administrator could only be appointed in an insolvent situation or where insolvency was inevitable. If only the Lord would protect us from parliamentary draftsmen! Surely the greatest menace to the community ever created!

After our report had been published on 30 April 1981 we heard nothing from the Government for two years. On 18 April 1983 in the House of Lords Lord Bruce of Donington asked the Government what action they proposed taking on it. In reply the Tory spokesman, Lord Lyell, said: 'Her Majesty's Government have accepted the general principles underlying the Cork Report.' Urgent consideration – which he declined to define as either within a month, a year or a century – was being given, he said, to the 'programme of legislation which would be needed to provide a modern body of insolvency law'. An unsatisfied Lord Bruce told Lord Lyell 'that in professional circles as well as in commercial circles there is very wide support for the main recommendations in the report' and called on the noble lord to urge the Government to make immediate efforts 'to stem the practices of dishonest liquidators in conjunction with dishonest directors to defraud their creditors'. Lord Lyell accounted the delay to the length of the report, 1,982 paragraphs in fifty-two chapters, and asked the House to be patient.

He also told their lordships that Sir Kenneth Cork had wished the entire report to be taken as a whole. I did indeed, and so did all my fellow-members. We would have preferred *in toto* to in principle. They ended by doing the very thing we asked them not to. They picked bits and pieces out of it so that they finished with a mish-mash of old and new. They 'complained' that as the report was so full and detailed – which is what we were asked to make it – there could never be enough parliamentary time to enact the whole thing. It was a pity they had not thought of that when they briefed us. But at least they did not pigeon-hole it as every other government had done since 1912. When a reporter asked me whether I thought they would merely put it on file and forget it, I chose words which I knew would obtain the maximum publicity in the popular press, and said the Government would be bloody bonkers if they did. No. They did not file it, but like every hotchpotch certain very important things were left out, so the general effect was lost.

As I indicated above, they accepted the idea of the administrator but made it more complicated than we would have liked. They said one could only be appointed when a company was insolvent or was in the process of becoming insolvent, which missed the whole point.

Instead of allowing any director, creditor or shareholder the right of applying to the court for the appointment of an administrator, they insisted that only creditors and the company in question could apply (after the passing of a formal resolution of the board of directors). We would have liked to see any individual director having a right to apply if he felt that was the right thing to do. I do not think the Government really understood what we meant. To them insolvency was insolvency; for them it was essential that a company went broke before anyone took action. Behind it lay the absurd theory that shareholders could always remove incompetent directors. But anyone who read a daily newspaper could not fail to realise that the most difficult thing for any company to do was to change its board. Owing to the proxy issue it was impossible to get co-ordinated voting. Directors who sent out proxies always had a large number returned. Many shareholders regarded it as a statutory duty to fill in a proxy form, and they were always in support of the chairman. So you had a silent majority voting for whatever the bit of paper asked them to. It is my firm belief that if you sent out a proxy form to half the shareholders in Britain stating 'I am an idiot and I am stupid to have bought these shares' they would sign it and send it back.

It is not at all easy to remove directors by a vote of the company. In any case the calling of the meeting and the trauma of the shouting ruin the company before it starts. At the news that a meeting has been called for that purpose, the shares go through the floor and the workforce go on strike. It just does not work. In theory yes, but not in practice. Whereas our way means that the shareholders go to the court to ask for the appointment of an administrator, saying 'This company is being run stupidly; the directors of what was an aircraft factory are now building breweries in Turkey; for God's sake stop them.' The directors would remain directors but lose their power of executive decision.

The silliest argument against the administrator idea was where would he get his financial support? If the company had assets, he would be in exactly the same position as a receiver. He would borrow from a bank and have the right to pledge the assets, like a receiver does, as security for his advances. Banks lend to a receiver because they think it is worth their while. They do not do it just to realise their debentures. They do not add a possible bad debt to make the situation worse. A receiver is always responsible personally for any borrowing he has from the bank which appointed him. We saw the administrator being in precisely the same position.

We hoped that the administrator idea would make insolvency more creditor-orientated, giving them a greater chance of getting their money back. Under the old law there was a most unfair distribution of the proceeds of a liquidator. The central part of the British financial system was the floating charge. Banks which had floating charges, and that was all of them, tended to go on lending much longer than they should. More often than not, by the time a receiver was appointed there was no money left for unsecured creditors. And then there was that queue of preferential claims – Inland Revenue for arrears of tax, twelve months PAYE, twelve months VAT, twelve months rates, holiday pay and the rest. Thus everybody was 'preferential' except the poor unsecured creditor. Some even thought preference should be given to money paid in advance by private individuals for goods they never received. It was a situation we wanted to redress in favour of the run-of-the-mill creditor. Our recommendation therefore was that *all* preferential claims should be abolished, with one exception. Preference should be given, we said, to trust money like PAYE and VAT which had been deducted on behalf of the Government, but even then only for as long a period as a diligent collector needed. We hoped to bring further aid to the creditor by ensuring that there was always money left for the liquidator, first of all hopefully to pay a dividend, but also to have funds for investigating and taking action against delinquent directors. It was no good introducing rules on how to make delinquent or dishonest directors responsible if there was no money available to investigate and prosecute or both. To provide this we suggested that 10 per cent of all realisations by a receiver or administrator should be left for the liquidator. We reckoned that by cutting out all preferential claims some 14 per cent of the realisations would be saved on average for the debenture holder. In that case we thought banks would not take too unkindly to having to hand over 10 per cent of them to the liquidator who could challenge whether the debenture was good or bad and take action or investigate where the directors had acted wrongly. With funds available to do the work, it was more likely that a private liquidator would be prepared to take it on.

Very little of this met with government approval. They refused to cut out preferential claims and they refused to bring in the Ten Per Cent Rule. This was their principal and, in our view, most unfortunate omission. Having taken away the *quid pro quo*, they could not penalise the debenture holders by taking 10 per cent away. Naturally enough, bankers declared the Ten Per Cent Rule to be utterly unacceptable, but realised later that they would be less criticised if there was in fact money available to challenge debenture holders. My view is that the Ten Per Cent Rule must come eventually, for without money or legal aid the liquidator's hands are tied. The law cannot work without money. If I was in charge of a company and decided to do things I should not do, I would make damn sure that there was not enough money left behind, after the debenture holders had been paid, to attack me. But obviously, to the Tory government, making this difficult or impossible was a low priority. They do not seem to understand that without money nothing happens and so matters are made worse. Subsequently, Parliament over-ruled the Government and abolished most preferential claims, but failed to bring in the 10 per cent.

Neither was the Government able to go along with our idea for a separate insolvency court with expert judges and counsel. The ordinary courts in Britain, we felt, were incapable of dealing with the complexities of insolvency. The failure of courts to come to grips with the kind of abstruse problems thrown up by insolvency was bringing the law into disrepute. The rarity of fraud ever being proved against directors of companies which became insolvent bordered on the scandalous. This was due to a large extent to the need to prove that the perpetrator intended to defraud, and to convince a jury that that had been the case. The Government apparently could not see any of this being changed by having a specialist court.

In my long experience of insolvency, as I have said, I can only count a few cases where there was actual intent to defraud. The principal one in which I was involved was that of John Bloom, and there was Emil Savundra. Most of the others had got themselves into fraud merely by continuing to trade when they ought to have stopped. When the twelve good men and true in the jury-box heard that kind of evidence they were not going to send a man to prison just because he had slipped into fraudulent trading. As a result there were some very large disasters in which the directors just walked away scot free.

It was a matter of fraud, too, when a smaller company started trading and went into liquidation, whereupon it appeared that the directors bought back the business and started trading all over again. This type of deliberate fraud was universally condemned. Cases of it were frequently featured on the BBC Television consumer protection series 'That's Life' presented by Esther Rantzen, whose team of researchers did an excellent job of exposure. Typical was the case of the company formed to provide a roof insulation service. The fraudsters found a dear old widow willing to hand over £500 to have her loft insulated, and never came to do the work. The non-action was prolonged and justified by correspondence giving specious reasons for the 'delay' typed on paper with an impressive letterhead, and then the company went broke. Two months later the victim received a letter from an insulation company with a similar name and similar directors once more offering to insulate her roof for £500. She fell for it again – and a third and fourth time. The racket was never stopped because small-time creditors never got round to taking legal action to put such companies into liquidation. So the directors always got away with it.

We also felt that there should be some tightening up of the Consumer Credit Law. Something needed to be done about the people who started a travel or mail-order firm with entirely inadequate capital – £100, say – took deposits on holidays or goods in advance, went bankrupt leaving consumer creditors unpaid, set up again in business and perpetrated the same fraud all over again.

More serious was the matter of 'retention of title' on which the Government also declined to accept our recommendation. We did not think we should interfere with the law when a creditor had taken steps to protect himself by stating on his invoice for all to see that he retained possession (title) of the goods he was selling until he was paid for them, even though he had 'sold' them and delivered them.

This he was able to do after the 1976 ruling in the Court of Appeal in the case of Aluminium Industrie Vaassen, a Dutch firm, versus the English company Romalpa Aluminium which had run into financial difficulty and been unable to pay AIV for the foil which they had sold and delivered to them. Romalpa's bank, which held a debenture, had appointed a receiver. The court ruled that AIV were entitled to the £35,000 in the receiver's bank account as the proceeds of foil sold by Romalpa to third parties. It confirmed the legality of the clause in AIV's contract of sale which stated that they were still the owners of the foil sold to a purchaser from which new objects had been made or had been mixed with other objects. This brought English law into line with the practice in Europe, in particular in Germany. But we did consider it unfair to others owed money by an insolvent company that part of the total assets they were seeking to have realised for distribution were deemed not to be assets at all since, though in his warehouse, they were not the debtor's property. We did not think it just that anyone should give a customer credit without knowing (because there was no evidence of the fact even on the company's balance sheet) that all the stock his customer had 'purchased' and was to be seen lying in his warehouse did not in fact belong to him at all. The security, in the form of the stock-in-hand on which the creditor based his willingness to give credit, was very much less secure than it was cracked up to be. The honest creditor who took his customer at his face value had no way of discovering so relevant a piece of information. We ran up against this when Cork Gully were appointed receiver of Brentford Nylons, a case I have already described (see page 90).

We on the Cork Committee recommended that retention of title should only apply to the original goods which a supplier sold to his customer – in the case of Brentford Nylons, the raw thread on bobbins – and not to what was made from them. We also stipulated that before other people's money was spent on employing labour and using power to convert these goods into finished products any company which had bought goods under retention of title should have the fact registered on their company file at the Department of Trade. In that case, any diligent creditor could say: 'Right, the whole of Brentford Nylons stock does not belong to them and therefore they will give no credit.' If the fact was registered and not kept secret, no company would accept goods on those terms because they have a marker on them that they are not trusted. If, on the other hand, it *was* registered and people were silly enough to give the company credit, then *caveat emptor*.

I got the impression that the Government only temporarily rejected our recommendation on this, intending to return to the matter of 'security in business' when they had the time, a heading under which it more properly fell. What did need immediate correction, however, was the too frequent attitude of public utilities like the gas and electricity corporations who blackmailed receivers and liquidators for the arrears which they had been too lazy to collect. When I was appointed liquidator of a glassworks where they had not paid their electricity bills for a year, the regional electricity board threatened to cut off the power unless I the liquidator paid the debt immediately. I told them I could not pay them the money as I had not got it. If you do cut off the supply, you will finish the glassworks, I told them. Just too bad, they said and threw the switch. Within hours the whole of the molten glass in the pipes and vessels had cooled and solidified. Talk of gumming up the works! The whole place was made useless, and any chance they had of getting their money disappeared in the bowels of that once sparkling translucent plant now a dark wrecked hovel which would take unbelievable time and money ever to rekindle into life.

Liquidators, too, could act just as irresponsibly. We were glad the Government implemented our suggestions for keeping out the cowboys. Only those with skill, qualification and insurance can now operate as insolvency practitioners. There were not many roughriders but enough to cause trouble. A favourite ploy was to insert a press advertisement telling vulnerable readers: 'You think you are bankrupt? Well, you are not!'

Another abuse which was used by the cowboy liquidators has now been stopped as a result of our report and subsequent legislation. This was the abuse made possible as a result of a legal ruling in a case known as Centrebind. It decided that if a company called instant meetings of creditors instead of after the statutory fourteen days' delay and went into liquidation, that and the appointment of the liquidator was valid, although the procedure was illegal.

This enabled the cowboys to have themselves appointed liquidators when no creditors were present! They would then sell the assets and business to the old directors or their associates for a peppercorn and decamp. When a proper liquidator was subsequently appointed by the creditors, all the assets were gone.

The new Act following our report stops this. It enacts that, although the appointment is valid, no assets can be sold until there is time to call a proper creditors' meeting, so that creditors can be consulted.

I must admit to being gratified at the extent to which our way of handling insolvency is now part of the nation's way. At the sessions of the committee, and through publication of the Cork Report, I have had a unique opportunity to put forward our principle that business is a national asset and, that being so, all insolvency schemes must be aimed at saving a business. I have been at pains to stress that when a business becomes insolvent it provides an occasion for a change of ownership from incompetent hands to people who not only have the wherewithal but also hopefully the competence, the imagination and the energy to save the business. Before the 1985 Act every insolvent business went into liquidation or receivership automatically. It was the kiss of death for them and the creator of unemployment. Whereas under the old law so many of our great industries were lost for ever, I trust that with the hope of life after Cork the number of liquidations, which totalled 14,895 in 1985 and bankruptcies 6,772 (compared with 4,537 and 3,500 in 1979), will start to decline. With the concept of the administrator and voluntary arrangements taking its place in Britain's insolvency law, the chances look bright for more and more businesses being saved in the years that lie ahead – *businesses* that is, not companies – and the value of the nation's assets growing in due proportion.

Part Four

Retirement?

Commercial Risk and Will Shakespeare

Bassanio: Have all his ventures fail'd? What, not one hit?
  From Tripolis, from Mexico and England,
  From Lisbon, Barbary and India?
  And not one vessel scape the dreadful touch
  Of merchant-marring rocks?

The Merchant of Venice

Chapter Eleven

Into Venture Capital for Business and Charity

Not everything across the Channel or the North Sea came in for criticism by the Harold Wilson Committee. Many regarded the national investment facilities available in France, the Netherlands and Sweden as greatly superior to anything we had in Britain. In their 'Note of Dissent' the trade union and Labour Party members of the Committee pointed to the *banques d'affaires*, National Investment Bank and investment reserve scheme in those countries as examples of the kind of facility we could well adopt in Britain. For them, the proposal which came nearest to these was that of the Trade Union Congress for a lending facility to which money would be assigned from life insurance and pension funds.

It was a matter which we on the committee discussed at length, and the majority opinion was that the situation could be adequately met by the present system. But I and three others – Andrew Graham, Professor Joan Mitchell and Hugh Stephenson – let it be known that the TUC proposal was unworkable. For us, the 'Note of Dissent' was based on a fundamental misconception of the rôle of money on the one hand and man and machines on the other. It was fallacious to think of the funds of institutions which were acting as financial intermediaries as idle resources which could and should be rescued from their idleness and put to work in a way that was doing society a service. The only real resources available in our view were underemployed and unemployed men and machines, which could only be brought into operation by creating more demand for them.

In a minority report we pointed out that the two factors which must determine the type of investment facility chosen were the high cost of capital relative to profitability, and the shortage of demand for finance. The institution created to run the new facility must have a progressive build-up, we said. It would not necessarily obtain all its funds from government. Its decisions would be separate from government, in the hands of people with expertise in assessing the long-term viability of commercial projects. It would promote and finance *new* companies with loan and equity capital as well as lending to existing companies. It would never prop up firms for social or political reasons. Indeed, being only partly financed by government, we were convinced that it would be able to take a more aggressive stance and bigger risks in supporting new industry, in spite of the scorn poured on the idea by the bankers.

A few months before I became Lord Mayor of London in November 1978, while such ideas were formulating in my mind (and those of my colleagues), I had a note from a friend of mine, Lord Cornwallis, asking me if I would be good enough to see two young men who he thought would benefit from my advice. These were an American, Peter Brooke, who had set up a very successful 'venture capital' system in America, T. A. Associates, and a Scot, David Cooksey, whose help he had enlisted to establish a similar system in Britain. The formula was to appoint managing agents to raise money and create a fund which had a separate board of directors and a separate chairman. The rôle of the managing agents was to find opportunities for investment, analyse them and write a report making recommendations to the fund's directors who would decide whether to invest in the project or let it go by. Peter Brooke's organisation had operated on these lines with the greatest success in America – for instance, he told me that in financing the huge Wang electronics business he was soon drawing 15 per cent profit from them. While he paid his managers for doing their job he also gave them 'for free' a stake in each project they recommended and the board decided to adopt. If the investment succeeded, they made a big profit on top of their salary; if it failed, they shared in the loss.

Peter Brooke had spent some time trying to sell the idea to British financiers and found it hard going. The City had been totally unreceptive. Our mutual friend Lord Cornwallis had suggested having a chat with me in the hope that I might recommend a new line of approach. All I could do at that first meeting, however, without giving the matter a bit more thought, was to tell them what an extremely good idea I thought it was, which I was certain would succeed. Would I actively join them in some rôle or other? That I said was impossible, since I was just about to take up my badge and gown for a twelve-month stint as Lord Mayor of London.

However, I would encourage them and give any help I could. Go ahead, I said, it is just what the country needs.

It took them three years to get their act together, and in 1981 they launched Advent Management Company Ltd, registered in the

Channel Islands, with David Cooksey as managing director, and the first fund – Advent Technology plc, which, as its name implied, was devoted primarily to investment in advanced technology ('hi-tech') projects. The managing agents they appointed to search out suitable projects for the investment of the fund's £10 million were all skilled in various aspects of engineering, electronics, chemicals, agriculture and the rest. To advise the fund's directors on the extent to which the process of the proposed project was technically sound and was unlikely to be overtaken within, say, the next decade, they had a panel of seven highly qualified professors, experts in their own field, as a technical advisory committee. Staff with commercial experience analysed the market for the product, reported on the probable demand and the risk of there being too little. They did not want to find themselves in the position of investing in a sure-fire cure for a disease which no more than one person in a million was ever likely to catch.

The following year they raised a second £10 million for another fund, Advent Eurofund Ltd. Half the money was put up by British universities, and half by the American multi-national Monsanto who insisted on its having a thoroughly independent chairman. By now my twelve months at the Mansion House was just a happy memory. At the beginning of 1980 I had returned to Guildhall House as senior partner of the firm which, as I have recounted, we then merged with the insolvency department of Coopers & Lybrand as Cork Gully. I helped put it into orbit by personally handling several joint receiverships with a Coopers & Lybrand partner. In making the announcement of the merger in April 1980 we mentioned that my brother Norman planned to retire on becoming seventy in November that year, and that I would retire in 1983.

I kept to this, and in April 1983 I resigned from Cork Gully and handed over as senior partner to Michael Jordan. To keep myself occupied, I set up a consultancy practice in another office building. I offered to resign as receiver of the DeLorean company – a personal appointment – but its major creditor, the British government, asked me to stay with the case until it was finally resolved. The Insolvency Law Reform Committee had presented its report ('Cork 2') to the Secretary of State for Trade and Industry in February 1982 so, apart from bludgeoning the Government to act on it, I was free.

In September 1981 I had agreed to form and become chairman of the new City branch of the Institute of Directors. As President of the Institute of Credit Management and of the Association Européenne des Practiciens des Procédures Collectives (AEPPC), which we formed, I had numerous speaking engagements talking to institutions on business and insolvency not only all over Britain but also in

Hong Kong, Singapore, Malaysia, Australia and New Zealand, when in addition I was able to advise Coopers & Lybrand managers on insolvency and take part in conferences. At home, however, I was changing the work I did and in the market for helping to create new businesses and keep them on the survival path rather than hauling them back to it after they had fallen off.

My brother Norman had started a syndicate in Malta which had built, and ran, a hotel and casino which had Ladbrokes and a group of German businessmen as the principal investors. His asking for my assistance in settling disagreements which arose between himself and his fellow-directors over how the place should be run brought me into sharp confrontation with Cyril Stein, the Ladbrokes chairman. Though we were on opposite sides in this particular tussle, we got to like each other, and on the return flight, when I sat next to him, he picked my brains on all kinds of matters regarding Ladbrokes, which was the start of a very different relationship. A few weeks later, when the smoke of the battle over Norman's Malta syndicate had blown away, Cyril Stein asked me to become a director of Ladbrokes, which I agreed to do. Their business then was almost entirely in betting shops, but in 1986 was involved in the leisure industry in a very much wider way and they had become the second-largest hotel-owner in Britain.

This and other directorships were offered to me, and I took only those where I thought I had something to offer.

My coming Mayoralty, as seen, had prevented me from joining Peter Brooke in setting up a venture capital system in Britain, but when David Cooksey renewed the invitation over lunch at my favourite hotel, the Stafford in St James's Street, just before Christmas 1983 the circumstances were very different. He brought with him Monsanto's chief representative in Europe, Constantine Anagnostopoulos, whom everyone called 'Costas'. In the course of the meal they would have discovered that I was likely to be a bit more independent an 'independent chairman' of their Advent Eurofund Ltd than they had envisaged, but they offered me the job none the less and I accepted it.

When in 1984 they formed a third fund after raising another £36 million, the largest single fund-raising exercise by any venture capital outfit in Britain, they asked me to be chairman of that as well. Monsanto took a smaller stake in this. Most of the money was raised from run-of-the-mill City financial institutions. Again it was for investing in selected and well-analysed hi-tech projects, not only electronics but bio-technology, graphics, you name it. As far as I was concerned, I may not have known what to invest in, but I hoped I had an instinct about what not to invest in. It all went extremely well, which was largely due to the brilliant David Cooksey who worked day and night in building the British system up into what I suppose is today the acknowledged leader in the provision of equity finance and management support to high-technology companies not only in Britain but also all over the world.

We learnt through experience not to take too large a percentage in any one project, since that would make us responsible for it and its management – the last thing we wanted. Being a majority share-holder would mean the company would have to become a subsidiary of ours, and we wished to avoid that. Our aim is eventually to float these so-called 'portfolio companies' as public companies and get our money back. To steer it in that direction we make a condition of our loan the placing of one of our people on their board to keep an eye on things. So often people who start companies lack the skill to manage them once they are operating. As soon as there are signs that a company in which we have invested is beginning to slide downhill, they take the initiative by removing any obviously ineffective direc-tor and replacing him by someone whom they themselves have recruited. Hopefully this will send it happily on its (upward) way.

The success of the operation depends to a large extent on the management company. I have taken a closer interest in this than I intended. I have no formal appointent in it, but I have been able to introduce David Cooksey to people in the City and in government whom he has now got to know well and deals with in his own right. For me my excursion into Britain's venture capital scene and my involvement with the Peter Brooke and David Cooksey 'Advent' enterprise, which has flourished beyond all expectations, has been extremely rewarding. After so long an entanglement with the nega-tive world of insolvency and business failure, finding myself pro-pelled forward on the crest of so much business success, caught up in the positive activity of setting things up instead of winding them down, has been an exciting way of starting my 'retirement'.

Venture capital is now a growth industry in Britain. In 1986 there were ninety-six members of a British Venture Capital Association with funding of £400 million, and altogether more than a hundred providers of this high-risk, high-yield capital. Banks like Schroders and Barings, who had frowned on such unorthodox schemes when we proposed them in our Harold Wilson Committee minority report, have jumped on the bandwagon. But Peter Brooke and David Cooksey paved the way. They and their high-powered, well-adjusted, technically qualified team of young managers of both sexes have introduced to the British industrial scene an investment facility, the lack of which we all deplored so vehemently as we talked our heads off under the chairmanship of that very astute and quick-witted ex-prime minister of Great Britain.

*

Success does not come easily. Few have the stomach for the risks which are involved. The sooner the next generation of businessmen learn to take responsibility the better. The risk of going bankrupt from incompetency should be a real one. In agreeing to become chairman of the Executive Committee of the Youth Enterprise Scheme which was providing venture capital for young people I saw the opportunity for practising what I had been preaching for so long.

I had taken little interest in the youth scene until, in 1978, Dennis Stevenson, the son-in-law of Sir Peter Vanneck whom in a few months I was to succeed at the Mansion House, asked me to be treasurer of the National Association of Youth Clubs. Giving financial advice to, and raising funds for, the NAYC just before my Mayoralty set me thinking about the charity which, along with all Lord Mayors, I would want to take under my wing. I decided that it should be youth-orientated. I tossed various ideas around with Stuart Cobley, a friend who had had considerable experience in running youth clubs. We came up with a scheme we called Practical Action which we took to the Manpower Services Commission of the Department of Employment for their advice and, hopefully, their approval. They agreed to fund it 50 per cent if I arranged funding of the balance. I promised to make it the principal charity of my Mayoralty. We embodied the idea in a charitable organisation attached to the National Association of Youth Clubs, to be run by Stuart Cobley with the assistance of Liz Rhodes as assistant director.

In formulating our scheme Stuart Cobley and I were anxious to create a charitable exercise which for once was not asking people for money. Industry gets bored with being asked for money, and it is boring asking for it. Practical Action set out to persuade companies to lend *equipment* to young people and to provide part-time instructors to teach them a trade or skill. I wrote to leaders of industry saying we did not want their money but hardware and people – tools and machinery on which children and teenagers could train in the Practical Action groups we formed all over Britain, and skilled operators prepared to hand on their skills. My appeal was well received. It was different and it was *practical*. Many did not read it properly and sent money; but, when we pointed out their mistake, they mostly said, 'Sorry, but keep it anyway.' It just shows how little people read charity letters.

The NAYC were delighted with the way Practical Action took off; it was one of the few charitable organisations set up by a Lord Mayor of London which continued after his year of office. It was an undoubted success, and it made the NAYC want to do something more for youth – a scheme which this time perhaps was designed to provide the young people who had acquired skills with the essential capital sum for setting up a venture in which they could employ their newly won expertise?

We discussed how best we could do this with Viscount Caldecote of Investors in Industry – the Three I's – the former International Credit and Finance Corporation set up by the clearing banks as their venture capital arm, and Sir David Lane, chairman of the NAYC. I insisted from the start that any organisation we might establish for providing seed capital should not do so by giving grants. No business would support such a scheme. The snag about giving young people grants is that they think they deserve it. A grant is a cosy umbrella to shelter under. The money comes in each week – £30 or so to help with running expenses – and after the first few weeks is taken for granted (how apt a phrase!). It does nothing to teach them to rely on themselves, which they will have to do if their enterprise is to succeed. We decided that what these enterprising but penniless young people needed was a venture capital scheme which at the same time was a charity fund. We would lend people capital from the charity fund if they had none of their own and then, in the right proportion, lend them support funds – 'banking money' – from a different fund. They would have to present us with a well thought out plan. Because interest was a killer, we proposed giving them an interest holiday for the first two or three years, provided we considered their plan workable and potentially profitable, and after that at a reduced rate. In this way young people would find out how to set up a business of their own and learn the difference between borrowed money and equity money. The essential point of our scheme was that they would *owe* both kinds of money and be responsible for paying it back. It was not a grant. They were never sure that, if they found themselves unable to repay it, we would not make them bankrupt.

We called the exercise the Youth Enterprise Scheme which had the useful acronym YES. The Honourable Angus Ogilvy, husband of Princess Alexandra, agreed to be chairman of the trustees and the advisory council; and I became chairman of the organisation that lent the money. Stuart Cobley was to run the scheme, once more assisted by the energetic Liz Rhodes; and we were to recruit a manager. When we came to form the necessary charitable foundation to put the idea into operation the Charity Commissioners told our lawyers that we could not have a charity which lent money; it would have to be grants, they said. On the contrary, I said, a charity *can* lend money. When they asked me how I knew I told them how, while I was Lord Mayor, I had come across a charity called Samuel Wilson's Loan Trust which had been lending money for 200 years or so. This was news to them. I had the City Corporation send them the deeds of the Trust which had been lending money at a pittance all that time and had hardly lost any money at all.

In his will of 26 October 1766, Samuel Wilson of Hatton Garden had left £20,000 to the Chamberlain of the City of London 'as a perpetual Fund, to be lent to young men who had been set up one year, or not more than two years, in some Trade or Manufacture in the City of London . . . and can give satisfactory security for the repayment of the Money so lent to them'.

No one was to have more than £300 or less than £100, nor for longer than five years. They paid interest at only 1 per cent a year for the first year and 2 per cent for the remaining four years. The borrower had to be a Protestant, and could not be an alehouse keeper, distiller or vendor of distilled liquors, but a young business-man of Honesty, Sobriety and Industry who had gained more from his business than he had lost by it. The fund was not to be subservient to any party views. The fund was confirmed by the Charity Commissioners as recently as September 1979, by which time the maximum loan had gone up to £5,000. It was a stroke of luck that I happened to know about the Samuel Wilson Loan Trust, and in the light of it we were given the go-ahead for the Youth Enterprise Scheme on the lines we had planned – no grants, only loans.

Having run the Northern Ireland Development Agency and discovered how difficult it was to lend money successfully, I was determined that YES should be as commercial as we could make it. Lord Caldecote got Investors in Industry to lend us £$\frac{1}{2}$ million banking money to prime the pump and establish the banking fund; Angus Ogilvy and the rest of us set about raising money for the charity fund. Angus Ogilvy put an enormous amount of work into it and was extremely successful in producing gifts in the region of £$1\frac{1}{2}$ million. Most of the industrialists approached congratulated us on getting the right scheme. A charity which helped the able-bodied and mentally alert, young men and women with brains and initiative but no money, was quite novel. To qualify for a YES loan they had to have not only a bright idea but also a specific and detailed plan setting out exactly how they saw the business operating, the amount of space they would require, the staff, the equipment. We had to have something concrete to assess for potential profitability, a plan on which we could pass judgement as worthy or unworthy of our attention.

There were other charities for helping the young deprived and handicapped to start and run a business, notably the Prince of Wales Trust, the Queen's Jubilee Trust and the Youth Business Initiative. But since they believed, as everyone else had done until we unearthed the Wilson Trust precedent, that the law prevented charities from lending money all these were purveyors of grants and nothing else. Pressure was brought on us to join forces with these organisations, but since under our discipline we could not give grants we had no wish to be associated with charities which did. I saw no objection to having the Prince of Wales as a Great Panjandrum over all four of us, and YES becoming one of the Prince of Wales's trusts, but we had to maintain our identity and unique way of working. I do not believe that the public who subscribe to charities are confused by several organisations doing 'the same thing'. If they are, they do not show it with their pockets, or with their requests for YES services.

Many of the trustees of YES were anxious that it should aim at large-scale growth in as short a time as possible. I counselled the very opposite. I wanted YES to grow very slowly. Learning the skill of lending money was going to take us time. We could not afford, in making a wild dash for growth, to make the mistakes and losses which would give us a bad debt record. If we allowed ourselves to get the reputation of backing losing horses, we would die an early death. The way to quick growth, said some, was to get financial help from the Government; but the Department of Employment, went this argument, was only likely to give support if all the 'similar' organisations combined. Personally I found this difficult to believe. In any case the Department of Employment was not responsible for the handicapped or deprived. They were looked after by the Department of Health or the Department of the Environment. I scotched this particular think-piece by going to see the Secretary of State for Employment, Lord Young, in mid-July 1986, and he made it abundantly clear that YES was the one he wanted to finance out of all possible youth business schemes, because it was in line with his department's disciplines. I told him we wanted to co-operate with the Prince of Wales's trusts and would be glad, for instance, to reduce administrative expenses by sharing a headquarters building and staff. We would very much like to have the Prince of Wales as our president. Caldecote and I told the leaders of the merger school of thought, Charles Villiers and Dr Alcon Copisarow, that we would be happy to see fund-raising for all of us undertaken by the YBI and the Prince of Wales Trust who would then allocate the sums raised downward to the various trusts. But it was clear that they would be satisfied with nothing less than amalgamation with the Youth Business Initiative, a takeover, which it seemed would mean the eventual smudging out of YES in name and method of operation.

We strengthened our ability to maintain our financial independence when, in 1986, YES joined up with the Fairbridge Society, a charity founded by Keith Fairbridge in 1909 as the Child

Emigration Society to pay for young people first of all to be educated
and then sent out to a job in one of the colonies. Under the
immigration laws introduced by Commonwealth countries such as
Australia and Canada in recent days, this is no longer possible. The
Fairbridge Society found itself with a bag of money and no idea how
to spend it. Angus Ogilvy heard of their plight, pointed out to them
the similarities of the aims of YES with Keith Fairbridge's objectives
of 1909, and persuaded them they could do no better than join us.
We became Fairbridge/YES, and our charity fund was swollen by
another £2 million.

To give the hard-won money in our YES charity fund the
maximum chance of being invested in a business idea which would
succeed and justify our faith in it, the plans submitted to us for our
judgement had to be as professional and succinct as those drafted by
the high-powered management agents of Advent Capital – well, as
near to them in form and clear thinking as possible. This was
something which most of the young people who had the ideas and
wanted the money to implement them would find exceedingly
difficult. But without plans of this calibre YES was likely to
flounder. Which is where the bright idea of using the Chartered
Accountants Livery Company came in.

It was arranged that the newly formed Chartered Accountants
Livery Company would provide a panel of accountants to advise and
help our young entrepreneurs. All went very well – too well in fact.
Everyone wanted to take it over and continue it with grant-making
charities. In the end they did succeed. I fought it as long as possible,
but so much pressure was put on the trustees that they gave in.
However, we managed to keep a Chartered Accountant from the
Livery Company (David Richards) as chairman of the loan-making
side. I am sure that he will do his best to make only responsible loans;
otherwise it will die. Having fought the takeover, I resigned, both
because I said I would and to make a point. Everyone tells me it is
now going well. I indeed hope so!

My anxiety to create new livery companies in London arose from the
threat from the GLC, to which I have already alluded, to 'take over'
the City. This threat was serious at the time but, like most attacks on
the City, it went away.

The City always looked to their liverymen for support in the event
of a socialist government or the GLC starting to make overtures. The
foundation of the power of the City of London was in fact the livery
companies. They were the organisations which created the wealth of
the City, starting in the early Middle Ages: the Butchers, the Bakers,
the Fishmongers, etc., controlled their trades, not only in London

but throughout the country. The liverymen were also Freemen of the City of London, and they had the voting power; only Freemen could vote and they elected the City Council, the Court of Aldermen, the Lord Mayor and the Queen's Sheriffs.

They also carried out great charitable duties, and many of the Oxford and Cambridge colleges and public schools were set up and organised by the livery companies. But in the late 1970s the majority of the old livery companies had lost their financial weight and one-time close connection with the City; few had any connection with their trade, craft or profession. Members of the Law Society certainly still practised the law, but only those who did so in London. There were other exceptions like the Furniture Makers who still made furniture, but by and large the Grocers Company no longer consisted of wholesale grocers and dealers; the members of the Mercers Company no longer went round mercing – dealing in textile fabrics. They promoted their trade and ran competitions, but such activity was minimal. The major livery companies like the Grocers had not produced a member of the Common Council or an alderman for a very long time, nor had Dick Whittington's company the Mercers. The Fishmongers had not had one of their basic members on the Corporation for many years, though Sir Peter Vanneck, my predecessor as Lord Mayor, became a member of the Fishmongers, but it was not his mother company.

I realised that if it only were to look for support from the livery companies in the 1970s it would have no backing, for very few of them had an actual trade or profession behind them of any importance. What were the equivalents today, I asked myself, to the old City merchants? Who were the people who now carried clout in the City? Who really had an interest in maintaining its independence? It was certainly not anyone who made horn drinking-cups like the members of my old livery company the Horners. Some of the members might be interested, but they would have no great influence.

There had been a few new livery companies in recent years. The Launderers, for instance, had been desperately trying to become a livery company for a long time. But to form one you had to be a guild and active for at least ten years, have a charitable fund and show you were upright, godly and respectable. Only after ten years would the Court of Aldermen accept you as a livery company, which to me seemed quite ridiculous. I suggested to Murray Fox that we should bring in the new professional bodies who already had charitable funds and could not possibly be asked to wait ten years. They had already accumulated prestige and good standing over a very much longer period, and most of them had their own halls. As livery companies they would give the City enormous strength.

So we proposed to the Court of Aldermen that there should be a new breed of livery company which could be brought into being instantly. Those who could show that they qualified by having the necessary power, influence and charitable funds, and were respectable in every way, should not have to go through the traditional process. The City officers were utterly opposed to the concept of instant livery companies in the beginning, and so was the chamber responsible for livery companies. But the Court of Aldermen jumped at the idea. They saw them as adding power to the office of Lord Mayor. In any future argument with government, a Lord Mayor could point to his Court of Aldermen containing members of the new professions who were giving him full support, and ask the Prime Minister whether he thought it in his interest to fall out with influential people of that calibre.

Certain members of the Corporation found such an argument 'political' and therefore unacceptable. But personally I found it a very cogent one. We did not try to sell the idea on that basis, however, but concentrated on emphasising the enormous influence organisations of this sort could bring to bear if they were behind the City Corporation. So we got the Court of Aldermen to agree that certain characteristics and disciplines would enable professions and crafts to apply for a livery, and that they would become the new instant livery companies, an exact replacement of the old ones, the powerhouses of the City, which had once wielded such power and influence to the good.

The professions I had in mind were the Chartered Secretaries, the insurers, the 80,000 Chartered Accountants, the Chartered Surveyors, the marketers, the bankers, the actuaries. All such had personal skills which had replaced the 'craft' skills of old. They were another kind of craft. Moreover they were people of standing and integrity, and supported by ample funds, for whom the City was designed. I wanted to keep the City as the One Square Mile where you could walk from one side to the other without getting into a car or run the risk of being knocked down by traffic pelting through a main road that ran through its centre. The City of London is a village, and I wanted to keep it that way. I like being able to walk from Lloyd's to Barclays Bank, from the Bank of England to the Stock Exchange and Mansion House, and go down Gresham Street to call on the various merchant banks. Such people as I envisaged forming the new instant livery companies had a vested interest in keeping the City intact, in keeping the aldermen and the Corporation free of the GLC and any political flavour it might have. So the City Corporation and Court of Aldermen agreed to waive the old rules for forming a livery company and to draw up new ones capable of creating them on the instant.

We set off on a recruiting campaign to sell the idea to the bankers, and get the Law Society to make themselves representative not only of London's lawyers but of those throughout the country. Indeed, we were anxious that *all* the professions did not regard themselves as representing merely the people who practised in London but professionals all over Britain. In this, too, we would be going back to the days when members of the Fishmongers Livery Company embraced the whole country and no one could sell fish in Hull or Bristol, so I believe, unless he had a licence to sell fish in the City of London. We wished for the City of London to be once more the centre of representation.

Many asked where the professional institute would end and the livery company begin. This presented no problem. The Chartered Accountants, for instance, ran the profession, but the Great and the Good joined the livery company, which gave them the facility to give service after they had ceased to serve on the Institute – senior and respected people, not necessarily retired, but probably still working in their firms. As liverymen they would influence their own profession and the Institute, while recognising that the independence of the City of London and of the Lord Mayor protected *their* independence.

I was keen for the Chartered Accountants, as one of them, to be the first instant livery company; and Murray Fox the surveyor wanted the Chartered Surveyors to have that honour. The accountants were first in drafting their charter and rules, but when they called a meeting to discuss them so many had ideas of their own on how the various problems should be resolved, and produced so many amendments, that the surveyors, who were more trusting of those who had drafted their rules, accepted the recommendations with little hesitation and pipped the accountants to the post. So, after spending so much time in arguing, the accountants were the second instant livery company. These were the 85th and 86th livery companies respectively. The third was the Chartered Secretaries of which I am an Honorary Freeman. The insurers, who treated me as the person instrumental in getting it off the ground, formed theirs; but so far the bankers, some of whom tend to regard the Goldsmiths as their livery company, have not got round to it. But I live in hope.

None of these new instant livery companies had money enough to found colleges or charities, but they all had big powerful organisations behind them, and they all had skills which they could use as charitable skills. If there were outside pressures to dismantle the City, the new livery companies would be in the forefront of holding on to the City tradition. A large number of the liverymen of the old livery companies from 1 to 84 were also liverymen of the new ones: I

myself, for instance, am a member both of the Horners and
Chartered Accountants. In this way the new livery companies get the
support of the old ones for the defence of the City and the Lord
Mayor. The creation of these instant livery companies brings the
City back to having the same kind of liverymen behind it that
protected it against the Crown at the time it was being created. The
only thing we no longer have in 1988 is a wall to keep the King's
troops out!

To what charity could members of the Chartered Accountants
Livery Company apply their accounting and management skills,
their knowledge of tax and insurance matters, their business
acumen? There was now an instant answer: the Youth Enterprise
Scheme. If any member who felt that the traditional wining and
dining of a livery company was not enough, felt an urge to give the
benefit of his experience to the inexperienced and impecunious for
no financial return, he could not do better, I told them, than help the
young self-employed who applied to YES for a loan, with the
preparation of those vital plans. I talked to the Court of the
Chartered Accountants Livery Company on the opportunity which
this presented to the unfulfilled liveryman. As Master I invited
Stuart Cobley, Liz Rhodes and Roddy Vernon, the man we had
recruited to act as national co-ordinator of YES, to the livery
company's banquets to meet members and spread the gospel. The
liverymen soon got the message. They appointed a leading member
to co-ordinate liaison with YES agencies throughout Britain, and in
no time we had forty or fifty fully qualified accountants volunteering
to spend time out of office hours vetting the plans of would-be
borrowers and then, if they were accepted, monitoring and supervising the resulting business to keep it on course.

Lord Benson, who helped to create Coopers & Lybrand, persuaded Lord Leverhulme to give us £¼ million for lending in the
Merseyside area. I tried to extend the services we could offer young
hopefuls by bringing in the Chartered Secretaries, but they were less
enthusiastic than their accounting brethren.

Few of the amounts of money we lent as seed capital were more
than £5,000, and the people we helped to start and run businesses of
their own were all under twenty-six. In its first two years the Youth
Enterprise Scheme had backed some 200 businesses giving employment to more than 300. Of the £380,000 invested up to 1986 only 5
per cent – about £19,000 – had to be written off, which in my

reckoning is not at all bad. For me it was a thoroughly satisfying and worthwhile exercise.

Since writing this the scheme has changed and YES is now closer to YBI and the Prince's Trust than I would wish, so I, as I have already told you, withdrew from active participation.

Chapter Twelve

Into Battle for Barbican, RSC and Arts Council

Retirement from W. H. Cork Gully & Co. gave me more time to deal with my venture capital involvement, which was an area of my profession which I had hitherto never encountered, but also ushered me into the strange new world of that section of the arts scene which is subsidised music and subsidised drama. What more fitting for one who had withdrawn from business, but from whom business had not withdrawn, than to devote his time and energy to charity! Under English law charities can be of two kinds: the foundation which benefits the poor, the sick and the disabled, and the educational body with 'charitable status' which is non-commercial and non-profit-making. I was lucky enough to be able to become involved in both.

Our first 'artistic activity' at Cork Gully began in 1955 with my brother Norman attending the creditors' meeting of a private commercial company run by a Polish gentleman, Julian Brunswick, which, at the suggestion of Alicia Markova, he called the Festival Ballet – it had been formed in 1951, the year of the South Bank Exhibition and Festival of Britain. Brunswick had brought his Paris-based Polish Ballet to London in 1939 and been marooned by the outbreak of war. In four years his new company, mainly of English dancers, had established a reputation with English audiences, but in 1955 it had just completed a disastrous American tour promoted by America's leading impresario, Sol Hurok, and was stranded in New York with no money to pay the fares home. It was broke. The principal creditors called a meeting in London, and Norman went along with the solicitor of one of them. As usual, all they could think of discussing was what assets there were and how much they would realise. It was too much for Norman. He pointed out that there could be little purpose in selling up a ballet company. The purchasers would only become the proud owners of sets of scenery, baskets of costumes and nothing else. Their sellable stock in trade was their talent for dancing. To bring the company to a halt and stop it ever performing again could not benefit anyone and, anyhow, most of the assets were in transit to Spain where they were to have their next tour.

They agreed to let Cork Gully work out a scheme. The world of show business was not Norman's world, and when he returned to his office he called one of the firm's partners on the internal telephone and told him of the meeting he had just left. 'I think this is more up your street than mine.' Gerry Weiss knew nothing about ballet, either, but he saw Norman's point. As he will tell you, that telephone call changed his life.

He agreed with Norman's diagnosis, but let it be known that Cork Gully could do nothing until the insolvent company returned to England. In the event, they persuaded Sol Hurok to lend them the money for the tickets and, while the dancers went on a well-earned holiday, Gerry and Julian Brunswick discussed the next move. The director-general's main asset was a three-year contract with the management of the Festival Hall for the Festival Ballet to perform there while the Promenade Concerts were being given at the Albert Hall. When the Festival Hall was built there was an unwritten agreement that only stage shows, and no concerts, should be presented on the South Bank during the summer Proms season in Kensington. It had been the stage director of the Festival Ballet Company who had designed the fit-up stage which transformed the Festival Hall from a concert hall into a theatre.

It was February, and the summer was still a long way off. Gerry Weiss told the Festival Hall management that they were in as much trouble as the Festival Ballet. If they broke the contract with Brunswick without complete certainty that the company could not appear, they ran the risk of being sued for breach of contract. If they did nothing and did not break the contract, there was a fair chance that the company would fail to turn up, and the Festival Hall would have nothing to offer the whole summer.

In our somewhat unofficial capacity of 'financial advisers' to the Festival Ballet, Cork Gully negotiated a bank loan to tide them over until the start of the summer season. The London County Council could not lend money; but as the landlords of the hall they guaranteed repayment of the loan to the bank out of the summer season's box-office receipts. After all, the LCC touched the money before the Festival Ballet did. They could make sure the loan was repaid, and see that what was left over was paid to the dancers. In fact the Festival Hall's finance officer, George Mann, on loan from the LCC, promised to give the members of the company their pay-packets personally – provided, that is to say, *pace* the creditors, there was a

show to pay them for. So many others had been clamouring for
payment for so long – choreographers, composers, designers, cos-
tume-makers, lighting-hirers and the rest – that they threatened to
obtain an injunction to stop the performances unless and until their
bills were settled. The Festival Hall management had no money;
they were going to pay everyone out of the box-office receipts. If the
creditors got their injunction, there would be no show and no money.
Gerry Weiss was away, so I told Julian Brunswick, who was
naturally aching to attend the opening night of his company at the
Festival Hall, to take himself off to Paris and stay there until the
season was over. For the creditors to stop that curtain rising they
would have to serve the writ on Brunswick personally. His 'non-
availability' would, I thought, spike their guns in a way that left them
incapable of acting until he reappeared. Protesting, Brunswick could
only do as he was told, take the ticket to Paris which I had brought
with me and the very next plane to France.

The Festival Ballet company were not in official liquidation or
receivership. It was just a voluntary arrangement which Cork Gully
were 'supervising'. Julian Brunswick kept going only by the credit-
ability of Cork Gully, and by the end of the second year we formally
withdrew our services as financial advisers, though Gerry, now
completely hooked on ballet, and Julian continued to talk on a
personal basis. Their main topic of conversation was how best to
obtain money from the Arts Council or the London County Council.
Gerry had fairly definite ideas, but the founder and director-general
was not at this stage prepared to fall in with them.

Things went from bad to worse, and in the early sixties Victor
Mischon (now Lord Mischon), a prominent member of the LCC and
a solicitor, asked if Cork Gully would resume its rôle as financial
adviser. Shortly afterwards the Festival Ballet finally went into
liquidation. At the creditors' meeting a liquidator was appointed
from the accountancy firm of Stoy Hayward & Co. who became the
owners of the costumes and scenery. Our advice to Brunswick was to
form a second company with an almost identical name. This new
Festival Ballet then made a hire-purchase contract with Davis, the
liquidator of the old company, to acquire its costumes and scenery so
it could carry on. In addition we arranged for the LCC to give the
new company financial help on an *ad hoc* basis – £5,000 at a time – as
the beginning of a subsidy. Finally we had the new company formed
into a non-profit-making charity – which is what Gerry Weiss had
advised Brunswick to do earlier.

The LCC were in a difficult position. They wanted to save this
excellent ballet company for London, but could not help a national–
international group on a permanent basis. That was for the Arts

Council to do, if they saw fit. Not even bridging finance was possible; it could only be temporary help while the Arts Council were making up their minds. It was a fraught period, entailing numerous battles, and our fighting them was not helped by the serious illness of Gerry Weiss in 1965 which kept him *hors de combat* for many months. I am glad to say he fully recovered, however, and was able to assume the position of chairman of the Festival Ballet Trust, and of another ballet company in Manchester. Julian Brunswick resigned. Anyone interested in his story should read his colourful *Brunswick's Ballet Scandals*. He was brilliant but difficult. As an accountant I have a very precise sense of timing, and I offended him enormously on one occasion when he was being particularly argumentative by telling him I would talk to him when he could get his dancers to dance in time with the music. The last time I had seen them they seemed to me to be always just ahead or just behind the beat. To him from then on I was the complete philistine. I must say, however, when Gerry Weiss took me to see the Festival Ballet perform Roland Petit's *Carmen* ballet in July 1986, by which time they had achieved international renown under their artistic director Peter Schaufuss, there was nothing the old philistine could fault by way of their precision timing or anything else. Coopers & Lybrand and Cork Gully were one of that summer season's evening sponsors, so I had special reason for being delighted to see how, after all those real-life dramas of its formative years, the company was achieving so high an all-round standard which was obviously a delight, too, to the enormous audience.

As I will recount later, years before Lord Drogheda had persuaded me to help form a trust and get the New Philharmonia Orchestra off the ground and solvent. It was through this and the help we were able to give the Festival Ballet that we realised how good it was that Cork Gully should be involved in something other than insolvency, and I took positively to encouraging partners to do so whenever they could. Gerry Weiss stayed with the Festival Ballet; Mike Jordan guided the Mermaid Theatre and Bernard Miles through its various problems; I was elected to the City Corporation's Music Committee and became responsible for the City's arts activities. When I was asked to chair the committee organising the St Cecilia's Day Concert, I co-opted one of our partners, Malcolm London, to do all the work, and when I later withdrew he remained the project's treasurer. Insolvency accountants left alone to do nothing else but insolvency work can become pretty dull creatures. While using their professional skill to organise arts events for people whose temperaments were seldom suited to the kind of disciplines required, they met Top People without asking them for anything. They made friends with people in the City on occasions when no one was 'talking business'. That apart, I firmly believed that, whatever it may have been when Morier Evans was writing in 1845, it was the duty of a business in 1986 not only to make money but to do something for the community.

I was extremely busy in the 1950s, and I am afraid I found regular attendance at Music Committee meetings quite beyond me. I was not of course an authority on matters musical, and in any event I was not the kind of person who liked to mix the time I gave to my business affairs with what I put in on other activities, however worthy and serious. I do not like being committee fodder. I prefer to do voluntary work in my spare time and if possible at home. It was not of course an attitude shared by the majority of Common Councillors, and inevitably the irregularity of my appearances at sessions of the Music Committee came to the attention of my alderman, Lionel Denny. He told me I was letting the side down.

Shortly after this reprimand, I had to be in Scotland on the day the Music Committee held its first meeting of the year and elected a chairman. It was to be a year of utmost importance for committee members since the Corporation was just about to wade into the uncharted waters of the Barbican Scheme.

At long last the Corporation had come to an agreement on how to use the 47-acre bombed site between Aldersgate and Moorfields which had been cleared after devastation by the Luftwaffe in 1941 and remained empty ever since. Neither factories nor offices would be built on it but a 'residential neighbourhood' including an arts centre to house the Guildhall School of Music and Drama which for almost a hundred years had been in John Carpenter Street on the Victoria Embankment. The move and the planning of the new school were going to need the closest supervision, and someone on that committee – I do not know whether to call him friend or foe – suggested it was a job for the absent Kenneth Cork. So, without my being there to say Yea or Nay, the Music Committee elected me their chairman for the ensuing year (1957). From being in the doghouse for non-attendance, I was given instant promotion to Boss Man. It was the cue to pay more attention to the arts in the future. My interest from being peripheral became deep and lasting.

Something which eased me into the unfamiliar arts world was having to help organise the first annual City Arts Festival, the brainchild of impresario Ian Hunter. It was an excellent idea, for it got people used to having the arts in a part of London which everyone associated solely with finance and business. Having performances of music and drama and art exhibitions in the livery company halls prepared them for the day when they would have a monster arts centre in the very midst of the banks and insurance offices.

My serving on the City Festival committee as the representative of the Corporation familiarised me with many of the kinds of problem which were going to arise over the Barbican. It also led to my meeting Lord Drogheda, the chief executive of the *Financial Times*, who was the committee's chairman. A great patron of the arts, particularly of opera, he had made history by persuading the directors of that pillar of the Establishment the *Financial Times* to start the collection of modern paintings which today is one of the most valuable in Britain. Shortly after our first committee meeting, he told me his advice had been sought by members of the Philharmonia Orchestra whose founder and owner, Walter Legge, had announced his intention of killing it off. Having got the orchestra to make gramophone records of all the main classical orchestral works, he had lost interest. What should they do now? they had asked Gareth Drogheda. On no account disband, he had said, but re-form yourselves as the New Philharmonia Orchestra. And go and see Kenneth Cork on how to set about it.

Previously Walter Legge *owned* the old Philharmonia Orchestra; I suggested that the players themselves should own the private limited company which was the New Philharmonia Orchestra – the more usual arrangement. The members of the orchestra were the only shareholders. From their number they elected a board of directors and a chairman, and hired a general manager/company secretary from outside. Lord Harewood agreed to become president. To finance the orchestra we created a separate NPO Trust and persuaded some dozen respected figures from the ranks of the Great and the Good to act as trustees and give the new orchestra integrity. I became a trustee myself, and I recruited my friend Charles Forte. Originally it was a trust of individuals, which meant each trustee had unlimited liability. But later we thought this was giving them too big a responsibility and changed it into a trust company limited by guarantee of one pound a head. That might sound a simple and desirable exercise, but for various abstruse reasons many of the old-type personal trustees resented having to change their status, and a lot of time and hot air were wasted making them see reason. We could not make the change without the agreement of every one of them.

If the musicians/shareholders disagreed with their general manager, they could always sack him – and no argument. He was their employee. But getting rid of an unpopular chairman always led to acrimony in which lack of administrative talent became irrationally linked with the poor man's shortcomings as a player – 'he's a rotten second trombone anyway!' But they survived, and the New

Philharmonia went on to become one of the finest orchestras in the kingdom.

This initiation into arts administration stood me in good stead for the battles that were to rage around the Barbican project. On my plate as chairman of the City Corporation's Music Committee I found the planning not only of how the Guildhall School would fit into the proposed Barbican Educational and Arts Centre, as it was first called, but how the theatre and concert hall, which would constitute the main part, would be used. The Music Committee invited Eric Cundell, the principal of the Guildhall School, to submit ideas on the kind of building and facilities he would like to see on the site. He drafted a brief for the architects in which he said he looked for a reproduction of what he had at John Carpenter Street but more modern. On the strength of this Chamberlin, Powell & Bon designed a tower-block packed with studio classrooms with a separate public concert hall and public theatre at ground level. The theatre was a small one, and the concert hall very much larger. The proposal was that both should be managed by the City Corporation, which I was convinced would be disastrous. I could not see the Corporation running a concert hall; a theatre had to be forward-looking and controversial, and have entrepreneurs who knew what they were up to. So I persuaded the Committee to commission Anthony Besch, who had had wide experience in running concert halls and theatres, to report on the situation and recommend how the Barbican Arts Centre should be run. In his comments on the suitability of Chamberlin's design, he said the theatre was too small; it should have at least 1,200 seats and the concert hall 2,000. His views were fed into the tortuous decision-making system at Guildhall and were examined by my Music Committee and the Barbican Development Committee of which I was not a member. My interest was mainly not what the centre would look like but who would run it. It was true that the Greater London Council were running the Royal Festival Hall quite efficiently, but they were constantly in debt. In any case, it seemed to me that the theatre and the concert hall should be treated separately. A theatre managed by the City Corporation would be hopeless. Every time they presented an exciting new play there was bound to be someone who said it was obscene or otherwise objectionable, and no self-respecting committee of the Corporation could tolerate being on the receiving end of that kind of thing. I gave the matter a lot of thought and came to the conclusion that what we needed was two tenants, one for the concert hall and one for the theatre. As the future occupiers they could brief the architect on the kind of hall and theatre which would suit their requirements.

In due course, and after much heart-searching, the Music Committee agreed, and then applied themselves to the trickier matter of *which* tenants – which orchestra and which theatre company.

My idea was to give one of the four London orchestras a place of residence at the Barbican. My first thought was naturally to invite the New Philharmonia Orchestra – of which I was a member of the Trust – but they decided it would be too big a responsibility for them. So we opened negotiations with the London Symphony Orchestra, which at least had the right name, on the lines that they should be the tenants of the concert hall and the Barbican Arts Centre resident orchestra. They would be responsible for arranging the whole twelve-month programme, booking other orchestras and artistes for the days when they were performing elsewhere. The LSO was run on the same lines as the NPO with the players as shareholders and directors. Ted Heath was their president. However, they were insufficiently funded, and they told us that regrettably they were not yet in a position to be our tenant. But could they make the Barbican their home, and would the City Corporation run them and the concert hall? And that is what was arranged.

Our first choice of tenant for the theatre was the Royal Shakespeare Company, which at that very moment were looking for somewhere which would give them a presence in London as well as at Stratford-upon-Avon. If players were to get lucrative parts in television, it was their performances in London not in faraway Stratford which would secure them. To make it worthwhile for actors to come to Stratford, Peter Hall, the director of the RSC, planned to have two companies playing one year out in Warwickshire and the next in London. Their plans for a London home were in fact already quite far advanced. They were negotiating with Ashley Dukes and his wife Marie Rambert to purchase a site opposite the Mercury Theatre in Notting Hill from their Mercury Theatre Trust. They had commissioned Sir Basil Spence, the leading architect of the day, to design them a theatre for this site and he had completed it. The land and the buildings were going to cost them a lot of money, and when it was finished the RSC would have to share it with the Ballet Rambert.

When I saw Sir Fordham Flower, chairman of the governors of the RSC, to tell him of our plans for a theatre in the Barbican Arts Centre, I said I was sure he and Peter Hall would not want to have half a theatre, with all the hassle of having to fit in with the ballet company's plans. Why not opt for the cheaper way of renting a theatre, custom-built to their exclusive requirements, instead of building and owning one out at Notting Hill with all the burden of maintenance of the fabric of the building of which they could not divest themselves except by selling it – if they could find a buyer.

It was not difficult to win them over. Both Fordham Flower and Peter Hall were soon excited at the prospect of making their London home at the Barbican, though it was only with difficulty that they were able to sell the change of plan at this late hour to the Governors of the RSC. They had the unenviable task, too, of informing Ashley Dukes and the Mercury Theatre Trust that they were no longer interested.

The new idea was that the RSC would be tenants of the City Corporation and be responsible for the whole twelve-month programme in the theatre. We were at pains to avoid the kind of arrangement which was being discussed for the National Theatre, to which Peter Hall had now transferred as Director. By this the National were to be tenants of the Greater London Council but responsible for the maintenance of the whole building, which meant they had to demand a subsidy far above what the Government found acceptable. It was a very onerous responsibility. In my opinion the National Theatre people should not have taken it on on those terms but told the GLC that, if they wanted them there, they would only go on terms which they could afford. They should have made a calculation setting out the sum they could reasonably expect from the Government by way of grant, estimated their income from all sources and arrived at the sum left over which would be what they could afford for rent and overheads. But they were all new to it, and of course Peter Hall was anxious to get into the building on the South Bank with as little fuss and delay as possible.

I was determined not to put the RSC in that position. In 1979 it was reckoned that building the Barbican Arts Centre was going to cost the Corporation around £55 million; though forecasting the effect of inflation over the next two years – it was still that long way away from opening, though the Guildhall School had gone into it in 1977 – the final cost was being put at £80 million. When quizzed on this by an interviewer for BBC Television I said, while people always estimated the increased cost of completion, they rarely estimated the increased cost of tickets. If there was 40 per cent inflation during the years before opening, I said, presumably ticket prices would go up by 40 per cent. Before building began the average best theatre seat cost £2, and in 1979 it cost £8. If you had estimated the current price of building when you started, and then the price of tickets, you would have said it was lunatic. The only time to build something like the Barbican Arts Centre, I said, was in times of inflation. After all, nobody knows today the original cost to the citizens of London of building Guildhall. When my interviewer asked me whether I thought there was a danger of our scheme running into disaster 'like the National', I said they had taken on their enormous building regardless. But their position was different. The public would subscribe to help a theatre in distress, but never to help a wealthy Corporation with the rent.

'If you don't get the right rent, you won't have the RSC in the Barbican?'

'That's right.'

It was after all open to the Music Committee to recommend another tenant, though it was a bit late for that now.

Sir Jeremy Morse, the chairman of Lloyds Bank, was busy making calculations of the probable income the RSC could make at the Barbican if we had them as our tenants, and feared there would be horrendous losses. It was September 1979, and they had not even got a date on which they could start to make bookings. I was of course coming to the end of my term as Lord Mayor of London, and I see that I told my diary on the day I received Jeremy's letter:

Of course the whole situation is ridiculous, the way it has escalated. It has gone on for years, and it is still going to take two years before it can open, and other people would have built the whole bag of tricks in about three or four years, or less, and at half the price. It really is a monument to our inefficiency.

We had not yet had any discussions with the RSC on their probable running costs, but they thought they would be able to pay us the same rent they were paying for the Aldwych Theatre but no more. If that was the case, that would be very reasonable, and we would have no problem.

When I took the sheriffs on a tour of the Arts Centre in October 1979:

My heart sank lower and lower. First of all, it is a long way from completion, and Maurice Laing [the contractor] was there and he clearly thinks we are mad. The concert hall was impressive but with an enormous amount of wasted space, all of which costs money to work and heat, and from which there is no income. How anybody can design a place which has so much covered space for which no proper use will be made! And then there is an enormous ramp for people to walk up which costs a fortune and will serve no purpose at all.

Then we went up and looked at the theatre. It is all right but some of the galleries only have two rows of seats, so the cost of having that gallery for just two rows of people is anyone's guess. And then there is no central gangway and the rows are at least 200 seats long, so everyone has to climb over each other. Then we've got a double fly tower so you can hold two sets of scenery one above the other. It is a bit like building a skyscraper; it's mad. Then of course there's voice projection. Won't the sound go whistling up there and not out into the auditorium with that amount of empty space up in the fly tower? The dressing rooms are upstairs, so the cast will have to come down to the stage in lifts and need to have closed circuit television to tell them where the play has got to. On the upper floors there is a huge covered glass area. In part of it I should think you could seat a couple of thousand; but the 'floor' consists of a domed skylight which forms the ceiling of the restaurant below. So all you can do with it is to fill it with trees and let them grow – and who is going to go up and look at them?

The design may look beautiful but it is a natural lunacy. I really can't think how we ever came to pass plans like these. I came back very depressed. It has been a great success so I must have been wrong.

The problems surrounding the Royal Shakespeare Company's ability to pay its way had been depressing me for much longer – since at least 1967 when George Farmer, the chairman of Rover Cars, who had become chairman of the RSC on the death of Fordham Flower, invited me to become a governor. They were having the greatest difficulty in getting the Arts Council to give them an adequate grant, and they thought that I could help them in this. I had got them the Barbican Theatre, said Farmer, but it was going to be of little use if by the time it was ready they had not survived. The Arts Council, it seemed, had turned down the sum they had requested as a grant, but told them they could have a lesser amount. Their answer had been to say in that case they would go broke. I told them what they should have done was to set down what effect the lower figure would have on their operation – having to close this theatre here, reduce the number of new productions there, reduce the season by three weeks and so on – and announce that all these cuts were the Arts Council's fault.

So we agreed to play it that way when we returned to the Arts Council to discuss the following year's grant. We spelt out in great detail precisely what the Arts Council would get for their £X million, and hinted that they might have to dispense with having a second company which played every other year at the Aldwych Theatre in London – which was preparing the way for performing in the Barbican Theatre. We made a strong point of there being a limit to the amount we could save yet maintain the standard which brought the customers in, and that we had reached that limit. The new tactic worked, and the Arts Council agreed to increase our grant.

But this, it seemed to me, was not enough to ensure survival. The Arts Council only did what we call 'deficit finance'; that is, you had to be broke before they gave you your money. They gave you a certain sum and then a guarantee against a deficit, which to me as an accountant was a very funny way of doing things. And it seemed to me that a way of mitigating the effect of this on the RSC was to create a separate fund of money which the Arts Council could not take into consideration when calculating the size of their grant. So we set up a charitable foundation called the Royal Shakespeare Theatre Trust, of which I was chairman, to which we invited industry, banks, insurance companies, individuals, to make gifts of money in return for a very grand illuminated Share Certificate resembling a Certificate of Merit which they could frame and hang on their wall. The objects of the Trust were primarily to raise money for the Royal Shakespeare Company, which is of course itself a charity established by royal charter in 1925, but we made sure to write into them others which enabled the trustees to give money to outside theatrical enterprises. If it had been solely to give money to the RSC, then the Arts Council would have been entitled to reduce its grant in the light of the amount raised. As it was, the total amount raised and the proportion of it given to the RSC were no business of the Arts Council, whose assessment of the grant they gave the company depended on the income shown in the RSC annual report which contained no account of the money received from the Trust. The response to our appeal for donations to the RST Trust was magnificent. There was no personal liability for a trustee of the Royal Shakespeare Theatre. In time we had more than a million pounds.

The fund was of the greatest value to the RSC. From it we bought equipment, costumes, scenery which the company could not afford on the Arts Council grant only, and made a present of them to the RSC. Like any charity receiving a grant, the RSC never knew the size of its Arts Council grant for the coming year, or indeed if it would get a grant at all, until the end of the previous year. So it had to plan the whole of its next year's programme and engage its artistes without knowing what subsidy they would get to help finance it. If the Government for some good reason suddenly decided to cancel your grant, you went bankrupt, and found yourself in breach of contract with your theatre managers and with your performers. It was all very dangerous, but having the RST Trust money behind them to give support whether the grant was big or small, existent or nonexistent, was a great boost to the morale of those who had to administer the company.

What, I had often thought in moments of fancy, about taking out a PPI policy for the support of the RSC? A 'Policy Proof of Interest' was Lloyd's way of getting round the rule of the insurance market that to insure anything you had to have an insurable interest. A gambling PPI policy at Lloyd's was itself proof of interest, but not a legally binding contract. If we had taken out a PPI policy insuring against a shortfall in the RSC's income, it would have been dishonest but in a good cause!

When George Farmer retired in 1975 to go and live in the Isle of Man, I was asked if I would succeed him as chairman of the governors of the RSC. The Flower family, who had founded the Stratford Memorial Theatre, had prior claim, I thought, and indeed one of them, Dennis Flower, was then deputy chairman. Should not he become chairman? When I was told he was not putting himself forward, I agreed to take over. The chairman of the RSC was also its chief fund-raiser; my reputation for this, I reckoned, was a main reason for their asking me. With no joy from the Arts Council or the Treasury, my thoughts turned to the section of the community I knew best, the City. I suggested trying to 'sell' whole productions of the RSC to commercial enterprises for exclusive sponsorship. This brought in considerable additional revenue. I myself was able to 'sell' two productions, one to the Midland Bank and another to Barclays Bank, and later to Ladbrokes and the National Westminster Bank. Cyril Stein saw that Ladbrokes became one of the principal supporters of theatre and the arts. The RST will always be grateful to them, but it was good for Ladbrokes, too.

I am sometimes asked if commercial sponsorship affects the choice of plays. Not in the least, is the answer. What the RSC – or any other company for that matter – do is choose the production and then look for sponsorship. I must say it raised my hackles when at a meeting of the RSC directors at which the Arts Council were represented at the time I was Lord Mayor

> they came up with this damn silly nonsense that the Arts Council needs acknowledgement on the programme. Told the Arts Council clearly that if there was any question of giving any acknowledgement other than to the Midland or Barclays or any other people I sell a production to, then it was out. I thought it was absolute nonsense, I told them, to give acknowledgement to the Arts Council for taxpayers' money. It is really quite childish. If they didn't like it and they said we would lose our grant, I could tell them to get stuffed and resign as chairman, which I am sure they would not like very much, and I told them the reason why. (Diary, 23 January 1979)

In the last years of my chairmanship of the Royal Shakespeare

Company, when inflation was running high, its expenditure got dangerously out of line with its grant. The Arts Council accused *me* of deficit financing – which any accountant would regard as immoral, let alone an insolvency accountant! If they did not give us the money we needed, what did they expect us to do? Close down? If it had come to that, I would have had enough RST Trust money to close without being insolvent. Though I never admitted it, that was my main reason for forming the Trust. It was the safety-net in the event of never receiving an adequate grant and having to go broke. None of us would have been directors of an insolvent company since the Trust fund would have rescued us. It was something of course you could only do once.

What rankled also was that even when the RSC had two companies, one at Stratford and one at the Aldwych Theatre in London, the Arts Council gave the National Theatre three times the size of our grant. At that time I was continually protesting to the Arts Council that since we were bigger than the National Theatre, and in my opinion better, we at least ought to have a similar grant. Yes, they would say, but you are *not* the National Theatre. But I could never get them to lift the RSC to the level of the National. The main stumbling-block was their insistence in returning again and again to the argument that they received a fixed sum of money from the Government each year and that it was their job to allocate it. If we give you more of it, they argued, who do we take it from? To me that was an extremely unfair argument. Did they not allocate their money on merit? I asked. No, they said. If they did that, they would have to close this theatre and that, and that was not their wish. They could not take away a grant from any of their grantees.

If that was the case, I told them, they were no earthly use to me. I was not interested in them. Survival of the RSC would have to depend on some other source of funding – as indeed, as I only learnt later after reading Sally Beauman's book, *The Royal Shakespeare Company: A History of Ten Decades* (Oxford University Press, 1982), had been the Arts Council intention when Peter Hall first mooted the formation of a second company in London in preparation for coming to the Barbican. When Peter Hall approached them he was told quite clearly that there was only one 'national' theatre company in Britain and that was the National Theatre to which alone they would make a grant. There would be no money to subsidise the Royal Shakespeare Company. So I started lobbying the Government.

Here we were going broke and the Arts Council was refusing to prevent it. With monotonous regularity I pounded away on these lines at every meeting of the four nationalised companies, English

National Opera, Covent Garden Opera, the National and ourselves, with the Minister of Arts. I made little headway. But I made sure that I only voiced such opinions within the privacy of official meetings – at meetings of the RSC board and of the Drama Panel of the Arts Council – never in public and never to the press. I would not allow any RSC staff or performers to hold protest meetings outside 10 Downing Street or abuse the Arts Council or, more important, the Government *in public*. All that would have done would have been to drive the Government into a corner so it was impossible for them to give way. If you bully government, they just have to stick it out and save face.

I made no headway whatsoever until, in 1982, Sir William Rees-Mogg, who had just retired as editor of *The Times*, was appointed chairman of the Arts Council and Louis Rittner the general manager and chief executive. Sir William had been told that sooner or later he would have to deal with the terrible Kenneth Cork, chairman of the Royal Shakespeare Company, who was quite impossible and always shouting at them. He decided to make up his own mind on that, however, and took the trouble to brief himself on the events of the last few years as regards the Arts Council's dealings with the RSC by reading through the minutes and correspondence. When he faced me over the luncheon-table at our first encounter he confessed at the outset to being warned that I was a terrible fellow and needed to be handled with care. On looking at the paperwork, however, he told me he had to admit that from my standpoint as chairman of the RSC he considered I was right in what I had been saying to the Arts Council. I had a legitimate grievance, and it was up to him and his colleagues to see how they could help. I told him they could only do so if they were prepared to stop saying that giving us more money meant depriving someone else, and whom should they deprive?

Paul Channon had always been a very pleasant man to talk to, but at every meeting had told me in the nicest way that he was quite unable to help the RSC. But when Lord Gowrie took over from him as Minister of Arts, a highly civilised man who thoroughly under-stood the arts and the problems of administration – as did also his wife – it became another ball game. For the first time I found a Minister for the Arts who knew what I was talking about. I had nothing new to say. I was still harping on the theme that the greatest Shakespearian company in the world was becoming more and more insolvent. But I was now able to add that if nothing was done about it we would have to close the London end of the enterprise, which was no longer the hired Aldwych Theatre but the custom-built Barbican Theatre which we had now occupied. I took Lord and Lady Gowrie to see performances of the company at Stratford and London, entertained them, had them meet our people and our backers, and I saw the penny gradually dropping. I do not know of course what he said to his masters at the Treasury or what they said to him. But I imagine his conclusion was on the lines of: If we are going to get these lunatic do-gooders off our backs the only thing is to hold an inquiry into the way they are running the business. That would prove that they could easily run these nationalised theatres properly if they wanted to, and show the public there is no need for the Government to subsidise an operation that could and should pay for itself. Be that as it may, the Minister for the Arts announced that he was prepared to appoint a government committee to enquire into the Royal Shakespeare Company, and while they were doing that to report, too, on the Covent Garden and English National Opera companies. A civil servant, Clive Priestley, who had been in the Prime Minister's private office and her 'think-tank', was to be chairman. I told Lord Gowrie I welcomed the inquiry. If the committee demonstrated that the RSC did not deserve money, then, as a Chartered Accountant, I would accept it. I would see that the RSC co-operated in every way.

Arnold Goodman and Max Rayne of the National Theatre were horrified. By allowing the Government to interfere in the running of the arts, as opposed merely to allocating grants, they said we were opening the door to their dictating what plays, music and ballets the national companies should perform, and that would be the end of their artistic freedom. We were letting the side down, they said. If they thought that, so be it, I told them. But if I did not 'let the side down', as they put it, the RSC would go broke. What did they expect me to do?

The Priestley Inquiry was a costly affair because it was very thorough, with groups of high-powered civil servants and accountants. I gave his team the run of the RSC, and allowed them to talk to anyone they wanted to, see how we operated, read through all the papers. I got the impression that Priestley thought I was just the nominal chairman, so I think he was surprised to find that I knew as much about the running of the company, its costs and expenses, as anyone down the line. Clive Priestley was a first-class businessman and a brilliant investigator. He spent a lot of his time with me, which gave me the opportunity to put across my case and explain why we needed the kind of money we had so long been asking for. I reiterated that since the Arts Council could not allocate funds on merit, which I considered an unfair position for them to be in, I would like to transfer the RSC's dependence on them to the Ministry of Arts, to whom I could make out a case for the company *deserving* the money I was asking for. To my great gratification, in their report to the Government, the Priestley Committee stated that there were only

minimal savings which we could make in the way we were running
the company, whereas they found there could be considerable
economies at Covent Garden and the Coliseum, home of the English
National Opera. So that confounded the critics, which presumably
included the Treasury, who were always saying that the only way to
stop going broke was to cut back on overheads. It was now
established by independent investigators that there was no wastage at
the RSC, whatever there might be elsewhere.

A criticism sometimes levelled at the RSC – and the National – is
that they stage too many glitzy 'popular' productions. I believe that a
national public theatre company should justify itself to all of the
public, not to just some of it, and should certainly do 'popular'
productions. They can't really just be described as moneyspinners –
the RSC's productions of Shakespeare are in fact extremely profitable. The RSC is for everyone, and should certainly produce a good
range of different kinds of play.

The musical *Poppy* came in for some flak. The RSC were accused
of producing it with one eye on Broadway, and I remember a review
in the press which criticised the elaborate costumes, saying 'Look
how they throw their money about.' In fact, *Poppy* was sponsored by
Ladbrokes and the production certainly paid off.

The RSC *should* take risks, in the kinds of play they put on and
with production aspects such as casting, set design and costume. It
should be innovative on *all* levels and appeal to the widest audience
possible. This means they should do different kinds of play (and why
should this not include musicals, which are enjoyed by a great many
people) and should also take the productions round the country. The
theatre should certainly not be confined to Stratford and London – it
is subsidised by the whole country, and should be seen by audiences
round the country.

When the Tory government read that the committee which they
had appointed recommended giving the RSC another million
pounds a year, they did not hesitate to allocate such a sum to the Arts
Council at once for specific payment to the RSC. We would still
receive a smaller subsidy than the National Theatre, but the total
government grant I now considered adequate, neither too little nor
too much.

On the other hand, I agree that the arts should not be over-funded.
Their hunger is insatiable, and they will go on demanding money,
however much you give them, but the well-run efficient companies,
which are an asset to the community, should be treated properly.
There was a particular crisis during Lord Gowrie's period as
Minister for the Arts – one of the best Ministers for the Arts which
the country has seen – and I was going to him and saying 'Please, can

we be directly funded by the Government, and not through the Arts Council? We can get nowhere with them.' The last thing Lord Gowrie wanted was to deal directly with the arts. The Arts Council is successful in one thing; it is a buffer between Government and the arts, and on the whole all the abuse for incorrect funding or any other thing is pushed on to the Arts Council, which otherwise would fall on the Government and the Minister.

I understand that a battle developed between the Priestley Committee and the Arts Council, and there was violent disagreement on certain of the recommendations which the Government had accepted. But, so far as the RSC were concerned, we came out of it adequately funded for the first time, which to me was justification for the campaign we had waged for so long in the face of so much incomprehension and no little vilification. We no longer would have to depend on being topped up by funds from the Royal Shakespeare Theatre Trust, which could be used for other purposes. I had now been chairman of the Royal Shakespeare Company for eleven years and felt the moment had come to make room for the person I had recruited to succeed me.

It is part of my business philosophy always to train a duplicate in any job entrusted to me, and for others in my team. Find a replacement for yourself early on and have him work with you, is my advice; do not try to be indispensable. The way to run a business, a theatre, a school, is to be dispensable. Trevor Nunn had taken over as artistic director of the RSC when Peter Hall succeeded Laurence Olivier as director of the National Theatre, and behind him stood Terry Hands whom we made joint artistic director. Behind David Brierley as general administrator of the RSC I had Bill Wilkinson. For my own replacement I recruited Geoffrey Cass, a management consultant who had once been a fellow-director on one of my companies, was chairman of Cambridge University Press, and was very interested in the arts. He became chairman of the Royal Shakespeare Theatre Trust when I had resigned that position on becoming chairman of the executive council of the Royal Shakespeare Company. I now brought him on to the RSC board or council, and had him take over from me the chairmanship of the finance committee.

I gradually lessened my influence until 1985 when I resigned as chairman enabling the governors to put Geoffrey Cass in my place. He will be a much more efficient chairman than me. He has a much more detailed and precise mind. I try to do things by instinct – by Guess and by God, and putting my finger into the wind. I became deputy president. Just about that time, Harold Wilson, who was the president, decided to resign, so the council asked if I would be the non-executive president of the RSC, an honour which I greatly appreciated.

To my surprise, when this happened, the Arts Council and the Minister suggested I might like to join that organisation. I thought it would be most interesting to see from the inside how the Arts Council worked, and to bring some of my ideas to the Arts Council, if that were possible, so I accepted. At the time, I had discussions with the new Minister for the Arts, Richard Luce, who indicated that he was very concerned, because nobody loved the Arts Council. The drama people did not like it; the music people did not like it; his colleagues in government did not like it; and Members of Parliament on both sides did not like it! They all wanted to get rid of it, and the Minister was very anxious not to get rid of it, because he thought it would be wrong, as I do, for the Government to allocate money directly to the whole of the arts world.

So I became a member of the Arts Council, and was greeted with great kindness by Sir William Rees-Mogg and Luke Ritner, Marghanita Laski, the deputy chairman, who was unbelievably kind, and the majority of the members. However, at the first meeting of the Council, my first fears were realised. All final decisions were made in the great boardroom. There were about twenty members of the Council, the representatives of Wales and Scotland, the directors of each discipline, music, drama, dance, etc., and the officers, the director-general and two of his assistants at least, and a whole lot of other advisers who sat at the back of the room.

There must have been about forty people in the meeting. Any discussion did not appear to be restricted to the members, but everybody joined in, and the meetings which started immediately after lunch could go on until about five o'clock. No one in his right senses would try to run an organisation with a committee of about thirty people. Nor do many modern companies put on their subsidiary company managing directors or chairmen on the main board, because they do not take a view of the overall position, but each looks to its own particular corner, and feels it has to fight it. This is exactly what happens in the Arts Council. All the disciplines are represented, and when any question of the allocation of money comes up each is fighting for its own corner. It is very difficult for them to fight on the basis of the overall good of what is upright, godly and needed. It is amazing how Sir William managed to control that meeting, and in many cases get his own way, but it took considerable restraint, good temper, persistence and charm, all of which he possessed.

The target for the taking away of money was always the Nationals, because they got more than anybody else, and the general idea was that if you want to do something they would not miss a bit! The fact that these were all professionally prepared budgets, and had been considered at a meeting at which the Arts Council's representative had been present and raised no objection, if not tacitly agreeing, made no difference to them. To give an example, when there was a problem with the *Sunday Times* lambasting the directors of the companies for taking too much out of the companies when their productions went commercial, one of the members who I had thought was more sensible than the others said, 'While they are vulnerable, now is the time to take some money off them,' at which point my respect disappeared immediately. What a way to run an organisation! If, indeed, you put a member of every discipline on the main council, what do you expect? Each will fight, in a way properly, for his own corner. A meeting which could have been cleared up in an hour and a half would last until late in the afternoon in most cases.

Later on, Marghanita Laski was due for retirement, and Sir William asked me if I would like to be the deputy chairman, and Richard Luce made the same request. I accepted, because the idea was that Sir William was going to retire fairly shortly; a new chairman would be appointed, and I would be able to tide over the time between the going of William and the settling in of the new chairman. This I thought was an excellent idea, and I felt that I could in fact guide the new chairman into having some changes in the constitution of the Arts Council. I was also asked if I would like to chair the drama panel, which I refused, because having had an involvement with the Royal Shakespeare Company I thought it was wrong. At the time I also thought the drama panel was quite toothless, and was unable to exercise any influence. The people in it had not the same authority and power as the people they were dealing with in the major companies. In any case, it would take a lot of time.

The other thing I was asked to do was to chair an inquiry into drama. This suited me very much, and I undertook to do it, provided I could choose my own committee. This I was allowed to do, and I chose Ian Brown as secretary – an excellent choice – and the following committee: Hugh Hudson-Davies (vice-chairman); Michael Billington; Diana Rigg; Peter Tod; and Clare Venables.

Hugh Hudson-Davies was one of the management consultants from Coopers & Lybrand who had done a report on the National Theatre for that organisation, and was extremely good. I thought we must have some consultancy expert who was used to investigating and reporting on a major operation such as drama.

All the members of the committee were very experienced in the theatre, and of course had strong ideas as to what should be done and what should not be done. The two ladies were strong supporters of the desire to increase female participation in management. It was a very friendly committee, and great fun. We all had different views, and we all argued our corner, but we got on with it. We had been asked to produce the report within six months, which was pretty hard going, so as to give the Arts Council ammunition to use in the argument with the Government about what the next grant to the Arts Council should be.

We did in fact produce it in time, but when the report, which was extremely well received, was presented to the Arts Council they dillied and dallied for months. When I spoke to the Minister and asked why he did not do certain things to implement the report his answer was: 'I can't until the Arts Council recommend it should be adopted.' As part of it was a criticism of the Arts Council, it was like saying you cannot hang somebody until you get a resolution of the candidates for hanging to agree to it!

To return to the committee, we decided in the short time available we should go and see personally as many of the drama organisations as we could, and to that end we divided ourselves up into little teams and set off round the country. I carefully kept away from the Royal Shakespeare Company, but I went to the National. When I went, I took Ian Brown with me, because I needed somebody with experience of other than a major company. We all found it extraordinarily interesting, and we found deep dissatisfaction with the Arts Council as to the way organisations were handled.

It was considered useless dealing with the drama panel because they had no authority. They had the same complaints that the Royal Shakespeare Company had about the Council, and there were an enormous number of complaints that, since they really had very little to do, they spent all their time interfering with things which did not concern them – things which should be done by the DHSS and the Equal Opportunities Commission. They tried to make grants dependent upon whether you had females on the board; how many ethnic minority were employed; and whether the theatre was suitable for handicapped people. All excellent things, but should be nothing to do with an Arts Council which was meant to be promoting drama.

There was great concern in the various companies (and this I knew beforehand) about the way when they did get one of their productions to go commercial there was very little money in it for them. The money all went to the designers and directors. They also believed, and I agree with them, too, that other people exploit the theatre. RADA and the theatre, without any help from such organisations as television, train and produce, in sweat and reasonable poverty, people and performances, and the television companies, for instance, are able to use them without having to run any training courses themselves. Every other industry has to teach people; the television people get it for nothing!

With regard to RADA the position was even more extraordinary. Although drama was a great part of British heritage, grants to students were not compulsory by local authorities, so that it was a case of whether local authorities liked to support them or not. Quite absurd! The other thing which I felt, and I believe the others agreed with me, was that those people who gave up a great deal of their time as governors or trustees, or supporters of the theatre, did it voluntarily, at a certain amount of cost to themselves, and yet when they talked to Government, or the Arts Council, they were frequently treated as grasping people, trying to make a job for themselves. Without this great independent support for the theatre, it would not last five minutes. A lot of these people give considerable sums of money to their theatres to keep them going. Although we were not enquiring into the opera, this particularly applied to opera.

No one believed that our report would be other than a whitewash of the Arts Council. I attended meetings at the Old Vic, in the North, and at Granada, and I told everybody that I would do my utmost to see that our recommendations were accepted. One of the major recommendations which we made was that we thought that good theatre, top class, should be available all over the country. Most of the excellence was in London, which if anything was over-supplied. We thought that centres of excellence should be within reasonable range of everybody in the country, and therefore after considerable debate we recommended that there should be created another six 'Nationals' which should be located strategically throughout the country.

The criteria for these new Nationals would be that they would have to put forward proposals and budgets showing that they could, with help from the central fund, produce the same quality as the existing Nationals. We knew this would make a great deal of difference to the problems of inner cities. You only have to go and look at Stratford-upon-Avon, or Chichester, which are thriving communities, full of life, and realise that without the Chichester Theatre, or the Royal Shakespeare Theatre at Stratford, nothing would be going on there at all. One can see Shakespeare's Birthplace in five minutes, and then what does one do? Go somewhere else. As it is there are about fifteen hotels around there, with all the trade which goes with them, linked to the Royal Shakespeare Company.

Again, there is no point in throwing money into inner cities. To have any effect you have to have industry there; to attract industry you have to have managers willing to live there, and to get managers willing to live there you have to have wives who are willing to go there, too. We consulted Henley College on the future of theatre, and their argument was that most people who were doing reasonably well had money. Money was no longer the primary demand; it was to be an expert in something or other – either in theatre, or in art, or in music – so as to have something to be proud of. Of these, theatre was the most likely one to appeal. Then people could talk with understanding, and impress their colleagues with their knowledge of theatre.

We also thought that the National theatres should in fact not just produce in London; they should produce all over the country, and their productions should be shared with one another, in order to save costs, so that if you had *Les Misérables* produced by the Royal Shakespeare Company, it would then go to the various other Nationals. All this required extra funding. This should be raised, we thought, first by the Arts Council becoming much more entrepreneurial. By being entrepreneurial I do not mean just taking the begging-bowl from the Government to industry, but actually doing deals with industry which would be of advantage to both. The same thing has been done with some of the charities with which I am involved, such as Youth Clubs UK, as part of the promotion of a product. The organisations help to sell the goods, and then there is a penny a tin or what have you, which went to the charity. My idea was that for promotions theatre tickets should be given, not just for the subsidised theatre but for any theatre. The commercial theatre equally requires support. I also thought the Arts Council should be equally interested in supporting the commercial theatre and amateur theatre as well as the subsidised theatre. In fact it would be the overriding authority for the great improvement in drama. The money was to come by the greater exploitation of the products of the subsidised theatre, which was probably the best theatre in the country, and also to get the television companies and other industries to pay for what they got for nothing – the training of their personnel – by a levy on those companies. If the levy was not accepted on the television companies, then the Government would have to find some other source. It would put the onus on them.

The report was produced on time. It also dealt with the problems which the *Sunday Times* had raised of the directors allegedly soaking their companies by taking great fees on the commercialisation of the theatres' productions. That was accepted to everybody's satisfaction. The report was extremely well received, attracted good publicity in all the newspapers, and gave the Arts Council a great deal of credibility for having produced a report which was not a whitewash and had constructive proposals. However, the Arts Council, having received the report, sat on it for about six months; implemented parts of it, although extremely slowly; and did not use it in their demands for funding.

The 'National' idea, which I think was one of the best ideas, and would have been of enormous help to the inner cities, thus assisting the Government with that problem, has never really got off the ground. The Council dismissed without any further question the idea of trying to obtain money from the television companies, and have not yet taken up the idea of the Arts Council being entrepreneurial, although I believe there is a rumour now that it will do so.

This made me even more disenchanted with the composition of the Arts Council. The Government meanwhile had been trying to find a new chairman, because Sir William was due to retire. Luce casually asked me if I would like to do it, and I said 'No', because I could not do four years, although I would not mind doing two years, and cause an investigation into the Arts Council by qualified management consultants with experience in the theatre, to decide what we did want as an Arts Council, which is certainly not what we have at the moment, but that was not taken up. I felt that, having borne the brunt of being chairman while the upheaval took place, a new chairman could come in, who had not caused the disturbance, and have an easy run in taking the Arts Council forward.

The idea was that I should be the link between the new chairman and the old. However, the Arts Council decided, because, I think, they could not find anybody prepared to take it on, that Sir William should remain for another two years, which meant that I would be off the Arts Council at the same time as he retired, so there was no point in my staying.

Meanwhile, the Royal Shakespeare Company, after my departure, partly owing to the Libyan bombing, and partly because they had a series of productions which were not really acceptable to the public, ran seriously into debt. It must be remembered that the Arts Council had never carried out the indication by the Government that the increased funding should continue. On the contrary, year by year, the grant was cut. I therefore decided that it was pointless for me to remain on the Arts Council, and I resigned. I was not prepared to attack an organisation while I was a member of it, and it was very important that I should go back to the Royal Shakespeare Company and be more active as president, in raising money. This I did, and with the help of the Council, Geoffrey Cass and the Trust we succeeded in raising £1 million for the RSC, which got it out of its immediate peril. With a friend of mine, Wafic Said, we are now in the process of setting up a fund in America. The Americans could not believe that a great company like the Royal Shakespeare Company would be starved of money by both the Arts Council and the

Government, so they are going to arrange a big campaign. Wafic Said is a very substantial businessman and film director, with a great interest in the arts. We anticipate this fund will give the RSC an adequate capital and thus make it less dependent upon the whims of Arts Councils and governments!

Once at Stratford with the RSC we were having one of our great occasions, and this time we sold a square foot of a garden to Americans. That way they 'owned' a bit of Stratford. As part of the general festivities, the Queen came, and I went down the river standing up on a barge next to her. It felt extremely perilous. We were wavering about, and there was nothing to hold on to. While I was debating whether or not to grab the Queen's chair to steady myself, the Queen said: 'Mr Cork, do you know what's written on that plaque down there?'

Well, I could hardly see it, let alone read it, so I had lamely to say no, I did not.

The Queen pointed out that it was to commemorate her mother travelling in the same barge.

Later, when I was a Sheriff in the City of London, the Queen came to a reception associated with the Women's Institute. Although Sheriffs are supposed to stay in the background, which I was diligently doing, one of her ladies-in-waiting said: 'Her Majesty would like to speak to you.'

'Mr Cork, do you know what these pictures are?'

They were pictures of buildings in the City, but to my increasing discomfort I couldn't recognise a single one of them. It was most bewildering – I'd been working in the City for years. Like an idiot, I looked at them and had to say no, I did not. I then had to scurry down the corridor and find out that the pictures were plans and designs for buildings that had never actually been built.

When I went back to tell the Queen this, she listened very politely and then said: 'Mr Cork, you never can answer my questions, can you?' (with a very nice smile).

I thought that was a very pleasant way of showing she remembered who I was!

One of the nicest things that happened when I retired from the Arts Council was the receipt of a letter from the drama panel much regretting my departure and thanking me for what I had done for theatre. But, then, the chairman of the panel was a professional, Sir Brian Rix. What a difference it makes when you deal with professionals!

I had promised everybody who wrote to me – and there were many who did when I left the Arts Council – that I would then lobby and do my best to get the whole constitution of the Arts Council changed, and try to obtain something which would promote the arts and be of real use. I did not wish to make all the suggestions myself, because I do not have the answer to all questions – even I do not think so! However, if we had an inquiry, then I would be prepared to give advice to it. Whether they accepted that advice would be up to the experts who were on that inquiry. The kind of thing I had in mind was that the Arts Council should consist of a small number of, say, seven eminent people, with excellent business records in their own professions or industries, and who had given considerable service to the arts. They would have the job, after taking advice, of deciding upon the distribution of finance between the different art forms. The various disciplines in the arts would have a director on the staff of the Arts Council and a panel of people involved and expert in that art, who would be responsible for recommending the distribution of the funds allocated to that art form amongst the clients.

The national companies should have a separate allocation of funds, and the panel would recommend to the Council the allocation to these companies, which would be judged on their standards and their importance in the national interest. They should be treated separately, with separate funds, so as to stop jealousy from the smaller clients.

The Council should be responsible for making itself entrepreneurial and have funds to invest in the proven successes created from the subsidised companies when these productions transferred to the private sector. This would create very considerable additional funds which would help to make the Council more self-supporting. Some of the best productions come from the subsidised companies, and the exploitation of them should help finance the Arts Council.

The policy should be to help and advise companies on how to become more entrepreneurial themselves, and create and concentrate on earning greater contributions to their own funds. The Council should also arrange schemes as do other charities, to raise monies for the Council itself from industry by promotions which would benefit both industry and the arts. I visualise the Arts Council being a kind of holding company for the arts, for the purpose of maximising the income and reducing the necessity of relying entirely on public money.

The Government has a legitimate grievance in that the arts do not do enough for themselves. The staff of the Arts Council should be of the calibre which is capable of running an organisation with a turnover of £150 million, and with that wide experience they should be paid accordingly and be encouraged to earn money for the Arts Council.

Contributions should be made to the Arts Council from those organisations which make use of the skills of the artistes, and productions which are subsidised by government funding – television, radio, etc.

It would be the responsibility of the Arts Council to create new 'National' companies, and they should receive local financial aid to help them do it, and see that there are centres of excellence other than London, throughout the country, so that subsidised excellence is made available to the whole population.

This would do more for the inner cities than merely throwing money at them, by creating an environment in which management and their families would be happy to live and thus create new industry in those areas.

However, other ideas should be put forward by interested parties to the inquiry. I do not claim that mine are the ideal ones. I would like to see the kinds of proposal which should make the United Kingdom into a major creative artistic environment and initiate innovation in the arts world. The benefit to tourism would be enormous, as would be the prestige to the country.

The reason, again, that I retired is that I thought I could do more for the arts outside the Arts Council than in it, in trying to get a new constitution created. I hope I can do it. I am certainly going to try! There are a lot of people who are only too anxious to support me, but the difficulty is finding the time to get it going. I am an optimist, so I hope one voice crying in the wilderness will be heard.

Envoi

I must go down to the seas again, to the vagrant gypsy life,
To the gull's way and the whale's way, where the wind's like a whetted
    knife;
And all I ask is a merry yarn from a laughing fellow rover,
And quiet sleep and a sweet dream when the long trick's over.

John Masefield, 'Sea-Fever'

I may have put a question mark after the title I gave Part Four, but in 1987 I really am retired as an insolvency accountant. I have not even been an insolvency consultant since 1983. For me at seventy-three the Long Trick is far from over. I must confess, however, to going down to the sea more frequently than before. My consultancy life today, with which I earn more money than I did as senior partner of Cork Gully and do not have to plough it back to finance the firm, consists of trusteeships; being a director of companies like Celestion, Ladbrokes, who own Hilton Hotels around the world, and Brent Walker, who are developing Brighton Marina; wrestling with the administrative problems of subsidised music and theatre as deputy chairman of the Arts Council, and giving lectures to accountants and others the world over who invite me in the belief, I suppose, that I know the Trick of How To Succeed In Business.

I cannot give them the Secret of Success but I try to pass on some of the lessons I have learnt along the way about guiding a business, or any enterprise for that matter, on lines which are more, rather than less, likely to lead to survival. As an insolvency accountant, my days were spent witnessing the havoc caused by mismanagement, being aghast at the cavalier attitude which so many untrained and unsuited amateurs brought to the extremely complicated business of management. It required the highest skill to make a reasonable profit in the seventies in the face of crippling VAT, Corporation Tax, high interest rates, inflating costs of raw materials, labour, energy, transport, promotion. There was no more accurate yardstick of the difficulty industrialists were having in finding an answer than the rising insolvency rate. The Department of Trade reported the courts had wound up more companies in 1974 than in any year since the Companies (Winding Up) Act was passed in 1890. In 1975, 5,398 companies were liquidated, an average of 104 a day. It was a 45 per cent increase over 1974, which was itself a record. In the ten years 1967 to 1976 the number of bankruptcies rose from 4,029 (with assets estimated by debtors at £4,700,000) to 6,700 (£22,500,000).

In such circumstances, to endure, to stave off insolvency, to achieve profitability, needed greater managerial skill than ever. For there were no universally accepted guidelines to success, no consensus of opinion on how best to climb, how best to prevent a fall. Government admitted there was no science about framing the nation's budget; the consequences of the measures prescribed, necessarily very long-term, could not be other than guesswork. The 'economists' continued to mouth incomprehensibilities. As Edward Heath said to Shirley Williams in their television conversation in October 1979, the seventies had regrettably thrown up 'no fresh economic thought'. Yet, if inflation was not controlled, many saw it as causing the complete collapse of the British way of life as we knew it – melodramatic perhaps, but not inconceivable.

Management was sailing in unchartered waters without a compass, and was not aware of it. Running a business was no longer a routine matter of watching overheads and profit margins. You had to stop working and start thinking. Any fool could work. Very few could think. Many believed capitalism had failed. Many more were convinced socialism had failed, chiefly because there was no way of limiting wage demands. For many years management considered workers expendable. It was good business sense to reduce the workforce when turnover dropped. But the Employment Protection Act has changed that. Then you could not reduce it even when you should.

Too little recognition was given to investment in a business represented by the workers and staff. They started at a low rate of pay, learnt their skill and prospered when the business prospered. That investment was as important as the shareholders. For those who worked in it, the collapse of a firm was infinitely worse, for though the shareholders lost their life savings the men on the floor lost their total means of supporting their families. Few managements were as answerable to the workers as they were to their shareholders. Until businessmen discovered a way of creating an ambience in which each man on the shop floor was as worried about the overdraft as the managing director, there was little chance of industry making a go of things.

Having done that, or perhaps as part of doing that, the management must feed the people on the floor with easily assimilated, true information week by week. But how few managements had the information themselves! Buckets of paper, yes – but information, no! You cannot think with what is on paper, but only with what is in your head. The kind of information you often get from a computer is 'Well, I never' information. Interesting but not particularly useful.

Every manager must have the basic facts about his business in his head and make mental adjustments to this basic information as each major event occurs. My profession has not done its job properly unless this can be achieved – basic facts such as weekly cash-flow limits, turnover, break-even figures and a mental running calculation of profit. A manager should only look at the figures produced by his accounts department to check the figures he already knows in his head. If one of my managers did not know, he would be for the high jump!

Many have learnt not to take fixed-price contracts, but how many in those days built 25 per cent inflation of wages and materials into their cash-flow, and worked out the peaks which would arrive over the next six months, and go *at once* to the bank to make the necessary arrangements? It is nearly always too late to do it if you are in the crisis. And remember that your business and your skill are one of the assets of this country. You will only succeed if it is run first for the benefit of the community, second for the benefit of your staff, and third and lastly for the benefit of yourself. The curious thing is that if you do it this way you will make more money than those people who do not.

But do not be deluded into thinking you can succeed without competition, from rivals both at home and abroad. It is living in Cloud-cuckoo-land to disregard the forces of competition, to complain of 'dumping' foreign cars as if the determining factor was having goods to sell and not the people who choose freely to buy them. It is even crazier to contract out of competition as the flour millers did with their Millers Mutual Association before they were advised that the Restrictive Practices Court was unlikely to consider it acted in the public interest. Industry does not exist to provide shareholders with dividends or workers with wages, but consumers and users with products and services. That is the target of industrial enterprise, and to try to aim it in any other direction or, worse still, continually chop and change its direction is making certain, in the words of Shakespeare's Richard II, which I was always quoting as Lord Mayor, that England will soon make 'a shameful conquest of itself'. In creating the services and goods, we create the wealth which enables the Government of the day to afford welfare services, police, army and the rest. We must return to making our own consumer goods. We are an under-developed country. We are being fed by Germany, Japan and Italy, to name but three. We are sucking in imports because Britain is a vacuum. We have people with more money to spend and not enough of our own goods for them to spend it on. The vacuum is filled by foreign goods coming in. By making our own consumer goods we will provide a reason for investment. The Tories say if you have a demand the market can fill it. The socialists say no one is investing, so investment should be directed. Neither of them has the answer. The socialists are establishing organisations to make goods, but they come up with the wrong price, the wrong technical ability and the wrong salesmanship. The Tories are wide of the mark, too. If there is a market for goods, it can be filled by people already in production, and those for the most part are foreigners. We have to do something to create our own goods.

The argument is finished that you can only make consumer goods if you have cheap labour. This is not true. If you can have a small amount of labour with high technological ability and high technology equipment, you can make your consumer goods and make them better than a non-skilled labour force. We could beat the Japanese at it if we wanted to, but we have got to get these enterprises started, and they have to have some encouragement.

One encouragement would of course be to designate certain items which, if manufactured, could get a 'tax holiday'. This ran into trouble, I know, with the Common Market rules, which said that we must not support our own industries. Our taxation system did not give us any advantage in earned income from our own company, whereas foreigners paid a much lesser rate of tax on what they themselves earned, so they were being encouraged to start where we were not.

Our taxation system made sure that the greater part of our spare money went not into industry but into pensions. The pension fund managers went to the share supermarket which was the Stock Exchange and bought what they hoped were safe bargains. Twice the amount of money entrusted to them chased the same shares round the Stock Exchange, all geared not to create investment. This was doubtless done for a very good reason, but if we did not create new industry, if we did not manufacture consumer goods, if when we paid the workers their increases they did not spend it on English goods, they would only inflate the Japanese, German, Italian and Singapore economies. They would not do ours any good at all.

The trouble was we had absolutely no plan. The country was just like a ship. The bosses and the trade unions and the Government kept tinkering with the works, and the socialists and the trade unions were saying everybody should travel in one class. There was no captain on the bridge and nobody knew where the ship was sailing – until we had a lady prime minister who did. And I reckon she came to the rescue just in the nick of time.

Now, this is the last story I'm going to tell you.

The great problem with young professionals is that when they are qualified they know it all and furthermore they maintain the strong belief that they are always right. I was certainly no exception.

I knew from law that the trustee in bankruptcy was an officer of the court and it was everyone's duty to help him, irrespective of who you were dealing with.

When I was dealing with the Lynskey Tribunal (famous at the time) it involved the character Tepper the tailor, who was alleged to have made very expensive suits in those days when you couldn't get suits for love or money. The other aspects of the case involved a Mr Price, who was either chairman or managing director of Stag-Russell. He had gone off to the South of France, and I wanted to get hold of him to find out where his assets were. I knew the Bank of England would have his address, so I wrote to them saying please could I have it. I received a very pompous letter back, saying the Bank of England didn't disclose such information.

I wrote back saying that unless they gave me, an officer of the court, the information I needed I would have the Governor of the Bank of England up for private examination for refusing to co-operate with an officer of the court. There was a deafening silence.

Later, I received a telephone call from a senior partner at Freshfields (lawyers for the Bank of England), who were enormously influential in the City, asking if I would go and see him. Duly flattered at being called up by an important person on some great matter, I went along. I was ushered up to his elegant office, he greeted me in a friendly way, and gave me coffee, and then we went on to discuss hunting, shooting and fishing (which I know nothing about) and sailing, which I did. Then he said: 'You know, your father was a difficult man, too. I hear that you are trying to have the Governor of the Bank of England up for private examination in front of the bankruptcy court. I don't think that's a very good idea.' I replied with the dignity of youth that I was entitled to do so. He smiled. 'I think we can arrive at a solution. Shortly, I will be called out of the office. On my desk you will find an address. If you are ungentlemanly enough to read it, you will obtain the information you want. In the City, we don't call the Governor of the Bank of England up in front of the Court, and it won't help your career very much.'

I never thought of doing it again. I have many friends in the Bank of England; it was extremely supportive during the crises of the 1970s. I am now satisfied that their ways of dealing with things are far better than any amount of legislation.

By the way, when I got to the South of France, Mr Price had left. I wonder who had tipped him off.

Index

Index

Picture Acknowledgements

Page 1: Author's Collection. Page 2: *Daily Mirror*/Syndication International (above). *Daily Mail*/Solo (below). Page 3: Heath/ *Sunday Times* (above) © Times Newspapers Limited, 1976. Richard Willson/*The Times* (below left) © Times Newspapers Limited, 1974. *Daily Telegraph* (below right). Page 4: Portrait by David Poole, President of the Royal Society of Portrait Painters. Page 5: The Keystone Collection. Page 6: Joe Cocks Studio, Stratford-upon-Avon (above). Page 7: © *Birmingham Post and Mail*.